CHINA'S EVOLVING MILITARY STRATEGY

Joe McReynolds
Editor

The JAMESTOWN
FOUNDATION

January 2017

THE JAMESTOWN FOUNDATION

Published in the United States by
The Jamestown Foundation
1310 L St. NW, Suite 810
Washington, DC 20005
http://www.jamestown.org

For more information on this report or The Jamestown Foundation, email: pubs@jamestown.org.

Jamestown's Mission

The Jamestown Foundation's mission is to inform and educate policymakers and the broader policy community about events and trends in those societies which are strategically or tactically important to the United States and which frequently restrict access to such information. Utilizing indigenous and primary sources, Jamestown's material is delivered without political bias, filter or agenda. It is often the only source of information which should be, but is not always, available through official or intelligence channels, especially in regard to Eurasia and terrorism.

Origins

Launched in 1984 by its founder William Geimer, The Jamestown Foundation has emerged as one of the leading providers of research and analysis on conflict and instability in Eurasia. The Jamestown Foundation has rapidly grown to become one of the leading sources of information on Eurasia, developing a global network of analytical expertise from the Baltic to the Horn of Africa. This core of intellectual talent includes former high-ranking government officials, journalists, research analysts, scholars and economists. Their insight contributes significantly to helping policymakers around the world understand the emerging trends and developments in many of the world's under-reported conflict zones in Eurasia.

TABLE OF CONTENTS

Section IV: China's Strategy Beyond Warfighting

LIST OF ACRONYMS

A2/AD   Anti-Access, Area Denial

AMS   Academy of Military Science

C4ISR   Command, Control, Communications, Computers, Intelligence, Surveillance and Reconnaissance

CCP   Chinese Communist Party

CMC   Central Military Commission

CMI   Civil-Military Integration

CNA   Computer Network Attack

CND   Computer Network Defense

CNO   Computer Network Operations

CNSA   China National Space Administration

DWP   Defense White Paper

GSD   General Staff Department

HGV   Hypersonic Glide Vehicle

ICBM   Intercontinental Ballistic Missile

INEW	Integrated Network and Electronic Warfare
KEW	Kinetic Energy weapons
KKV	Kinetic Kill Vehicle
LSIO	*Lectures on the Science of Information Operations*
MCF	Military-Civilian Fusion
MIIT	Ministry of Industry and Information Technology
MIRV	Multiple Independently Targetable Reentry Vehicles
MOOTW	Military Operations Other Than War
MPS	Ministry of Public Security
MSS	Ministry of State Security
NDU	National Defense University
NHM	"New Historic Missions"
NFU	"No First Use"
PAP	People's Armed Police

PBSC	Politburo Standing Committee
PLA	People's Liberation Army
PLAAF	People's Liberation Army Air Force
PLAN	People's Liberation Army Navy
PLARF	People's Liberation Army Rocket Force
PLASSF	People's Liberation Army Strategic Support Force
PRC	People's Republic of China
SMS	*Science of Military Strategy*
SNDMC	State National Defense Mobilization Committee

Preface

For over two decades, the People's Republic of China has been engaged in a grand project to transform its military into a modernized fighting force capable of defeating major foreign powers. After the first Gulf War saw the United States use precision-guided munitions and C4ISR technologies to decisively defeat Iraq's aging, mechanized forces, Chinese military thinkers concluded that a similar fate would likely befall the People's Liberation Army in combat unless drastic changes were made. From that point onward, readying the PLA to fight in modern warfare has been firmly enshrined as one of the country's highest policy priorities.

Each successive leader has left their own imprint not only on the PLA's force structure, but also on its strategic guidance. Jiang Zemin's initial focus on developing the PLA's ability to win a "local war under high-tech conditions" gradually morphed into Hu Jintao's emphasis on building an "informatized" force capable of surviving and winning at modern information warfare, as well as enabling the PLA to carry out what Hu termed the "New Historic Missions," which emphasized for the first time the importance of Military Operations Other Than Warfare (MOOTW). As the PLA moves into the era of Xi's leadership, the evolution of its guiding military-strategic thought will continue alongside Xi's major changes to the PLA's force structure and China's expanding conception of its "core interests" in the South China Sea and elsewhere.

China's modernization of its military forces and continued points of sharp difference with the United States on foreign policy in the Asia-Pacific have increasingly forced the U.S. military and policy communities to prepare for the possibility of a serious confrontation with China. Although we do not face a "new Cold War," as the United States and China are at peace with one another and are economically intertwined to an extent entirely unlike the U.S.-Soviet military rivalry of old, numerous flashpoints of contention exist that could bring China into a serious military conflict with either the United States or her allies. It is vital to understand both the capabilities of China's modernizing military and the military thinking of China's leadership when formulating policy or responding to China's actions.

However, despite the great attention that has been devoted to cataloguing the PLA's advances in its military platforms and technology, there is little in the way of comprehensive information available to analysts and policymakers regarding recent developments in Chinese strategic thought. China's military-strategic bodies publish a variety of influential and authoritative works explaining recent trends and debates, but few Western China analysts possess both the subject-matter expertise and Chinese language ability to absorb and contextualize this output and convey its central insights to a Western policy audience. When information does reach Western policymakers, it does so after an extreme delay; authoritative Chinese publications on strategy often take years to prepare, and then additional time elapses before Western analysts begin to integrate the new materials into their assessments. This time lag of years complicates efforts at mutual strategic understanding in what is arguably the world's most important bilateral national security relationship. As a result, foreign discussions of Chinese military behavior generally center on observing new military hardware as it is introduced into service and parsing the public declarations and actions of the Chinese leadership, neither of which are sufficient for predicting Chinese military and civilian decision-making in the event of a crisis.

This gap in understanding warps the U.S. debate over China policy in several important ways. First, it creates a bias toward treating the few Chinese-authored works on military strategy with English translations as being of great importance, even when they are neither authoritative nor representative. Second, it degrades the ability of Western analysts to contextualize observed changes in the PLA's force structure and operations for policymakers. Without access to current writings on Chinese military strategy, analysts and policymakers are forced to rely on a combination of out-of-date translated writings and official PLA communiques. In the absence of fuller information, analysts and policymakers are prone to engaging in mirror-imaging, erroneously assuming the PLA's approach to strategy is essentially the same as ours would be, were we in their position. Finally, it pushes U.S. defense planners toward a reactive, rather than proactive, approach to planning for how the United States will respond militarily to China's rise. Without information regarding leading indicators of deep strategic change, Western analysts are more likely to be caught unaware by shifts in policy or unanticipated Chinese military actions.

China's Evolving Military Strategy aims to address these challenges by offering sector-by-sector expert assessments of important recent developments in Chinese strategic thought to the Western foreign policy community. The first two chapters, by Timothy Heath and Taylor Fravel, grapple with big-picture questions of the sources and forms of PLA strategy and broad trends in the evolution of Chinese strategic thought. Cristina Garafola, Andrew Erickson, and Michael Chase then address recent shifts in strategic thinking in the "conventional" services of the Air Force, Navy, and Rocket Forces. The discussion then turns to the "non-traditional" domains of information warfare, with John Costello, Peter Mattis, Joe McReynolds, Kevin Pollpeter, and Jonathan Ray examining China's strategic approach to electromagnetic warfare, network warfare, and space warfare in detail. The final three chapters by Dennis Blasko, Morgan Clemens, and Dan Alderman discuss the PLA's strategic approach to peacetime, covering deterrence, non-warfare military operations, and civil-military integration in China's defense modernization efforts. Collectively, the editor and authors hope that offering a comprehensive picture of current trends in Chinese strategic thought will equip Western analysts and policymakers with an improved conceptual and practical framework for assessing Chinese intentions and determining how best to respond to Chinese actions.

This project could not have succeeded without the assistance of many friends and colleagues in the China analyst community, and the authors of this volume would like to acknowledge their generous contributions. Kenneth Allen has lent his time and his wealth of knowledge to multiple chapter authors. Peter Wood at the Jamestown Foundation has done superb editing work in shepherding this volume to print. Glen Howard has championed this project at an executive level from its early stages. The editor and the Jamestown Foundation are grateful for the support of the Smith Richardson Foundation for this volume. Finally, the editor would like to thank Mike Green, Lonnie Henley, James Mulvenon, and Bob Sutter for serving as mentors from the start of his career as a China analyst; without their support (and patience) in training new generations of China analysts, projects such as this would not be possible.

SECTION I: CHINA'S OVERALL APPROACH TO MILITARY STRATEGY

Chapter 1: An Overview of China's National Military Strategy

Timothy R. Heath

A country's national military strategy represents the intersection between national and military levels of strategy. A common definition regards strategy as a general plan of action to realize objectives (ends) through a particular employment (ways) of the resources available (means). National military strategies link the military's ends, ways, and means to national objectives. They are expressed in the form of broad directives to guide both military planning and the conduct of operations and campaigns. In addition to serving as authoritative sources of strategic guidance, they also typically provide assessments and contextual information to explain and justify the strategy.[1]

The study of China's national military strategy as a sub-topic within the larger category of "military strategy" is important for several reasons. Because it is so intimately tied to higher order national strategic objectives, studying China's national military strategy can provide insight into the leadership's intentions regarding the use of military power. Moreover, familiarity with China's national military strategy provides critical context for the study of the PLA's ambitions regarding its own modernization and operations.

This chapter aims to guide the reader in the study of China's equivalent of a national military strategy. China does not issue a "national military strategy" document in the manner of the

United States. Nevertheless, virtually all modern states rely on something equivalent in function to a national military strategy to guide the construction and employment of military power. After reviewing the state of scholarship on the topic, this chapter will offer a framework for analyzing China's national military strategy through the study of key party and military documents. It will then review China's most current national military strategy.

Western Scholarship on the Study of China's National Military Strategy

The most important Western studies of China's national military strategies in the post- Deng Xiaoping era have been those written by David Finkelstein and Taylor Fravel. In 1999, Finkelstein broke ground with one of the first serious efforts to analyze China's national military strategy in the Jiang Zemin era.[2] Taylor Fravel considerably enriched the study of the topic with his analysis of the 1987 and 1999 editions of the book, *Science of Military Strategy* (战略学). Drawing from these sources, Fravel presented military strategy from the Chinese perspective and introduced a rich array of Chinese terms, frameworks, and concepts to a non-Chinese audience. In that study, he introduced what he referred to as the "military strategic guidelines" (军事战略方针), which he described as an important part of the country's military strategy.[3] In 2007, Finkelstein expanded and enriched the study of China's national military strategy with his now classic work, "China's National Military Strategy: An Overview of the 'Military Strategic Guidelines.'"[4] Because this analysis has largely defined the state of thinking in the field, it merits a closer look.

Finkelstein's article put forward the argument that the "military strategic guidelines" found in PLA literature served as the functional equivalent of a national military strategy. As he pointed out, the Central Military Commission (CMC) issues the guidelines, thus establishing their authoritative status. PLA sources also clearly regard them as a guide to the construction and employment of military force. Finkelstein cited a research department of the National Defense University, which defined the guidelines as the "overall guiding principles for planning and for guiding the development and use of the armed forces."[5]

Other features of the guidelines appeared to underscore their importance. Revisions and changes occurred infrequently— indeed, Finkelstein noted that authorities had only implemented four major changes since the founding of the People's Republic of China (PRC). Finkelstein highlighted in particular the importance of the "strategic guiding thought" (战略指导思想), which he explained provide "official judgments" underlying the military strategic guidelines for any particular period. The strategic guiding thoughts provided the "core" upon which the guidelines flesh out details for the "ends, ways, and means" of China's national military strategy. Finkelstein described the military strategic guidelines as having six component parts, consisting of: 1) strategic assessment; 2) adjustment of the content of the "active defense strategy"; 3) articulation of strategic missions and objectives; 4) guidance for military combat preparations; 5) identification of the main 'strategic directions'; and 6) determination of the focus for army building.[6] Hailing the guidelines as the framework that can explain "what is driving the PLA's modernization," Finkelstein declared that "every modernization program, every reform initiative, and every significant change that the PLA has undergone, and which foreign observers have been writing about for over a decade, are the results of some of the fundamental decisions made when the new guidelines were promulgated in 1993."[7]

It is difficult to overstate the impact of Finkelstein's study in the field of PLA studies. Prior to its publication, analysts lacked a way to reliably identify China's national military strategy. Finkelstein's work offered a simple, seemingly authoritative template that appeared to be readily corroborated by numerous references to "military strategic guidelines" in publicly available Chinese sources. Not content to rely on the second-hand reporting provided by Western scholars of this apparently critical source of information on the PLA, U.S. authorities immediately began to seek out a copy of the military strategic guidelines. In 2009, the China Military Report to Congress, published by the Department of Defense, declared that "China relies on a body of overall principles and guidance known as the 'military strategic guidelines' to plan and manage the development of the armed forces," but noted the contents had not been made publicly available.[8] Similar language appeared in the reports from 2007 through 2012.[9] Indeed, Finkelstein's insights continue to dominate scholarship of China's national military strategy, with Taylor Fravel affirming in 2015 that the guidelines "represent China's national military strategy."[10]

While this work by Finkelstein has justly earned plaudits for its breakthroughs, his focus on the "military strategic guidelines" as a unitary coherent entity has also raised puzzling questions. The first is that no official Chinese document by the name of "military strategic guidelines" has yet been uncovered. While this is not necessarily a problem in the sense that China employs policy formats different from the West, the absence suggests that the comparison with a true "national military strategy" could be misleading. Some observers regard the elusive guidelines as something of a secret strategy document, despite a lack of hard evidence that this is the form that the guidelines take. The executive branch's China Military Power reports from 2006 to 2012 have each declared, for example, that the "PLA has not made the contents of the guidelines available to the public."[11]

Second, Chinese sources generally describe the guidelines not as an equivalent of a national military strategy, but as a subset of military strategy. The 2015 military strategy Defense White Paper, PLA books on military strategy, and numerous articles in military media consistently describe the guidelines in connection with the concept of "active defense," (积极防御) yet Western scholars have tended to either downplay the link or dismiss it altogether. Finkelstein, for his part, acknowledged in his 2007 study that the relationship between the "active defense strategy" and the "military strategic guidelines of active defense" appeared "so intimate" as to be "nearly indistinguishable in the minds of the PLA." However, he argued that the principles of "active defense" remain "too general" to be useful, a "near empty construct" that required fleshing out with specifics from the guidelines.[12] This conclusion appeared to reverse Finkelstein's point in the same article that "strategic thoughts" like "active defense," provided the "core content and meaning" for the "framework" of the military strategic guidelines.

Third, the military strategic guidelines framework has ironically had difficulty accounting for major developments in national strategic guidance to the military. The difficulty of incorporating analysis of the "New Historic Missions" (新历史

使命, or NHM) concept, discussed below, exemplifies the problem. Issued in 2004, the NHM concept clearly plays an important role in defining the military's strategic mission and thus should play a central role in any post-2004 analysis of the PLA's national military strategy. Yet despite voluminous publication in Chinese official sources, Western scholarship has struggled to explain how the concept fits within the military strategic guidelines.[13]

A closer look at Chinese military terminology provides some insight into the meaning and purpose of the military strategic guidelines. Finkelstein and others translate the Chinese term *fangzhen* (方针) as "guidelines" in the phrase "military strategic guidelines." In English, the term "guidelines" evokes a discrete corpus of instructions, generally in written form. The Chinese term *fangzhen*, however, does not carry the same connotation. The 2011 edition of the PLA's authoritative dictionary (commonly known as the 军语 or *junyu*) consistently describes *fangzhen* as encompassing "frameworks and principles" (纲领和原则), which leaves a greater degree of ambiguity as to their actual form than the term "guidelines" take. Indeed, it is worth bearing in mind that the Chinese regularly employ *fangzhen* for virtually all policy topics as a way for authorities to guide the overall conduct of policy, and that in many cases these consist of a handful of general directives whose application and meaning requires considerable exposition by scholars. For example, Chinese officials regard Deng Xiaoping's famous "24 character" set of foreign policy directives, which includes the well-known imperative to "hide your capabilities, bide your time" (韬光养晦), as a "foreign relations strategic *fangzhen*" (外交战略方针).[14] There is no known document called "foreign relations strategic *fangzhen*," and experts acknowledge that these directives form but one aspect of China's foreign policy.

Within the community of Western PLA watchers, it has long been understood that grappling with difficult or ambiguous Chinese concepts and terms of art on their own terms is preferable to attempting to shoehorn Chinese concepts into one-to-one pairings with Western equivalent terms. Such pairings often end up being reductive, obscuring more than they elucidate and eliminating nuance. For example, PLA watchers generally refer to the sensitive policy planning documents known as *gangyao* (纲要) simply by Romanizing, rather than translating the term of art literally as "planning document" or some other approximation. The result has been a sharper shared understanding of the precise role of *gangyao* within the Chinese system.

In the case of the "military strategic guidelines," which are often discussed as a single coherent entity with a degree of certainty that is higher than what the evidence supports, it would behoove us to do the same. In this spirit, rather than using the term "military strategic guidelines," this chapter henceforth references "military strategic *fangzhen*" in its efforts to explain their place in the broader PLA strategic context and reinforce the idea that the military's use of *fangzhen* follows a practice widely observed in all of China's bureaucracies.

How the PLA's Leninist Characteristics Influence Strategy Formulation

Part of the difficulty of deducing China's "national military strategy" is that such a strategy by definition must straddle both political and military topics. At such, it sits awkwardly astride the responsibilities of two important bureaucratic actors: the central leadership and the military leadership. China's central leadership is comprised of the collective party-state leadership in Beijing. The most important players are the General Secretary and the Politburo Standing Committee (PBSC), but the broader Politburo, various central leading groups, the Central Committee and affiliated organs, and the State Council also play important roles. These are the decision makers responsible for issuing national level strategic guidance. The military leadership consists principally of the Central Military Commission, which in the post-Deng era has been headed by the CMC Chair, who has served concurrently as CCP General Secretary and President of the People's Republic of China (PRC). The topics addressed in a national military strategy must be covered in directions issued by the central leadership, the military leadership, or some combination of the two.

Unique features of China's Leninist political system provide important clues as to how to how these levels of leadership articulate a functional equivalent of a national military strategy. Considerable scholarship has documented how the PLA's Leninist identity shapes its organization and activity. The PLA is a "party army" that serves the CCP, not a national army in service of the state, for example. Party members form the key decision making cells in virtually every military unit, and the PLA continues to rely on political commissars as equals to military commanders to provide motivation, morale, and political discipline (though in practice they appear to defer to commanders in wartime decision-making). These features are well documented and described in Western scholarly writings on the PLA. Less well explored, however, are the ways China's

Leninist political system affects the process by which the military receives and issues strategic direction. Some of the most pertinent principles underlying this process merit review:

- *The party controls strategy.* A fundamental Leninist principle grants exclusive control of the formulation of strategic guidance to the ruling CCP. In the case of the PLA, the party controls strategy, not the military, though military leaders may, in their dual role as high-level party members with representation in the party CMC, involve themselves in the formulation of policy and represent their respective bureaucratic interests in intra-party debates.

- *Party organizations incorporate higher-level direction.* Party cells and committees in the military are compelled to incorporate higher-level direction. They must also ensure any guidance originating from party leaders in the military (i.e., the CMC) reinforces and supports directions from central authorities.

- *Central leaders use guidance to control the military.* Central authorities exert political control in part by guiding the work of the military. Central leaders entrust only the most specialized and technical details of policy formulation to military officials. As a corollary, whenever central authorities change national strategic guidance, the military revises its guidance accordingly.

- *Publication of central direction enhances control.* Central leaders may rely on secrecy to communicate sensitive information, but the imperative to demonstrate the central leadership's political foresight, wisdom, and authority provides a powerful incentive to publish many details of strategic guidance to all elements of state power. Incessant publication of relevant guidance reinforces to the public, and, more importantly to the military, the PLA's subordination to central authority.

- *Concern for legitimacy informs the format of guidance.* In terms of format, the military generally expresses guidance in terms similar to those used by central leaders and other bureaucracies. Thus, the military replicates the central leadership's reliance on theory, directives, and guiding principles, etc., to express strategic guidance and uses these in a manner that would be intelligible to both central leaders and other bureaucracies, even if the non-military actors do not necessarily grasp the more technical details.

These observations provide important clues as to where the observer should look for insight into China's national military strategy. First, one should expect the central leadership to issue the most important guidance and the military to augment and reinforce that guidance with specialized and more technical details. A good rule of thumb is that if there is any type of guidance that could possibly carry implications for the conduct of national strategy, it will be the central leadership that ultimately controls its expression, not the military. Second, the central and military leadership will publish many aspects of the national military strategy in publicly available documents. Third, the national military strategy will be expressed in a manner that can be understood by both central and military authorities (i.e., through the use of strategic concepts, party theory, directives, guiding principles, etc.).

What is China's National Military Strategy?

The above discussion concluded that the study of China's national military strategy should begin with documents issued by central authorities, rather than those issued by military leaders. A review of available public documents suggests that the most important parts of China's national military strategy belong can be found in documents related to national level strategy and its sub-components, the national security strategy and defense policy. Study of these sources provides essential context for interpreting the more specialized and detailed strategic guidance issued by military authorities.

National Strategy

National strategy provides authoritative direction for all elements of national power regarding the achievement of national level goals and objectives set by the central leadership. China does not consistently use the term "national strategy," but central authorities provide a functional equivalent in what they regard as the "socialist path with Chinese characteristics." The functional equivalent to a national strategy may be found in Party Congress work reports and key Central Committee plenary documents. Commentary in official news outlets like Xinhua and *People's Daily*, and scholarly analysis in journals associated with the Central Committee, such as *Outlook* and *Study Times*, provide useful exposition that can help us interpret the meaning and significance of guidance provided in these documents. Since at least 2002, China's national strategy has sought to elevate the standard of living of its people and realize the nation's revitalization as a great power by the mid-21st century.[15]

For the military, the national strategy is important for several reasons. First, it provides the underlying strategic assessment that guides the work of all bureaucracies, including the military. The PLA may tailor the assessment to fit its bureaucratic needs, but the military threat assessment must follow the logic and intent of the central leadership's overarching assessment. Second, the central leadership defines the military's role in the national strategy. Military thinkers and analysts expound on the meaning and implications of this definition, and undoubtedly carry out much of the analysis that informs any concrete formulation of their role, but the central leadership provides the official delineation of this role in Party Congress reports and related documents. Third, the central leadership defines the broadest parameters of strategic concepts and guidance regarding the meaning of "security" and "defense," and even regarding the construction and operation of military power. The logic is that the central leadership has a vested interest in ensuring that the activities of the military (and all other ministries) conform to the spirit and purposes of the national strategy. The military may add detail and expand on the direction provided by the central leadership, but they may not undermine or contradict the national level direction.

National Security Strategy

China's national security strategy exists as a subset and "important part" of its national strategy. The 2011 version of the PLA dictionary defines the national security strategy as the set of *fangzhen* (方针) and tactics (策略) that "guide actions to ensure comprehensive security for the nation's survival and development." [16] China's security strategy outlines at the broadest level how security should be conceived and how it is to be realized to support the national strategy. For years, China did not have a formal national security strategy nor an organization dedicated to formulating one. In earlier years, the Central Committee developed policy ideals for security, such as the "new security concept" (新安全观), and directed relevant ministries and bureaucracies to implement their policies accordingly. However, without a bureaucracy to sustain and manage the process, it is unclear how effectively central leaders held ministries accountable for successful implementation. In 2015, Chinese leaders established a National Security Commission (国家安全委员会). That year, they also issued the first national security strategy, although its contents remain only indirectly known. [17] The central leadership's definition of "security" and provision of key directives may be found in the Party Congress report as well as Defense White Papers. For the military, the national security strategy is important because it defines "security" and provides general guidance on how all ministries should provide security for the nation's development.

Defense Policy

Also falling under the purview of the central leadership's responsibility is the issuance of a defense policy. China's "defense policy" provides the "basic norms governing the conduct of all activities undertaken to meet national defense responsibilities for a prescribed period," and is an "important part of national policy." [18] However, China does not issue a document called a "defense policy," and indeed officials generally characterize the defense policy in a few sentences. Instead, China's defense policy is described in the Party Congress report, Defense White Papers, and other authoritative sources. For the military, defense policy provides a critical mechanism for the central leadership to govern the general spirit of the military's posture, construction, and activities.[19]

Military Strategy

The Central Military Commission provides the more specialized, granular details of the national military strategy, which is often referred to as China's "military strategy." The 2011 PLA dictionary defines "military strategy" as the "set of *fangzhen* and stratagems (策略) that guides the comprehensive war effort."[20] The 2013 *Science of Military Strategy* similarly defines "military strategy" as the "*fangzhen* and stratagems for planning and guiding the overall construction and employment of military power, centered on war."[21] These definitions make clear that the purview of the military strategy lies principally in guiding military modernization and military activities to support national objectives in peace and war. Indeed, the 2013 *Science of Military Strategy* states that "military strategy proceeds from international strategy and the general situation of national development," and thus "must be subservient to and serve the general situation of national development."[22]

China's military strategy consists of a number of directives that blend judgments about the nature of warfare and threat assessments with key strategic concepts and precepts drawn from the party's military thought. Because the military strategy must conform to higher level direction, it often summarizes and incorporates relevant higher-level assessments, strategic objectives, and directives. This is why it is often described as the "concentrated embodiment of the military policy of the party and the state."[23] But the context provided by the recapitulation of higher order directives should not be confused for the military strategy itself. Misunderstandings over which level of authority is responsible for which part of the national military strategy lie at the heart of the most commonly encountered mistakes in analyses of China's national military strategy. The military strategy's principal contribution is to translate the strategic guidance provided by central authorities into a format usable for military planners.

Figure 1: Levels of strategy in the Xi Jinping era

Strategy Level	Key Concept	Primary Sources	Guidance Focus
National strategy	"Chinese dream"	Party Congress report; Central Committee plenary documents	General guidance to all party, government, military on ends, ways, means to realize national revitalization
Security strategy [part of national strategy]	Holistic security concept	Party Congress report; national security strategy	How to achieve domestic and international security environments needed to support above
Defense policy [part of national strategy]	"Defensive" defense policy	Party Congress report; Defense White Paper	How to construct and carry out defense-related activity to support above
Military strategy	"Active Defense"	Defense White Paper; speeches by CMC members	How to construct and operate military forces to support above

Putting it Together: China's National Military Strategy

Both the central and military leadership employ directives, strategic concepts, party theory, and guiding principles to articulate strategic guidance. Each of these forms of political expression serves an important role in providing policy direction, educating, reinforcing party authority, and inculcating loyalty and identification with the party. Directives are the authoritative instructions to carry out a particular policy or action. Directives (指导) differ from orders (命令) in that the former are designed to guide the spirit of policy action, while the latter direct specific action. Strategic concepts (战略思想) are the "basic viewpoints for guiding and planning the overall military situation." [24] These provide the most fundamental principles and ideas that underpin all strategic guidance. Military examples include the concepts of "active defense" and "people's war."

Party theory provides the underlying logic and analysis that links strategic concepts to directives. The party's military guiding theory (党的军事指导理论) is the party's "scientific theory" system regarding the construction and operation of military force. It encompasses all the theoretical contributions of preceding leaders, namely Mao Zedong, Deng Xiaoping, Jiang Zemin, and Hu Jintao.[25] Guiding *fangzhen* (指导方针) provide the framework (纲领) and basic principles (原则) to guide activity regarding a particular topic. The most relevant for the military are "military strategic guiding *fangzhen*," also known as military strategic *fangzhen*.

The particular components of military strategy that are relevant to the study of China's national military strategy consists of the following: 1) strategic and military threat assessment; 2) designation of military strategic role and tasks; 3) guidance on the construction of military force; and 4) guidance on the employment of military force.

Strategic Assessment and Military Threat Assessment

"Strategic assessments" made by China's central leaders describe the overarching trends that both threaten and favor the country's survival and development. The assessments inform the work of every ministry and bureaucracy. The PLA refines the central leadership's strategic assessment by describing in more detail the military nature of threats and relevant trends in warfighting that it observes worldwide. China's military leadership has traditionally designated "main and secondary strategic directions" to orient the military's preparations for conflict. In the past, the term "*strategic direction*" has referred principally to major threats to the nation's survival or unity that the military must orient itself toward. As a result, the designation of "strategic directions" represented the military application of strategic assessments by the top leadership regarding the international situation.

The relationship between strategic assessments by central leaders and the translation by military authorities of the assessment into strategic directions can be seen repeatedly in China's recent history. For example, in the 1950s and 1960s, Mao regarded the United States as China's main strategic threat. Military leaders accordingly defined the "main strategic direction" in terms of possible attack from the "east" (Taiwan and the Pacific Ocean). In the 1960s, Mao saw threats from both the Soviet Union and the capitalist West. The military thus identified the main strategic direction in terms of attack from the "north" and "west" from the Soviets, and from the "east" from the United States. In the 1970s, acrimonious relations led Beijing to label Moscow the main threat, with the military in turn designating the potential for large-scale Soviet invasion from the "north" and "west" as the "main strategic direction".[26] In 1985, Deng Xiaoping declared that China no longer faced a threat of large-scale invasion, and that the main danger stemmed from possible localized conflicts along the borders and including Taiwan. Following this conclusion, the military did not identify a primary enemy as the main strategic direction. Instead it adopted a coastal concept with no specific enemy identified and called for "attaching importance to managing and maneuvering on the high seas and maintaining our maritime rights and interests."[27]

Military Strategic Role and Tasks

While the central leadership outlines the strategic role of the military to support national strategy, the military translates this information into strategic tasks and responsibilities around which it can plan the construction and use of military power. The official conception of these tasks has shifted over time, and since 2004 senior leaders have invoked the term "historic missions of the armed forces in the new period of the new century," often referred to by the shortened term "New Historic Missions" (新历史使命), to describe this role. The NHM concept outline four responsibilities, which call on the PLA to: 1) provide an important guarantee of strength for the party to consolidate its ruling position; 2) provide a strong security guarantee for safeguarding the period of important strategic opportunity for national development; 3) provide a powerful strategic support for safeguarding national interests; and 4) play an important role in safeguarding world peace and promoting common development.[28] The CMC has in turn translated this directive into numerous military tasks (军事任务) that guide the planning of operations and campaigns.

Guidance on Construction of the Force

The "construction of armed forces" (军队建设) is a PLA term of art that includes direction regarding: 1) the development, procurement, and acquisition, of weapons, platforms, and equipment; 2) developments in the command and organization of the military, as well as institutional and personnel reform; and 3) doctrine, training, and education. The central authorities set the tone for the general orientation of the military's construction to ensure conformity with the party's overall agenda. In particular, leaders frequently employ the phrase "base point for preparations for military struggle" to define the fundamental type of conflict for which the military must prepare.

As in the case of threat assessments, the central leadership defines the overall mode of development and modernization which in turn informs the military's approach. In the 1950s and 1960s, for example, the party's revolutionary focus informed the military's egalitarian organization, rank structure, and doctrinal focus. In the 1960s and 1970s, Mao's choice to undertake the Cultural Revolution resulted in a PLA in which radical politics dominated military professionalism. Only when Deng assumed power and directed a national turn toward modernization did the military recover its own focus on modernization. In 1985, the military translated Deng's directives into a focus on creating a modern military capable of prevailing in "localized conflicts." In 1992, following the conclusion of the Gulf War and the lopsided victory of the United States due in part to its high-tech "Revolution in Military Affairs," the PLA refined that directive to preparing a military capable of fighting a "localized war under high-tech conditions." In 2004, the central leadership's decision to pursue a national "scientific development concept" raised the importance of national "informatization" (信息化; broadly, the development and pervasive utilization of information technologies) as a driver of growth.[29] The military, recognizing the importance of these technologies in its own domain, refined guidance on the construction military accordingly by directing the creation of a military capable of "winning localized war under informatized conditions."

"Active Defense" and Guidance on the Use of Military Force

Guidance on how to use military power to achieve the political and strategic goals outlined by central leaders lies at the heart of China's military strategy. Central authorities provide broad guidance to govern the PLA's use of force in service of strategic objectives. This interaction between central and military authority can be seen clearly in this realm of strategic guidance as with the others. During the revolutionary era, the party's political focus on mass mobilization coincided with the central leadership's advocacy of the military tactics of "people's war" that similarly relied on mass mobilization. Similarly, in the 2000s, the central leadership's focus on elevating the role of science and technology to drive economic growth led them to revise the idea of "people's war" to emphasize qualities of "high technology" and educated, skilled personnel rather than the mobilization of poorly educated rural conscripts.

The PLA translates generalized central guidance into a more specialized form featuring an authoritative set of precepts, maxims, and guiding principles informed by key strategic concepts, the most important of which is "active defense." Indeed, China's recent military strategy white paper calls the "strategic concept of active defense" the "essence of the party's military thought." The white paper defines *active defense* as the "unity between strategic defense and operational and tactical offense," encompassing numerous related and subordinate precepts and principles. The 2013 *Science of Military Strategy* explained that the goal of the strategic concept of active defense is to "defend the nation's sovereignty, security, and territorial integrity." Its basic posture is that of "self-defense," which directs the military to "strike back" but does "not preclude preemptive strikes in campaigns and combat."[30] This definition may be contrasted with the view present in the 1998 defense white paper, which defined "active defense" as a "self-defense" posture in which China seeks to "gain mastery by striking only after the enemy has struck." By defining the guiding principle in terms meant to guide the defense of the homeland, the military's conception of active defense of that time faithfully reflected the defense policy of that time.[31]

The Central Military Commission (CMC) codifies general directives based on the broad concept of active defense and its applied meanings as the "military strategic *fangzhen*" of "active defense." Chinese sources consistently describe these guiding principles as a subset of military strategy, frequently describing the military strategic *fangzhen* as principles that apply the strategic concept of "active defense." The military strategic *fangzhen* are thus best understood less as a secret "Rosetta Stone" document that if uncovered would unlock an entirely new understanding of Chinese motives and military actions, and more as an authoritative set of guiding principles that guide the construction and employment of military force in support of national objectives in accordance with the strategic concept of "active defense."

National Military Strategy under Xi Jinping

This chapter argues that each level of strategy recapitulates relevant portions of higher-level strategies for context and authoritative direction. Thus, it is generally more insightful and fruitful to begin study of China's national military strategy by examining the manner that the military receives and develops strategic guidance, i.e., "from top down." One can apply this insight to the study of China's national military strategy under Xi Jinping by first reviewing key relevant concepts. Drawn principally from the national levels of strategy, these ideas provide critical context for understanding the national military strategy. After reviewing the relevant key concepts, the analyst is then better prepared to review the levels of national strategy, security strategy, and defense policy.

Context: Key concepts under Xi

China's leadership continues to orient all national strategic guidance toward the realization of "national rejuvenation," an ideal that has been recast as the "China dream" under Xi Jinping. However, significant changes in concepts related to national security strategy and defense policy have profoundly influenced the country's national military strategy.

While China nominally adheres to a "defensive" policy, the focus has shifted since around 2010 from homeland defense to what may be characterized as a policy of coercive, but "non-violent expansion." Like its predecessors, China's most recent of its biennial Defense White Papers, published in 2015, upholds the "defensive nature" of the country's national defense policy and states that China will "never seek hegemony or expansion." However, it also acknowledges that China's evolving situation has set "new requirements" for the military to help build a "favorable strategic posture" and "guarantee the country's peaceful development." In particular, it highlights the need to better protect the country's "growing strategic interests." To shape the international order, the paper outlines goals of "actively expand[ing] military and security cooperation" and "promot[ing] the establishment of a regional framework for security and cooperation."[32] These directives evoke an ambition to build a stable, peaceful Asian security environment in which China plays a leading role and in which countries lack the ability or motivation to militarily challenge China over its "core" interests.

There are several noteworthy shifts in China's security strategy and defense policy on display here. First, the vision of security has expanded to include virtually all policy domains and to include the open ocean, space, and cyberspace. Second, the intermingling of military and non-military actors and policy concerns has elevated the need for centralized civilian decision-making. Third, the inherent tension with the United States raised by the policy shift has increased the importance of crisis management and deterrence.

Expansion in Security Concept and Domains

The recent adoption of an "overall" or "holistic" security concept exemplifies the expanding scope of the country's security strategy and defense policy. According to the military strategy white paper, the expanded concept combines both domestic and international security; security for the homeland with security for overseas citizens, enterprises, and other interests; and interests related to the nation's survival with those needed for its development. Security now encompasses eleven fields, including not only the political, economic, and military spheres but also territorial, cultural, social, scientific and technological, informational, ecological, financial, and nuclear domains.[33] Moreover, security is required for the interests that have expanded into the open ocean, outer space, and cyberspace.

Increased Need for Centralized Control

This changing view of security has somewhat blurred the lines between civilian and military tasks and actors. To support these broader security requirements, the military must carry out both war and non-war missions. As the military steps up its involvement in non-war activities, non-military assets have become more involved in actions formerly reserved for the military. This can be seen in the maritime domain, where the Chinese Coast Guard was created from disparate maritime agencies in 2014, in part to defend Chinese maritime territory, and has now formed into a paramilitary service. [34] The increasing complexity of security, and of military-civilian coordination, has raised the demand for centralized security-related decision making. The creation of the National Security

Commission and the issuance of a National Security Strategy in 2015 underscore the importance with which Chinese leaders regard the task of calibrating policy to balance competing security objectives and control risk.[35]

Increased Need for Crisis Management and Deterrence

The shift toward a coercive, but non-violent expansion of influence inherently raises tensions with the United States and its allies because China's expansion is premised, to some extent, on the contraction of influence by the United States and its allies. Military officials judge that this has elevated the likelihood of tensions with the United States. Sun Jianguo, PLA Deputy Chief of the General Staff, explained that "without struggle, it will be impossible for the United States to respect our core interests."[36] This, in turn, elevates the importance of finding ways to manage bilateral relations to reduce the risk of conflict, manage crisis, and deter adversaries. In 2013, President Xi Jinping urged the United States to adopt a "new type of great power relationship" (新型大国关系) premised largely on U.S. strategic concessions as a way to reduce the risk of conflict.[37] Chinese willingness to establish rules for use of a military hotline, and to conclude confidence-building measures governing maritime and air-to-air military encounters, similarly reflects an underlying anxiety about the potential for militarized crises.[38] The elevation of the status of China's strategic missile force through the creation of the PLA Rocket Force as a full independent service similarly signals, in part, the growing importance placed on strategic deterrence to influence the response of the United States and its allies to China's coercive, but non-violent expansion of influence.[39]

These discussions provide critical context for understanding how China's central and military leadership approach topics related to national military strategy. The subsequent sections analyze in more detail the national and military elements of the national military strategy as developed in the era of Xi Jinping.

National Element of National Military Strategy under Xi Jinping

It may be tempting to attribute the dramatic changes in China's policies to Xi Jinping's personal preferences, since they have largely coincided with his ascent. But while Xi has undoubtedly played an important role in directing policy, the principal drivers of the policy changes—in many cases, the most significant since the start of reform and opening up—lies with the changing requirements for national development within the shifting domestic and international conditions of the first two decades of the 21st century, labeled as the "period of strategic opportunity" by Chinese authorities as its geopolitical characteristics are seen as being favorable to China. Focused on ensuring the nation's revival as a great power and the continued elevation in the standard of living for the people, Beijing has for some time regarded the second decade of the period of strategic opportunity (which coincides roughly with Xi's ascent) as one that will require a more active, assertive set of policies.[40]

Despite the importance of China's shift toward a defense policy of non-violent expansion, however, its limited, largely opportunistic nature deserves emphasis. Although it accepts coercion as a legitimate means, China's pursuit of nonviolent expansion does not seek to invade and subjugate people in the manner of classic imperialists. Nor has China signaled a desire to contest U.S. global leadership—such an ambition is infeasible in any case. Beijing's aim is to reshape elements of the regional and international order and to expand control over core national interests in the least destabilizing manner possible, while ensuring preparation for contingencies. These new requirements have driven important changes to military strategy and to the military's missions and tasks.

Figure 2: Summary of National Military Strategy during the Xi Jinping Era

Aspect	National Level Guidance	Military Level Guidance
Strategic assessment	International trends, threats to development	Military threat assessment
Strategic roles and missions	PLA's role in national strategy (historic missions)	PLA tasks (diversified tasks)
Construction of the armed forces	Incorporate information technology into modernization	Base point for military struggle: Localized war under informatized conditions
Employment of armed forces	Holistic security concept, defense policy, active defense	Military strategic guidelines of active defense

Under Xi Jinping, the central leadership has issued national level strategic guidance for the following parts of the national military strategy: 1) strategic assessment; 2) military strategic role in national strategy; 3) construction of the armed forces; and 4) employment of armed forces.

Strategic Assessment

The 18th Party Congress report established the overarching strategic assessment to guide the work of the military and all other ministries. It noted perceived international threats to national development, such as that the world remains "far from peaceful" and that threats stem from "increasing hegemonism, power politics, and neo-interventionism;" "local turmoil," and "global issues such as food, energy, resource, and network security." It also noted that in the security domain, China faces "interwoven problems affecting its survival and development as well as traditional and nontraditional threats."

The PLA's Strategic Role in National Strategy

The 18th Party Congress report affirmed that the New Historic Missions continue to define the PLA's role in national strategy. The report stated that the military would "carry out the historic missions of the armed forces to meet the new requirements for national development."

Construction of the Armed Forces

The 18th Party Congress report directed the military to modernize in a manner that incorporates more information technology. It stated, for example, that officials should "intensify efforts to accomplish the dual historic tasks of military mechanization and full informatization, striving to basically complete military mechanization and make major progress in full military informatization by 2020." It stated that military modernization should focus on enabling the military to fight "localized wars under conditions of informatization."

Employment of the Armed Forces

According to the 18th Party Congress report, the central leadership has outlined a holistic concept of defense policy, and designated "active defense" as the key concept to guide the work of the military in carrying out its assigned duties. The report stated, for example, that all officials must "take a holistic approach to our work related to... national defense." It directed the military to "implement the military strategy of active defense," as well as guidance regarding the use of military power in space, the network domain, and ocean domains, as well as in peacetime and other war and non-war conditions.

Military Element of National Military Strategy under Xi Jinping

Developments in national strategy, security strategy, and defense policy provides critical context for understanding China's national military strategy. These developments have shaped the military's contribution to the national military strategy under Xi Jinping, in particular regarding: 1) threat assessments; 2) the military's strategic role and tasks; 3) construction of the armed forces; and 4) the employment of military force.

Threat Assessment

The shift in defense policy toward non-violent expansion has dramatically changed the meaning of "threat." Military leaders now view threats in terms of dangers posed to the country's sustained development and to the realization of national revitalization. The definition of threat in these terms explains the military strategy white paper's otherwise puzzling claim (in light of China's strength and security) that "national security issues facing China encompass far more subjects, extend over a greater range, and cover a longer time span *than any time in the country's history*" [emphasis added]. The main strategic direction should thus be regarded more as the "first among equals" among a broad menu of threats for which the PLA must prepare in the modern era, rather than the near-exclusive driver of military strategy. Although official statements on the issue remain scarce, one may deduce from military writings that the main strategic direction continues to emanate from the maritime regions. An article by one PLA expert in 2009 identified the southeast maritime area as "still the main direction."[41] The threat from this direction stems from potential Taiwan separatism, but also from possible clashes and crises related to maritime disputes, including Vietnam and the Philippines. The expert regarded Japan as a secondary direction, due to the festering dispute over the Senkaku Islands and other issues. Potential intervention by the United States on behalf of its allies also underscores the importance of the maritime direction.

The 2015 military strategy white paper lends support to this interpretation. In its review of threats, the paper principally focuses on dangers emanating from China's maritime direction, namely the U.S. rebalance to Asia, Taiwan, Japan, and disputes with neighbors over "China's maritime rights and interests." The paper also states that preparations for military struggles now "highlight maritime military struggle" in particular. Underscoring this point, it prioritizes the development of a "modern maritime military force structure" capable of "safeguarding" China's "national sovereignty and maritime rights and interests."[42] But the maritime region is not the only source of threats. Instability in the western regions poses the danger of separatism and terrorism. The diverse array of threats to China's economic interests abroad, including international instability, piracy, natural disasters, and international terrorism, also require the military to ready potential responses. Additional threats are apparent in the cyber and space domains. China thus faces "various threats and challenges in *all* its strategic directions and security domains," as the 2015 defense white paper noted.

Missions and Tasks

The military's principal missions aim to address this broad array of threats. The military strategy white paper affirms that the PLA's strategic role remains defined by the New Historic Missions announced by Hu Jintao. To carry out this strategic role, military authorities have elaborated a number of strategic tasks. The 2015 military strategy white paper names eight such tasks, including: (1) "safeguarding China's security and interests in new domains," which includes the task of protecting interests in the open oceans as well as in cyber and outer space; (2) "safeguarding the security of China's overseas interests," which directs the military to protect assets that may be in other countries; (3) "participating in regional and international security cooperation and maintain regional and world peace," which directs participation in multi-lateral efforts to promote international stability; and (4) "performing such tasks as emergency rescue and disaster relief, rights and interests protection, guard duties, and support for national and economic development," which requires the military to prepare for humanitarian missions both domestic and foreign; (5) "dealing with a wide range of emergencies and military threats and effectively safeguard the sovereignty and security of China's territorial land, air, and sea"; (6) "resolutely safeguarding the unification of the motherland"; (7) "maintaining strategic deterrence and carry out nuclear counterattack"; and (8) "strengthening efforts in operations against infiltration, separatism, and terrorism to maintain political security and social stability."

Guidance on the Construction of Military Forces

Military authorities revised the "base point for military struggle" in 2004 to focus on "local war under conditions of informatization" as the most likely type of conflict. Modernization efforts have accordingly emphasized qualities of power projection, rapid movement of troops, employment of networks of weapons and sensors, and joint operations. The 2015 white paper briefly describes changes expected of the services accordingly. It states that the army will "reorient from theater defense to trans-theater mobility" and "elevate its capabilities for precise, multi-dimensional, trans-theater, multi-function, and sustainable ops." The PLA Navy will "shift its focus from offshore waters defense to the combination of offshore waters defense and 'distant sea protection' and build a combined, multi-function, and efficient maritime combat structure." The PLA Air Force will shift from "territorial air defense to both defense and offensive operations, and build an air-space defense force structure that can meet the requirements for informatized operations." The PLA's strategic missile force will strengthen its capabilities for strategic deterrence and nuclear counterattack as well as medium and long-range conventional precision strikes. [43] More recently, authorities announced the elevation of the strategic missile force, now designated the "Rocket Force," to a status coequal to that of the other services. Authorities also announced the formation of a "Strategic Support Force" responsible for managing defense assets in space and cyberspace, reflecting China's growing emphasis on securing its interests in those domains and the PLA's judgment that the struggle for information dominance will be central in future wars.[44]

Guidance on the Employment of Military Force

The 2015 military strategy white paper acknowledges that the "national security and development strategies" and new "tasks" of the military have raised requirements to "enrich" the concept of active defense and "enhance" the military strategic guidelines accordingly.

Because the principal reason for the issuance of military strategic guiding principles lies in ensuring that the military operates in a manner that directly supports the central leadership's strategic objectives, one should expect changes in the guidelines to closely mirror the spirit and intent of the shift toward "non-violent expansion" in the national defense policy. The military strategy white paper validates this expectation. Changes in military guidance emphasize qualities of strategic foresight, coordination with non-military efforts to enhance security, and the military's role in shaping the peacetime international system, crisis management, deterrence, and expeditionary activity.

The white paper explains that the military strategic *fangzhen* highlight "strategic vision" and direct the military to be "more forward looking." The *fangzhen* underscore the importance of "subordination to and service of national strategic objectives," directing the military to "closely coordinate political, military, economic, and diplomatic work." Reflecting the shifting focus of military activity, guidance "balances" traditional precepts with new ones designed to support non-violent expansion. The military strategy white paper listed *fangzhen* that "balances war preparation and war prevention, stability maintenance and rights protection, warfighting and deterrence, operations in wartime and the employment of military force in peacetime." Underscoring the importance of expeditionary activity, it directs the military to "strengthen international security cooperation in areas crucially related to China's overseas interests to ensure the security of its interests" and calls on the military to "deal with threats" in the network and space domains "in a manner that maintains the common security of the world."[45]

Conclusion

The idea that China has a unitary "national military strategy" may be regarded in some ways as an artifice that awkwardly imposes a Western construct on China's Leninist politics. Yet this idea is not without merit. Identifying the functional equivalent of a national military strategy offers the analyst the potential to gain authoritative insight into Beijing's intentions regarding the construction and employment of military power. Moreover, as an advanced industrial state, the expectation that China needs some equivalent to the functions of a national military strategy is hardly unreasonable.

In fact, analysis of publicly available documents suggests that China does have a functional equivalent, but accessing the relevant information requires a study of both national level and military strategic guidance and familiarity with key features of China's political system. This approach carries an obvious drawback. The sheer volume of official documents and explanatory analysis, the complexity of China's political system, and the difficulties of the political language of a nominally Marxist party-army (to say nothing of the added complexity of the Chinese language and unique culture) imposes a formidable obstacle.

It is understandable why Western analysts may seek a single, authoritative presentation of China's national military strategy, as it would provide a simple clarity on these matters. But the temptation should be resisted. The PLA's identity as a party army, and the division of responsibility between central and military authorities, makes any such simplistic characterization invariably problematic. In China, the formulation of national military strategy is split between the work of central and military leaders, with the former controlling the core content and the latter providing more detailed and specialized guidance. China also expresses its national military strategy through a polymorphous and often bewildering language of strategic concepts, socialist theory, directives, and guiding principles. No single concept, directive, or guiding principle accurately captures the sum of Chinese national military strategy.

The PLA may characterize its "military strategy" or "military strategic guidance" as the "concentrated expression of the military policy of the party and state." But it is worth bearing in mind that PLA officers who read these shorthand descriptions undergo considerable training in the logic and meaning of strategic guidance outlined in documents and writings issued by central authorities. Thus, Chinese documents on military strategy frequently assume considerable familiarity with the basics of the Leninist system and of many aspects of central strategic guidance. Western readers who do not familiarize themselves with this same material put themselves at risk of taking information out of context and misinterpreting the significance of particular concepts or directives. The confusion over the meaning and significance of the military strategic *fangzhen* illustrates this point.

The best way to understand the PLA's national military strategy, in short, is to learn it the way the Chinese military officer does: through the study of central strategic guidance complemented by the study of the military's more specialized, detailed guidance. The process can be shortened somewhat by familiarizing themselves with the most salient aspects of guidance at both levels. However, there should be no illusions; considerable labor is required for analysts to understand China's distinct and unique approach to articulating national military strategy. Considering the significance of the topic, especially amid signs of increasing military tensions between China and the United States and its allies, the investment of the necessary labor to gain an accurate grasp of Beijing's perspective seems one well worth making.

NOTES

[1] Alan G. Stolberg, "How Nations Craft National Security Strategies," *SSI*, October 2012, p. 23.

[2] David Finkelstein, "China's National Military Strategy," *The People's Liberation Army in the Information Age*, James Mulvenon and Richard Yang (ed.), RAND Corporation: Santa Monica, CA (1999), pp. 99–145.

[3] Taylor Fravel, "The Evolution of China's Military Strategy: Comparing the 1987 and 1999 Editions of *Zhanluexue*," *China's Revolution in Doctrinal Affairs: Emerging Trends in the Operational Art of the Chinese People's Liberation Army*, James Mulvenon and David Finkelstein (ed.), CNA Corp.: Alexandria, VA (2005), pp. 79–99.

[4] David M. Finkelstein, "China's National Military Strategy: An Overview of the 'Military Strategic Guidelines'," in Andrew Scobell and Roy Kamphausen, eds., *Right Sizing the People's Liberation Army: Exploring the Contours of China's Military*, (Carlisle, PA: Army War College Press, 2007), pp. 69–140.

[5] Finkelstein (2007), p. 82.

[6] Finkelstein (2007), p. 86.

[7] Finkelstein (2007), p. 130.

[8] Department of Defense, "Annual Report to Congress: Military Power of the People's Republic of China," 2009., http://www.defense.gov/Portals/1/Documents/pubs/China_Military_Power_Report_2009.pdf

[9] Department of Defense, "Annual Report to Congress: Military and Security Developments Involving the People's Republic of China 2012," May, 2012., http://www.defense.gov/Portals/1/Documents/pubs/2012_CMPR_Final.pdf

[10] Taylor Fravel, "China's New Military Strategy: 'Winning Informationized Local Wars,'" *China Brief*, June 23, 2015., https://jamestown.org/program/chinas-new-military-strategy-winning-informationized-local-wars/

[11] Department of Defense (2009).

[12] Finkelstein (2007), p. 89.

[13] Timothy R. Heath, "Why PLA Watchers Keep Missing Changes to China's Military Strategy," *American Intelligence Journal*, October 2009.

[14] "Comrade Deng Xiaoping's 'Hide your Capabilities, Bide Your Time' Concept: Was it Expediency?," *People's Daily* [人民日报], April 7, 2010.

[15] Timothy R. Heath, "What Does China Want? Discerning the PRC's National Strategy," *Asian Security*, March 2012, pp. 54–72.

[16] *Military Dictionary* [军语], PLA Press, 2011, p. 51.

[17] Xinhua, "China Warns of Unprecedented National Security Challenges," January 23, 2015, http://news.xinhuanet.com/english/china/2015-01/23/c_133942451.htm.

[18] *Military Dictionary* [军语], PLA Press, 2011, p. 18.

[19] Chen Zhou, "China's National Defense Policy," *China Military Science* [中国军事科学], September 2009.

[20] *Military Dictionary* [军语], PLA Press, 2011, p. 50.

[21] Sun Zhaoli et al., *Science of Military Strategy* [战略学], (Beijing: Academy of Military Sciences Press, 2013), p. 3.

[22] Sun Zhaoli, p. 10.

[23] Luo Zhen, "An Interpretation of the New National Defense White Paper: Interview with Chen Zhou," *PLA Daily*, May 27, 2015, p. 5.

[24] Science of Military Strategy (战略学), (Beijing: National Defense University Press, 1999), p. 61.

[25] Military Dictionary, p. 3.

[26] Sun Zhaoli, pp. 44–46.

[27] David M. Finkelstein, "China's National Military Strategy: An Overview of the 'Military Strategic Guidelines,'" in Andrew Scobell and Roy Kamphausen, eds., *Right Sizing the People's Liberation Army: Exploring the Contours of China's Military*, Carlisle, Penn.: U.S. Army War College, 2007, pp. 69–140.

[28] "Full Text of the 17th Party Congress report," Xinhua, October 24, 2007.

[29] For more information, see Joe McReynolds and James Mulvenon, "The Role of Informatization in the People's Liberation Army under Hu Jintao," in *Assessing the People's Liberation Army in the Hu Jintao Era*, Roy Kamphausen, et al, eds., (Carlisle, PA: Army War College Press, April 2014).

[30] Sun Zhaoli, p. 47.

[31] "Full Text of Defense White Paper," Xinhua, July 27, 1998.

[32] "Full Text: China's Military Strategy," *Xinhua*, May 26, 2015.

[33] "Xi Jinping Speaks at Politburo Study Session on Security," Xinhua, April 15, 2014.

[34] Ryan Martinson, "The Militarization of China's Coast Guard," *The Diplomat*, November 21, 2014.

[35] Zhao Kejin, "China's National Security Commission," Carnegie-Tsinghua Center for Global Policy, July 14, 2015. As of January 13, 2016: http://carnegietsinghua.org/2015/07/09/china-s-national-security-commission/id7i

[36] Sun Jianguo, *Seeking Truth* [求实], March 1, 2015. As of January 13, 2016, http://www.qstheory.cn/dukan/qs/2015-02/28/c_1114428331.htm

[37] Jane Perlez, "China's 'New Type' of Ties Fails to Persuade Obama," *New York Times*, November 9, 2014.

[38] Phil Stewart, "U.S., China Agree on Rules for Air-to-Air Military Encounters," *Reuters*, September 25, 2015.

[39] Ministry of National Defense of the People's Republic of China, "China Establishes Rocket Force and Strategic Support Force," January 1, 2016, http://eng.mod.gov.cn/ArmedForces/second.htm.

[40] Timothy Heath, "Xi's Bold Foreign Policy Agenda: Beijing's Pursuit of Global Influence and the Growing Risk of Sino-U.S. Rivalry," *China Brief*, March 19, 2015. https://jamestown.org/program/xis-bold-foreign-policy-agenda-beijings-pursuit-of-global-influence-and-the-growing-risk-of-sino-u-s-rivalry/.

[41] Fan Zhenjiang, "A Study of Strategic Military Guidance in the New Period of the New Century," *China Military Science*, March 2009, pp. 36–44.

[42] China's Military Strategy [中国的军事战略] State Council Information Office [中华人民共和国国务院新闻办公室], May 29, 2015. http://www.scio.gov.cn/zfbps/gfbps/Document/1435341/1435341.htm.

[43] Ibid.

[44] Ministry of National Defense of the People's Republic of China, "China Establishes Rocket Force and Strategic Support Force," January 1, 2016.

[45] "Full Text: China's Military Strategy," *Xinhua*, May 26, 2015.

Chapter 2: China's Changing Approach to Military Strategy: The Science of Military Strategy from 2001 and 2013

M. Taylor Fravel[1]

In November 2015, Xi Jinping announced a series of sweeping and unprecedented organizational reforms designed to improve the PLA's military effectiveness. These reforms constitute the most significant restructuring of the People's Liberation Army (PLA) since the general staff system and military region structure were adopted in the early 1950s.[2] The broad scope of the reforms highlights China's commitment to developing a modern and capable military that matches its status as one of the largest economies in the world. The reforms also underscore the importance of understanding China's approach to military strategy, which may help illuminate how a restructured PLA will be employed. Specifically, the reforms beg questions about the content of China's military strategy. What wars might China fight? How would it fight them? What capabilities do Chinese strategists believe are needed to win such wars?

Definitive answers to questions about China's military strategy are hard to find, especially when key Chinese-language sources on the topic are not readily available in English. Although China issues biannual defense white papers, and Chinese leaders give speeches that sometimes address questions of military strategy, important military topics are discussed in only a broad and general way. In Chinese-language sources, however, PLA officers and scholars publish a wide range of opinions on

military affairs, but generally they speak only for themselves and
will often disagree strongly with one another on questions of
strategy. When individuals within these debates are selectively
translated into English, they can be mistakenly viewed as
representing an authoritative view of the PLA. The
quintessential example comes from a 1999 book, *Unrestricted
Warfare*.[3] Despite being authored by two senior colonels from
the PLA Air Force who specialized in political work and not
strategic analysis, it was translated into English with the subtitle
"China's Master Plan to Destroy America," and was erroneously
understood as such by many within the Western media and
policymaking communities. (The actual subtitle of the Chinese
original was "Two Air Force Senior Colonels on Scenarios for
War and the Operational Art in an Era of Globalization.")

Within this context, the 2013 publication of the *Science of
Military Strategy* is an essential source for understanding how
China's thinking about military strategy is changing.[4] Replacing
an edition published twelve years earlier, the 2013 edition of the
Science of Military Strategy reveals how some of the PLA's top
strategists assess China's security environment, how military
force should be used to secure China's interests, and what kinds
of military capabilities the PLA should develop in the future.
Analyzing and disseminating the content of the this edition of
the *Science of Military Strategy* is important for deepening
understanding of China's approach to military strategy.

To examine how China's approach to military strategy is
changing, this chapter compares the 2013 edition of the *Science
of Military Strategy* with the 2001 edition. The chapter reaches
two conclusions. First, the 2013 edition represents an evolution
of China's approach to thinking about military strategy. It does

not contain a description of a revolutionary new approach to China's military strategy. Instead, it examines changes in China's security environment through traditional concepts that have underpinned the PLA's approach to strategy, such as "active defense," by modifying or adjusting these ideas based on new circumstances. Second, a main theme throughout the text is how new and expanding interests overseas, along with worldwide advances in military technology and the posture of potential adversaries, are expanding the battlespace in which the PLA will need to operate and the importance of greater strategic depth. Thus, much of the book can be interpreted as examining how the PLA should respond to these new conditions based on its traditional approach to strategy.

This chapter first reviews how to read or interpret books on military strategy published as part of the PLA's professional military literature. Importantly, the 2013 edition of the *Science of Military Strategy* does not contain China's official military strategy or its military strategic guidelines (军事战略方针), nor does it contain a detailed discussion of the PLA's current operational doctrine. Instead, it conveys the views of strategists at the Academy of Military Science (军事科学研究院, or AMS), an organization that houses some of the PLA's most important military thinkers, some of whom who play a much more direct role in the development of China's military strategy than their counterparts do in Western military educational institutions. The chapter then examines the key differences between the 2001 and 2013 editions of the *Science of Military Strategy*. Overall, the 2013 edition is more practical and applied (and thus less theoretical and conceptual) than the 2001 edition, with a heavy emphasis on the "system of military power with Chinese characteristics" and key capabilities that China needs to develop in the coming decades to defend its territory and interests. The chapter then examines new concepts introduced in the 2013 edition that were absent or downplayed in the 2001 edition, which are linked to the expansion of the battlespace and need for greater strategic depth. These concepts are forward defense, strategic space, effective control, and strategic posture. The conclusion discusses ways in which future research using the 2013 edition can help to deepen understanding of China's approach to military strategy.

How to Read Chinese Writings on Military Strategy

The 2013 edition of the *Science of Military Strategy* represents the apex of the PLA's professional military literature on the study of war. China's approach to military science divides the study of war into the three levels of strategy, campaigns, and tactics. Although not widely used in Western militaries, the phrase "science of strategy" is a term of art within the PLA.[5] Publications with the title "science of strategy" examine either overall military strategy or strategy for the services.[6] The PLA's own glossary of military terms defines the science of strategy as "the discipline of studying the overall situation and rules of war, national defense, and army building."[7] As a result, the purpose of such books is to improve understanding of the characteristics of war at any point time and the associated implications for how such wars should be prevented or fought, also known as "strategic guidance" (战略指导).

To date, research institutes associated with the PLA have published five books with the same title of *Science of Military Strategy*. The Academy of Military Sciences (AMS) has published three editions of the *Science of Military Strategy*, in

1987, 2001 and 2013.[8] The Deputy Commandant of AMS led the drafting of the 1987 volume, while the AMS Department of Military Strategy Studies authored the 2001 and 2013 editions.[9] AMS has also published two textbooks on the science of military strategy, in 2001 and 2013, whose content closely resembles the 2001 and 2013 editions. The PLA's National Defense University (国防大学, or NDU) has separately published two editions of the *Science of Military Strategy*, in 1999 and 2015.[10] The Deputy Commandant of the PLA's NDU supervised the drafting of both volumes, with specific chapters authored by individual scholars. In addition, the PLA's NDU has published closely related books on military strategy, such as the 2007 *Theory of Military Strategy*.[11] The AMS editions are authoritative because they play a direct role in the formulation of the PLA's strategy and operational doctrine, while the NDU editions are authoritative because they are edited by one of the organization's top two leaders. Only one edition of these books has been translated into English. In 2005, AMS published an English translation of its 2001 edition, which is one reason why this edition is most widely known and widely used by those outside China.

The primary audience for these books are officers in the PLA, not foreign observers interested in China's military affairs. The books are often used in graduate courses at both AMS and NDU, though the edition can vary by the institution and by the instructor. The purpose of assigning these books is to teach officers in the PLA how to think about strategy and strategic issues. In this way, such books can indirectly influence the formulation of China's military strategy.

Although these volumes examine military strategy, they do not contain China's military strategic guidelines, China's official military strategy, or the PLA's military doctrine more broadly. The military strategic guidelines （军事战略方针） are introduced in internal speeches by China's top party or military leaders, usually at an enlarged meeting of the Central Military Commission. Nine of these guidelines have been issued since 1949 and they most closely approximate China's national military strategy.[12] The publication of the AMS editions of the *Science of Military Strategy*, however, significantly lags behind the introduction of new strategic guidelines. The 2001 edition, for example, was published eight years after the 1993 guidelines, while the 2013 edition was published nine years after the adjustment of the strategic guidelines in 2004. High-level authoritative statements of China's military strategy based on the guidelines are usually contained in the biannual white papers on national defense. In fact, the 2015 white paper focused extensively on military strategy.[13] Likewise, in some contexts, a recent volume on national defense and military modernization published in a series of training materials for party cadres may come closer to offering an authoritative statement on specific aspects of current military strategy than recent editions of the *Science of Military Strategy*.[14] Finally, China does not have a concept of military doctrine directly analogous to that used by Western militaries, but what Western observers might view as doctrine is codified in documents such as campaign or operational outlines (战役作战纲要) or combat regulations (作战条令). These documents, which outline how campaigns or specific operations should be conducted, are classified as secret and not openly circulated.

Even though the various editions of the *Science of Military Strategy* do not reflect China's official military strategy, military strategic guidelines, or military doctrine, they do highlight the views of many of the PLA's leading strategists, some of whom are involved in the formulation of strategy or operational doctrine. In the case of the 2013 edition of the *Science of Military Strategy*, it was authored collectively by the Department of Military Strategy at AMS. AMS is one of the two most important research institutes in the PLA and reports directly to the Central Military Commission (CMC). Historically, this department has played an important role in assessments of China's security environment and especially China's assessment of the "shape" or "form" of war (战争形态) at any point in time. Lead by Major General Shou Xiaosong (寿晓松), the writing team for the 2013 edition included thirty-five individuals. Major General Shou joined the PLA in 1969, serving in the former Lanzhou Military Region's 61st Division before moving to AMS in 1981.[15] Although the strategy department does not speak or write on behalf of the PLA as an institution, their views are quite influential within the PLA and should be taken seriously by outsider observers seeking to better understand China's approach to military strategy. Books like the 2013 edition of the *Science of Military Strategy* are thus informative and illuminating but not completely authoritative or definitive statements of official strategy such as those contained in classified documents.[16]

A final point to note is the timing of the drafting process for the 2013 edition. Although published in December 2013, more than a year into Xi Jinping's leadership of the Chinese Communist Party (CCP), the concepts and formulations (提法) in the volume reflect mostly those developed in the Hu Jintao era. The decision to draft a new edition was made in 2010 and the actual drafting occurred in 2011 and 2012. In December 2012, a meeting held to review the draft that resulted in several changes

and the AMS leadership finally approved the final draft in April
2013.[17] Although one can find references to Xi Jinping's formula
of a "strong army," the text should not be viewed as representing
Xi's own thoughts or influence on military affairs and strategy.
Instead, it reflects the culmination of developments in PLA
thinking about strategy during the period of Hu Jintao's
leadership of the CCP.[18]

Key Differences between the 2001 and 2013 Editions

Although this chapter emphasizes the differences between the
2001 and 2013 editions of the *Science of Military Strategy*, an
important similarity must be emphasized at the outset that
underscores the PLA's evolutionary approach to thinking about
military strategy. This similarity is the shared embrace of
China's foundational strategic concept of "active defense" (积极
防御). The concept of active defense in Chinese strategic
thought can be traced back to the 1930s and has been
incorporated into each military strategic guideline since 1949.[19]
The essence of active defense is that China adopts a strategically
defensive posture, in which China will not "fire the first shot"
but will use offensive actions to achieve defensive goals. Other
important elements of active defense include seeking to deter
war, if possible, and mobilizing national support under the idea
of "People's War" (人民战争).[20]

The authors of the 2013 edition make clear that active defense
remains the foundation for thinking about China's military
strategy. The book describes active defense as "the overall
master guide for planning and guiding the development and use
of armed forces with war as the core."[21] The book then identifies
several components of the idea's "basic spirit," the most

important of which is "adhering to the position of self-defense and upholding striking after the enemy has struck" (严守自卫立场, 坚持后发制人). The book then invokes Mao's statement that "We will not attack unless we are attacked; if we are attacked, we will certainly counterattack." Other components highlighted by the book include combining strategic defense with offense at the tactical and operational levels, preventing or containing war if possible, and the role of People's War.[22]

The shared embrace of active defense establishes the context for examining the differences between the 2001 and 2013 editions, including the definition of military strategy, emphasis on force development, descriptions of future wars, emphasis on functional domains and its prescriptive focus. These differences can be summarized as 1) a broader definition of military strategy, 2) a much more practical and applied focus, 3) a shift in the military conflicts China will face, 4) the role of the functional domains of nuclear, space, and cyber, 5) a forward-looking perspective and emphasis on advocacy, and 6) challenging the dominance of the ground forces.

The first difference between the two books is in their definition of military strategy itself. The 2001 edition defined strategy narrowly as "planning and guiding the 'overall situation of war.'"[23] The 2013 edition, however, contains a much broader definition of military strategy as the "overall planning and guidance for the development and employment of armed forces, which take war as the core."[24] This broader definition of strategy is also somewhat ironic, as it mirrors the definition from the NDU's 1999 edition that scholars from AMS criticized at the time as being overly broad and not focused enough on the essence of military strategy or how to fight wars.[25]

The 2013 edition's broader definition of strategy carries several implications. First, it expands the scope of strategy beyond a narrower focus on only how to wage war. Instead, it addresses strategic planning and guidance for military forces in peacetime, including deterrence actions, crisis management and control, and non-war actions, such as peacekeeping and disaster relief. In this way, the definition of strategy in the 2013 edition reflects the non-war goals for developing and employing military forces, especially those that were raised as part of the PLA's "New Historic Missions" (新历史使命) in the Hu Jintao era.[26] In particular, the 2013 edition identifies deterrence actions and non-war military actions as two of the three "basic methods of using military power" along with actual warfighting. In other words, the 2013 edition identifies non-combat uses of military power as equal to warfighting. Second, it focuses more explicitly on force development (建 设), examining the kinds of capabilities that the PLA should have in the future and how these forces should be organized. The 2001 edition did not address force development, while the 2013 edition includes one chapter on how to develop a "military power system" (军事力 量 体 系) and another chapter that examines the force development goals for each of the services.

A second difference is the thematic orientation. Although the 2001 edition had a strong theoretical focus, the 2013 edition largely ignores questions of how to conceptualize strategy and is much more practical and applied. As noted in its preface, the 2013 edition "does not rigidly adhere to the style and content of the two previous editions of the Science of Military Strategy and does not think grandiosely or attend to every aspect."[27] Instead, the goal of the new edition is to "grasp firmly the major strategic issues of our military's development and employment at the new stage of the new century."[28] Later, the preface notes that the book "insists on combining theory and practice so that it has strategic height, theoretical depth and *strong practical focus* (强烈的现实针对性), and can theoretically explain and answer the major issues for the strategic guidance of our army under the new situation" [emphasis added].[29]

One consequence of this difference in orientation is that analysts must be somewhat cautious about automatically interpreting any particular omission of content from the 2001 edition in the 2013 edition as reflecting a change in Chinese thinking. In recent years, for example, each edition of China's biannual defense white paper has adopted a specific thematic emphasis, which resulted in some outside observers incorrectly speculating at the time that policies going unmentioned in a given edition (such as China's "no first use" nuclear policy) were perhaps being abandoned. When analyzing successive editions of important PLA texts, an absence of evidence is not necessarily evidence of absence.

The length and organization of the two volumes reflects the practical orientation of the 2013 edition. The 2013 edition is about forty percent shorter in length than the 2001 edition. The 2001 edition endeavored to produce a detailed theoretical framework for conceptualizing all the dimensions of military strategy, while the 2013 edition avoids such a comprehensive examination and instead stresses the nature of the threats and wars that China will face, the operations and actions that should be conducted in response to those threats, and the force development required to enable those actions. Reflecting these differences, the 2001 edition contained chapters on strategic

decision-making, war preparations, war control, strategic
deterrence, principles for strategic actions, strategic offense,
strategic defense, strategic maneuver, strategic air raids and
counter-air raids, strategic information operations, and
strategic support. By contrast, the 2013 edition lacks chapters
that cover these topics, with the sole exception of a chapter on
strategic guidance for military deterrence actions.

Likewise, the two editions differ in their level of detail regarding
the "form of warfare" (战争形态). The 2001 edition contains
three chapters to the subject, reviewing the characteristics of
high-tech local wars. The 2013 edition, however, devotes only
part of one chapter to these same issues under the updated
conceptual framework of "informatized" local wars.[30] The 2013
edition also examines topics not covered or not covered in detail
in the 2001 edition, including the functional domains of nuclear,
space and cyber, strategy for the services and theaters of
operation (战区) as well as new concepts discussed later in this
chapter.

A third difference is how the 2013 edition describes the future
wars that China may face. To start, the portrayal of China's
security environment in the 2013 edition can only described as
dim, hostile, and basically zero-sum. In particular, the book
identifies five challenges to China's peaceful development. The
first is that "Western nations lead by the United States carrying
out strategic encirclement against our country," listing
everything from U.S. efforts to integrate China into the existing
(U.S.-led) international order to the rebalance and Air-Sea
Battle as policies that treat China as America's main adversary.[31]
Another threat is "increasing resistance to [China's] expanding
national interests,"[32] with the authors arguing that Western

monopolies control the majority of the world's natural resources and that the United States controls the world's major strategic channels (通道). Likewise, deep sea, polar, outer space and cyber areas where China has growing interests are described as having been seized decisively by other great powers, constricting the expansion of China's interests. [33] Other challenges include "increasing security risks and dangers" in China's periphery, obstacles to Taiwan's unification, and growing domestic instability. In addition, the 2013 edition notably contains numerous direct or implied references to the United States as China's chief adversary (对手), while similar references were much less common in the 2001 edition.

The 2001 edition only briefly describes the specific kinds of wars that China might face in the future. Specifically, it refers to the possibility of a local war of invasion and a war over Taiwan's unification. By contrast, the 2013 edition outlines four kinds of potential conflicts, including not only a large-scale invasion of China or a war over Taiwan, but also conflicts over disputed territories or instability in neighboring states along with non-war actions such as counter-terrorism or sea-lane protection. In addition, the book offers an overall judgment about the key features of China's more complicated security environment. The book stresses the importance of the eastern and maritime directions, the role of new functional domains such as space and the electromagnetic spectrum, and the possibility of operations beyond China's borders over the traditional western and land directions and in traditional domains. Likewise, given ongoing disputes in the South and East China Seas, the book assesses that the most likely kind of war for China is "a limited military conflict in the maritime domain," while the most important war to prepare to wage "is a relatively larger and high intensity local war under nuclear conditions in the maritime direction."[34] This characterization of China's future war preparation goals significantly elevates the importance of the maritime domain when compared with the 2001 edition, and reflects the PLA's shifting budgetary and force development priorities over that time period.

A fourth difference is the emphasis in 2013 edition on the functional domains of nuclear, space, and computer networks. Nuclear likely received greater attention in the 2013 edition because China has become much more open in relative terms to discussing nuclear issues, including the official discussions of China's nuclear policy and strategy in the white papers as well as publications by individual Chinese scholars, both military and civilian.[35] The space and network domains, however, were not nearly as prominent as strategic concerns when the 2001 edition was being drafted and were also areas where China at the time lacked the sort of substantial military capabilities that it possessed in the nuclear domain. The 2013 edition emphasizes how modern war is now "five dimensional" (五维一体), characterized by contests for supremacy in the ground, sea, air, space, and information domains, with the characteristics of these domains and the interconnections among them carrying major implications for force structure as well as command and control.

A fifth difference is that the 2013 *Science of Military Strategy* is much more forward-looking than the 2001 edition. The 2013 edition contains many sections where the book is clearly making suggestions and offering the collective advice of AMS's military strategy department regarding China's future military strategy. For this reason, the 2013 edition is fascinating to read and offers much clearer insights into how the PLA's leading strategic thinkers envision the relationship between ways, means, and ends. Yet for the same reason, the 2013 cannot be viewed as representing China's current military strategy, though some of the recommendations may be adopted as China adjusts its strategy in the future. Likewise, as the book was drafted by members of the PLA and recommends many changes that all involve enhancing the PLA's capabilities, it unsurprisingly helps the PLA to advocate for continued high rates of increases in China's military budget despite an overall slowdown in the civilian economy.

A final difference is how much the content of the 2013 edition challenged the existing organizational structure of the PLA at the time it was written. The volume attacks many of the traditional sacred cows of the PLA, starting with the dominance of the ground forces and all the institutional features that have followed from ground force dominance, such as the four general departments and the military region structure and the primacy of the ground forces in what are ostensibly joint command structures. The book criticizes "'big army' thinking" ('大陆军' 概念), the focus on defending homeland territory, the treatment of strategic directions and theaters of operation (战区) as independent or autonomous spheres or areas, and other features of the PLA that are associated with the long-standing dominance of the army. Likewise, as mentioned earlier, the book stresses the importance of new domains in conventional warfighting, calling for a more equal focus on the ground, air, sea, space and cyber domains.

New Strategic Concepts

Although other chapters of this book explore the content of the *Science of Military Strategy* within specific domains and subject-matter areas in greater depth, several new high-level strategic concepts are introduced in the 2013 edition that provide important context for more specific analysis. These concepts are forward defense, strategic space, effective control, and strategic posture.

Forward Defense

Perhaps one of the most important concepts introduced in the 2013 edition is "forward defense" (前沿防卫) or expanding the battlespace beyond China's borders to increase China's strategic depth.[36] The concept is introduced as part of an effort to redefine the foundational concept of China's military strategy, "active defense" (积极防御). The book notes that the content of China's active defense strategy has been adjusted several times in the past, but always as a part of "a defensive strategy for national territory" or a strategy that envisioned fighting within Chinese territory or on its borders but not beyond them. By contrast, the 2013 edition states that "in terms of content, [our] military strategy must breakthrough simplistic traditional strategic thinking of guarding borders and defending territory, and actively and reliably realize the enlargement of the defense of national territory to forward defense."[37] Later, the volume urges its readers that "we strategically are obliged (有必要) to establish forward defense as guiding thought" because of the need to "support the omni-directional expansion of national interests and win future wars [we] might face."[38] If the 2001 edition envisioned China's borders and coasts as the strategic "first line" (一线) or front line in a war, the concept of "forward defense" in the 2013 edition calls for pushing the first line away from China's borders and coasts to ensure that combat occurs beyond China's homeland territory, not on or within it. In this way, China's borders and coasts are now viewed as interior lines in a conflict, not exterior ones.

The emphasis on forward defense reflects several changes in China's approach to strategic questions over the past decade. The first is the expansion or enlargement (拓展) of China's national interests. Although China's interests have expanded peacefully, the volume portrays them as facing resistance from the West, thus resulting in serious threats to China's interests beyond its borders cannot be eliminated. As the book observes, "our country's national interests already go beyond the traditional scope of national territory, territorial waters, and territorial airspace, and continuously spread toward the periphery and the world in a continuous extension to maritime, outer space, and electromagnetic space."[39] As a result, the book highlights the importance of "struggle and control" in interstate conflict over the maritime, polar, space, and network domain global commons.

The second change is the assessment that the global trend toward informatized long-range combat systems requires China to expand the space for defense further from its shores to ensure sufficient strategic depth. Although China's risk of being invaded is low, the book observes that "the main way of threat has already changed from a traditional land invasion to space, air-sea and network-air integrated non-contact strikes and our in-depth national territory is under the cover of the enemy's medium and long range fire power."[40] In a thinly veiled

reference the United States, the volume describes a "strong
adversary" with "comprehensive distant war superiority in the
maritime direction" that can strike China without itself being
attacked. As a result, "the difficulty of using 'our land to defend
our land' and 'using the near seas to defend the near seas' has
greatly increased, and we are even perhaps unable to ensure
victory. Therefore, [we] must consider expanding the scope [of
warfare] for the implementation of outwardly oriented
defensive operations."[41] In the past, the main threats to Chinese
interests overlapped with direct threats to national territory. At
present and looking to the future, however, China's interests
have expanded beyond China's national boundaries, while
advances in military technology and the maritime area of
conflict are more prominent concerns. As a result, China will
need to prepare to counter these threats by operating beyond its
borders to create the necessary strategic depth.

Offering the concept of forward defense as a basis for adjusting
the content of active defense carries several important
implications. First, it requires a "new-type concept of strategic
space" that is "internal and external, multidimensional" (内外
兼顾, 多维立体). This concept is discussed in greater detail
below. Second, it requires adjustments to the scope of China's
strategic directions (战略方向) and theaters of operation (战
区). For example, the scope of the strategic directions should be
expanded to combine areas inside and outside China's borders.
Inland theaters should be extended beyond China's land
borders, while coastal theaters should expand further toward the
sea. Moreover, the book urges that "when conditions are ripe,
consider establishing an independent maritime theater to better
plan as a whole advancing into the oceans and managing the
oceans."[42] Third, it requires that China "have strategic attack

capabilities" (战略攻击能力) and create a "strategic attack posture" (态势).[43] The main reason is that since the 1990s, the trend is that "offense and defense are increasing integrated and the distinction between the two is increasingly vague," while "great power militaries increasingly emphasize offensive operations."[44] As a result, the book states that "while our military maintains 'striking after the enemy as struck' strategically...strategic offense should be an important operational type for active defense." Fourth, China "should view joint distant warfare (联合远战) based on our territory as an important form of operations (作战形式)."[45] The authors view China's homeland territory and near seas as interior lines and the Pacific Ocean as exterior lines. The basic idea they advocate is using "forces and weapons for long-range warfare" deployed on Chinese territory or in the near seas to strike targets on the periphery, increasing the survivability of China's forces by leveraging China's sheer size. In essence, they write, the "character" of joint distant warfare is "integrated joint operations" (一体化联合作战). Integrated joint operations is a PLA term of art that generally refers to joint operations as they are understood in the West, whereas the Chinese term for joint operations generally refers to what would elsewhere be considered mere combined arms.[46]

Strategic Space

The 2013 edition of the *Science of Military Strategy* defines "strategic space" (战略空间) as "the area required by a nation (民族) or state to resist foreign interference and aggression, and safeguard their own survival and development."[47] Although similar to forward defense, the main difference between the two concepts appears to revolve around the scope of combat

operations. The concept of forward defense is linked clearly to
the areas where China should be able to conduct military future
military operations, namely, the idea of pushing out or
extending the front line from along China's borders and coasts
into its periphery. By contrast, strategic space captures areas that
China would want to influence with its military capabilities,
including non-war operations and presence more generally, but
not combat operations.

Of all the new concepts in the book, strategic space is perhaps
the most ambiguous. It conveys the idea that China's interests
extend far beyond its borders, in multiple dimensions, and thus
military capabilities in all these dimensions will be needed to
defend China's interests. The extent of strategic space is defined
as follows: "Its outer edge is determined by the expanded scope
of national interests and determined even more by the distance
in which military power can be projected."[48] The book deems
strategic space as "brand new topic in the process of China's
rise."[49] The rationale for the idea of strategic space comes from
the recent "profound changes" in China's development and
security environments, "especially the threat of war from
multidimensional spaces."[50]

Following a discussion of the changing nature of strategic space
in the 21st century, the book then describes what is required for
China. It offers a new formula of "national territory as the
support, the two oceans as the key point, space and networks as
the key" as an outline for expanding China's strategic space. The
basic idea is that China should "moderately expand strategic
space" from its homeland territory (本土) into areas that will
have a direct impact on China's security environment. The two
oceans refers to an expansive conception of the Indo-Pacific that

comprises all littoral areas, including Africa, North America, South America, Oceania, and Antarctica—fifty percent of the world's oceans. This reflects the need to further protect China's maritime rights and interests and defend them if a crisis erupts.[51] Outer space refers to concerns about the United States, which is viewed as "plotting for outer space dominance." China's expansion into space is described as "inadequate" at a time when threats from space are seen as only increasing.[52] Finally, the reference to information networks refers to China's view that it is pervasively vulnerable to network attacks and information technology supply chain infiltration by "some Western nations," and that China's lacks of indigenous development of core technologies limits its ability to defend against such attacks.[53]

Effective Control

A third concept introduced in the 2013 edition of the *Science of Military Strategy* is "effective control" (有效控制) of conflict situations. Although the concept of "war control" (战争控制) featured prominently in the 2001 edition, the concept of effective control is broader because it encompasses the deterrent, crisis management, and non-war uses of military power in addition to warfighting. Effective control refers to preventing wars from occurring (遏制战争) and managing crises, if possible, while also protecting or defending Chinese interests.

The starting point for effective control is a clear acknowledgment of China's current limitations and weaknesses. As the book notes, "our country is presently in the key phase of becoming rich and strong. [Our] comprehensive national power has clearly increased, but our strategic capabilities and especially our capabilities for military actions abroad (境外) are still limited." [54] As a result, the book endorses the late 2000s modification of Deng's guideline to "persist in biding time while actively achieving something." [55] Given the imperative of peaceful development, "the employment of military power must reflect even more the spirit of 'soft weapons' (弱武), displaying the strategic functions of support, awe, and persistence to achieve the strategic goals of controlling situations and stabilizing the overall situation."[56] The book notes that despite the increase in China's warfighting power and potential over the past thirty years, China's warfighting endurance capability (战争承受能力) has declined, which places a premium on fighting short wars or even avoiding wars that would have the potential to escalate and become protracted. Thus, the book notes that even the local wars that China prepares to fight must be actively controlled "to reduce as much as possible the risks of war and destructiveness of war."[57]

More generally, effective control seeks to change the means by which strategic goals may be achieved short of war. The book notes that core of effective control contains three shifts in approach: 1) from "emphasizing 'defense' (防) to emphasizing 'control' (控)," 2) from "emphasizing 'war' (战) to emphasizing 'power' (势)," and 3) from "seeking 'victory' (战胜) to 'winning first' (先胜)."[58] In other words, effective control seeks to achieve the same goals as war, but without needing to resort to combat if possible, and restricting the intensity of conflict if hostilities do occur.

According to the book, the concept of effective control includes three components. The first is "creating situations" (营造态势).

The authors define this as "creating a strategic situation advantageous for internal stability and external expansion and a long period of order and security. The core lies in strategic balance, a stable periphery, and opposing separatism to promote unity."[59] Strategic balance refers to how China should deal the "hegemon's" efforts to "contain and control" (遏控) China. The book notes that China should avoid being provoked, prevent political, economic, or diplomatic issues from becoming strategic conflicts, prevent U.S. alliances from treating China as the adversary, and increase the "risk and price for an opponent to carry out strategic deterrence and control or armed intervention against us."[60] The book also discusses creating a favorable posture for China in the region and over Taiwan. The former includes all of China's "good neighborly" engagement policies along with the means to effectively control crises to strive for a region "without war and with less chaos" (不战少乱).[61] The latter refers to continuing with the long-standing strategy started by Jiang Zemin of "attacking with the pen and defending with the sword" (文功武备), or seeking to deter Taiwan's independence militarily while pursuing unification politically.[62]

The second component of effective control is preventing and controlling crises (防控危机). The book notes that China remains in a period of "strategic opportunity," which is also a period of "strategic danger". As the book states, "as soon as a crisis is inappropriately handled, it can create serious interference and destruction of the overall situation of the nation's development and security, even affecting the historical process of China's rise."[63] Thus, the book calls for strengthening crisis management and "especially using appropriate military deterrence and non-war military actions to prevent small disturbances from creating great suffering and prevent crises from escalating to wars."[64] At the same time, the book suggests that crises can be exploited to "seize opportunities so as to implement some strategic measures that would have been difficult to resolutely push during peacetime."[65] Although the example used in the book is the implementation of "democratic reforms" in Tibet after the outbreak of the rebellion in Lhasa in 1959, such advice might also resonate with China's seizure of effective control of Scarborough Shoal during a crisis with the Philippines in April 2012. The book does not describe how to balance these different elements of effective control, but the implication is that opportunistic behavior should be pursued when the risk of further escalation is low.

The third component of effective control is "controlling war situations" (控制战局). Control of war situations occurs after "the overall situation of peace and development is damaged," but in many ways repeats ideas from the 2001 edition on war control. These would include ensuring that military goals support political goals, ensuring a favorable situation on the battlefield does not expand political goals and escalate the war, only starting a war once completely prepared, and ending a war in a controlled manner.[66]

Strategic Posture

"Strategic posture" (战略布局) is defined as "carrying out overall deployment activities of strategic forces (力量) and resources to achieve strategic goals."[67] According to the book, the objective of strategic posture is using the overall deployment of military capabilities "to form a favorable strategic situation (态势)" and "compete for the strategic initiative" (战略主动).[68]

In this way, the book calls for a holistic approach to the deployment of Chinese forces in a way that will enable China to control "key nodes" (关节点).[69] The implication is that China lacks sufficient overall planning and deployment, largely because of rigidity introduced by the idea of independent and mutually exclusive strategic directions and military regions. The complexity of China's security environment, and its varied objectives for the use of military power, require a more holistic and integrated approach to how forces are deployed.

In the past, the book notes, the deployment of China's forces according to the "primary strategic direction" was an example of strategic posture in action. By concentrating forces against the primary strategic direction, the goal was to create a favorable strategic situation to prevent a possible invasion. Consistent with the book's theme of moving beyond territorial defense, the authors note that changes in China's security threats, strategic goals, strategic tasks, military capabilities, the form of war, and geographic conditions all "require the optimization and adjustment of the military strategic layout."[70] Changes in China's security situation (安全形势), including the increasing links between traditional and nontraditional security threats, requires that China improve its capabilities for dealing with its main strategic adversaries and operational targets (主要战略对手与作战对象). This preparation is considered particularly important due to the possibility of "chain reactions" or the simultaneous occurrence of multiple crises or conflicts.[71] In addition, on a global level, national interests are gradually transcending national borders. The authors refer to rights and interest in the maritime, space, and information domains as examples of this trend, along with overseas economic and security interests. Finally, the speed of changes in the "form of

war" is accelerating. Informatized warfare requires China to
abandon its traditional emphasis on ground war (陆战性), close
war (进战性), and territorial defense (国土防御性) in favor of
joint, long distance, and offensive-focused (联合, 远战, 攻势)
approaches.[72]

The 2013 *Science of Military Strategy* identifies the "four
transformations" that are needed to optimize China's strategic
posture as "functional versatility, multidimensional integration,
internal and external unity, and integrated coordination."
Functional versatility (功能多样) refers to a shift from
"emphasizing security" to "safeguarding security and
supporting development." This creates a strategic posture that
can deal with old domains and new ones, traditional threats and
nontraditional ones, to create "a peaceful and stabile internal
and external environment for the nation's peaceful
development." This includes cultivating a strategic deterrence
posture in peacetime and a rapid reaction capability when a
crisis occurs to prevent escalation, while in wartime it requires
the ability to seize the strategic initiative. Multidimensional
integration (多维一体) refers to the transformation from
emphasizing the ground forces to an "omni-directional, multi-
dimensional, and multi-domain" posture.[73] The book again
criticizes "big army" thinking to emphasize the networked
integration of the ground, maritime, air, space, and network
spaces. Internal and external unity (内外结合) refers to creating
a strategic posture that combines internal and external elements
to shift form homeland defense to forward defense. Internally,
this means moving to a more forward deployment of forces
within China by shifting forces from the interior to coastal areas.
Externally, this means creating overseas strategic support points
(支点) to support overseas military actions. Integrated

coordination (整体协调) refers to the transformation from compartmentalization of functions to the combination of centralization and decentralization that would improve the responsiveness of the PLA. The main target of this transformation is the stove-piped approach to planning for the services and theaters of operation that has hindered the flexibility of the force in the past.

The book contains three guiding principles for how to optimize China's strategic posture. These principles again reflect the forward-looking nature of the 2013 edition. The first is adjusting the strategic posture for land-based strategic directions to create "an outwardly extending strategic posture with effective strategic depth, mutual reliance and sufficient capability."[74] The second is "enriching" the maritime direction to create a strategic posture that can "effectively support near seas defense (防御) and far seas defense (防卫)."[75] The third is creating a strategic layout for space, which is described as its own strategic direction.

The *Science of Military Strategy* and the Future of the PLA

The 2013 edition of the SMS is an important book that should be read by anyone with an interest in China's approach to thinking about military strategy. Although it does not constitute China's official military strategy or doctrine, it captures the views and insights of a group of prominent strategists within the PLA on China's current security environment and future military strategy. Moreover, it provides an important baseline for further study and examination of how Chinese strategists approach questions of strategy and how China's own military strategy might evolve in the future.

Looking forward, future research to deepen understanding of China's military strategy might focus on three areas. The first would be to compare the 2013 edition of the *Science of Military Strategy* with the 2015 Defense White Paper on military strategy and the organizational reforms outlined in November 2015. Such a comparison would help identify which the ideas from the 2013 edition are reflected in China's official military strategy. For example, the emphasis on functional domains and theaters of operation in the white paper track closely with the discussion of these subjects in the 2013 edition of the *Science of Military Strategy*. At the same time, the white paper lacks any references to the concepts of forward defense, effective control, or strategic space. Likewise, the 2013 edition of the *Science of Military Strategy* notes the importance of improving joint command and downplaying the ground forces that reflect one basic thrust of the reforms, which includes the creation of a Joint Staff Department (联合作战部) under the CMC and the creation of an army headquarters equivalent in rank with the other services. At the same time, the 2013 edition calls for the PLA Air Force to focus on space, which in the reforms were centralized across several different organizations including the new Strategic Support Force. In other words, the 2015 white paper and reforms offer an ideal opportunity to see which ideas have been adopted and which have not, at least yet.

The second area would be to compare the 2013 edition of the *Science of Military Strategy* published by AMS with the 2015 edition published by the PLA's NDU. Such a comparison would help to highlight differences among PLA strategists on the question of military strategy. In the late 1990s, for example, AMS and NDU engaged in a debate over the meaning of military strategy with dueling editions of books with the same title. The near simultaneous publication of two volumes on the same topic by different institutes within the PLA permits yet again a detailed analysis of different approaches in China to the same questions of how to formulate and execute military strategy.

The third area for future research would be to track the use of the key concepts and ideas contained in the 2013 edition. Although it does not reflect China's official military strategy or doctrine, the book's ideas could play an important role in how China's strategy develops in the future. One way to examine the influence of the book would be to examine the degree to which the concepts it introduces are embraced by other publications and documents in the future.

NOTES

[1] The author thanks Dennis Blasko, Fiona Cunningham, David Finkelstein, Eric Heginbotham and Joe McReynolds for helpful comments and suggestions.

[2] For a review of the reforms and their potential significance, see David M. Finkelstein, *Initial Thoughts on the Reorganization and Reform of the PLA*, CNA China Studies, January 15, 2016; Kenneth Allen, Dennis J. Blasko, and John F. Corbett, "The PLA's New Organizational Structure: What is Known, Unknown and Speculation (Part 1)," *China Brief*, February 4, 2016, https://jamestown.org/program/the-plas-new-organizational-structure-what-is-known-unknown-and-speculation-part-1/; Kenneth Allen, Dennis J. Blasko, and John F. Corbett, "The PLA's New Organizational Structure: What is Known, Unknown and Speculation (Part 2)," *China Brief*, February 23, 2016, https://jamestown.org/program/the-plas-new-organizational-structure-what-is-known-unknown-and-speculation-part-2/.

[3] Qiao Liang and Wang Xiangsui [乔良，王湘穗], *Unrestricted Warfare: Two Air Force, Senior Colonels on Scenarios for War and the Operational*

Art in the Era of Globalization, [超限战: 两个空军大校对全球化时代与 战法的想订], (Beijing: PLA Literature Press, 1999).

[4] Shou Xiaosong, ed., *The Science of Military Strategy* [战略学], (Beijing: Military Sciences Press, 2013). Hereafter cited as SMS.

[5] Books published in China with the character "*xue*" (学) refer to the study of a subject. For example, "*shuxue*" (数学) is mathematics or the study of numbers. "*Zhanlue xue*" (战略学) is thus the study of strategy and, in a military context, the study of military strategy.

[6] On services, see, for example, Dai Jinyu, ed., *The Science of Air Force Strategy* [空军战略学] (Beijing: National Defense University Press, 1995).

[7] Junshi kexue yuan, ed., *Military Terminology of the Chinese People's Liberation Army* [中国人民解放军 军语], (Beijing: Military Sciences Press [internal circulation], 2011), p. 12.

[8] SMS 2013; Gao Rui, ed., *The Science of Military Strategy* [战略学] (Beijing: Academy of Military Sciences Press [internal circulation], 1987); Peng Guangqian and Yao Youzhi [彭光谦、姚有志], eds., *Science of Military Strategy* [战略学], (Beijing: Military Sciences Press, 2001).

[9] In the past fifteen years, this department has been called the strategic studies department, the war theory and strategic studies department, and military strategy studies department.

[10] Wang Wenrong, ed., *The Science of Military Strategy* [战略学] (Beijing: National Defense University Press, 1999); Xiao Tianliang, ed., *The Science of Military Strategy* [战略学], (Beijing: National Defense University Press, 2015).

[11] Fan Zhenjiang and Ma Baoan, eds., *On Military Strategy* [军事战略论], (Beijing: National Defense University Press, 2007).

[12] For a detailed study of China's strategic guidelines, see M. Taylor Fravel, *Active Defense: Explaining the Evolution of China's Military Strategy* (book manuscript under advance contract with Princeton University Press). The most recent guideline adopted in 2014, see M. Taylor Fravel, "China's New Military Strategy: 'Winning Local Informationized Wars'," *China Brief,* June 23, 2015, https://jamestown.org/program/chinas-new-military-strategy-winning-informationized-local-wars/.

[13] *China's Military Strategy* [中国的军事战略] State Council Information Office [中华人民共和国国务院新闻办公室], May 29, 2015. http://www.scio.gov.cn/zfbps/gfbps/Document/1435341/1435341.htm. In previous research a decade ago on the 1999 NDU *Science of Military Strategy*, I overstated the degree to which such volumes are authoritative and reflect official military strategy. See M. Taylor Fravel, "The Evolution of China's Military Strategy: Comparing the 1987 and 1999 Editions of *Zhanlue Xue*," in David M. Finkelstein and James Mulvenon, eds., *The Revolution in Doctrinal Affairs: Emerging Trends in the Operational Art of the Chinese People's Liberation Army* (Alexandria, Va.: Center for Naval Analyses, 2005), pp. 79–100.

[14] Zhang Yang, ed., *Accelerate and Promote National Defense and Armed Forces Modernization* [加快推进国防和军队现代化], (Beijing: People's Press, 2015). The chief compiler for this volume was General Zhang Yang, Director of the General Political Department. Scholars from the National Defense Policy Research Center at AMS played a role in the drafting of this volume. Individuals from the same center also participate in the drafting of China's biennial white papers on defense.

[15] "寿晓松," *Baidu Baike*, [accessed March 15, 2016], http://baike.baidu.com/view/1183279.htm.

[16] Also, expertise in the strategy department is not evenly distributed across all areas in the volume. For example, none of the authors listed are recognized experts in either nuclear strategy or cyber strategy.

[17] On the drafting, see SMS 2013 p. 275.

[18] Herein lies one of the central challenges of understanding the evolution of China's military strategy: even somewhat authoritative Chinese publications often take years to prepare, and then additional time elapses before Western analysts of the PLA (many of whom do not read Chinese) begin to integrate the new materials into their assessments. This time lag of years complicates efforts at mutual strategic understanding in what is arguably the world's most important bilateral national security relationship.

[19] On the evolution of China's military strategic guidelines, see Fravel, *Active Defense*.

[20] For a detailed review of active defense, see Dennis Blasko, "The Evolution of Core Concepts: People's War, Active Defense, and Offshore Defense, in

Roy Kamphausen, David Lai and Travis Tanner, eds., *Assessing the People's Liberation Army in the Hu Jintao Era* (Carlisle, PA: Army War College Press, 2014), pp. 81–128.

[21] SMS 2013, p. 42.

[22] SMS 2013, pp. 48–50.

[23] Peng Guangqian and Yao Youzhi [彭光谦、姚有志], eds., *Science of Military Strategy* [战略学], (Beijing: Military Sciences Press, 2001), p. 15.

[24] "对以战争为核心武装力量建设与运用全局的筹划指导." See SMS 2013, p.4.

[25] Yao Youzhi and Zhao Dexi, "The Broadening, Conservation and Development of 'Strategy', ['战略'的繁华，守恒与发展]," *China Military Science*, No. 4 (2001), pp. 120–127.

[26] For a discussion of the new historic missions, see Daniel Harnett, "The 'New Historic Missions': Reflections on Hu Jintao's Military Legacy," in Roy Kamphausen, David Lai and Travis Tanner, eds., *Assessing the People's Liberation Army in the Hu Jintao Era* (Carlisle, PA: Army War College Press, 2014), pp. 31–80; M. Taylor Fravel, "Economic Growth, Regime Insecurity, and Military Strategy: Explaining the Rise of Noncombat Operations in China," *Asian Security*, Vol. 7, No. 3 (2011), pp. 177–200.

[27] SMS 2013, preface 1.

[28] Ibid.

[29] Ibid.

[30] For more information on the PLA's use of the "informatization" concept, see Joe McReynolds and James Mulvenon, "The Role of Informatization in the People's Liberation Army under Hu Jintao," in Roy Kamphausen, David Lai and Travis Tanner, eds., *Assessing the People's Liberation Army in the Hu Jintao Era* (Carlisle, PA: Army War College Press, 2014), pp. 207–256.

[31] SMS 2013, p. 79.

[32] SMS 2013, p. 81.

[33] Ibid.

[34] SMS 2013, p. 100.

---

[35] For an example of research based on these new sources, see Fiona S. Cunningham and M. Taylor Fravel, "Assuring Assured Retaliation: China's Nuclear Posture and U.S.-China Strategic Stability," *International Security*, Vol. 40, No. 2 (Fall 2015), pp. 7–50.

[36] This could also be translated as "frontline defense."

[37] SMS 2013, p. 104.

[38] SMS 2013, p. 105. This is one clear example where the authors, by the language they use, are advocating for a position, not reflecting official policy. Indeed, the concept of forward defense does not appear in the official 2015 white paper on national defense and only a single entry can be found in the *Liberation Army Daily* newspaper, to an article published in 2014.

[39] SMS 2013, p. 105.

[40] SMS 2013, p. 106.

[41] SMS 2013, p. 106.

[42] SMS 2013, p. 107.

[43] Ibid.

[44] Ibid.

[45] SMS 2013, p. 108.

[46] SMS 2013, p. 109.

[47] SMS 2013, p. 241.

[48] Ibid.

[49] Ibid.

[50] Ibid.

[51] SMS 2013, pp. 246–247.

[52] SMS 2013, p. 247.

[53] SMS 2013, p. 248.

[54] SMS 2013, p. 110.

[55] SMS 2013, p. 110.

[56] SMS 2013, p. 111.

[57] SMS 2013, p. 111.

[58] SMS 2013, p. 112.

[59] SMS 2013, p. 113.

[60] SMS 2013, p. 113. However, the 2013 edition of *The Science of Military Strategy* does not offer an explicit strategy of "counter-intervention." See M. Taylor Fravel and Christopher P. Twomey, "Projecting Strategy: The Myth of Chinese Counter-Intervention," *The Washington Quarterly*, Vol. 37, No. 4 (2015), pp. 171–187. For an opposing view, see Timothy Heath and Andrew Erickson, "Is China Pursuing Counter-Intervention?," *The Washington Quarterly*, Vol. 38, No. 3 (2015), pp. 143–156.

[61] SMS 2013, p. 113.

[62] SMS 2013, p. 113.

[63] SMS 2013, p. 114.

[64] SMS 2013, p. 114.

[65] SMS 2013, p. 115.

[66] SMS 2013, pp. 115–117.

[67] SMS 2013, p. 244. This could also be translated as "strategic layout," but as used in this part of the book, "posture" in terms of how forces are arranged and deployed better captures the meaning of the Chinese term than layout.

[68] SMS 2013, p. 250.

[69] SMS 2013, p. 251.

[70] SMS 2013, p. 252.

[71] On concerns about a multiple simultaneous conflicts, see M. Taylor Fravel, "Securing Borders: China's Doctrine and Force Structure for Frontier Defense," *Journal of Strategic Studies*, Vol. 30, No. 4–5 (2007), pp. 705–737.

[72] SMS 2013, p. 252.

[73] SMS 2013, p. 254.

[74] SMS 2013, p. 255.

[75] SMS 2013, p. 255.

SECTION II: CHINA'S STRATEGY FOR CONVENTIONAL AND NUCLEAR WARFARE

Chapter 3: The Evolution of PLAAF Mission, Roles and Requirements

Cristina L. Garafola

Every Chinese leader since Deng Xiaoping has called on the People's Liberation Army Air Force (PLAAF) to strengthen its capabilities, modernize its aircraft, and shoulder an increasingly outward-looking mission set. Jiang Zemin, for example, highlighted the need to "build a powerful, modernized air force that is simultaneously prepared for offensive and defensive operations" (攻防兼备) in a 1999 speech on the topic.[1] In more recent years, the PLAAF's role has expanded even further, with the PLAAF commander being granted a seat on the Central Military Commission (CMC) along with the PLAN and PLASAF commanders since 2004. That year also saw the creation of both the PLAAF's service-specific strategy, a major milestone confirming the service's importance to China's leadership and its growing clout, and the "strategic air force" concept, which describes the PLAAF as having both offensive and defensive capabilities and integrating air and space capabilities.

This evolution is reflected in the major works on the PLA's strategic thought that have been issued over this period. Changes in the discussion of the PLAAF from 2001 to recent works, including the 2013 version of *Science of Military Strategy* and other authoritative sources, highlight the increasing responsibilities of the PLAAF as a "strategic service" able to provide decisive impact during a conflict. These sources portray a shift from a campaign-focused approach, adopted as the

PLAAF was still absorbing the lessons of the 1991 Gulf War, to a strategic-level focus that is capable of conducting offensive and defensive operations, deterrence missions, layered air defense, protection of China's border and maritime "rights and interests," and MOOTW activities.

The PLAAF's Changing Status, Mission and Roles

Until only recently, the PLAAF's standing and missions have reflected its status largely as a supporting service to the PLA Army (PLAA). A recent authoritative publication describes the PLAAF's development in three separate phases since the PLAAF was established on November 11, 1949. During the first period (1949 to 1955), the focus was on "building an Air Force on the Army's foundation," figuring out how to employ the PLAAF in combat during the Korean War, and establishing an aviation industry.[2]

During the second period (1956 through the 1980s), the PLAAF suffered both in terms of its warfighting capability and also politically. Subpar education and training negatively impacted the PLAAF during the Cultural Revolution, and the 1971 "Lin Biao incident"—in which Minister of Defense Lin Biao, who had strong ties to the PLAAF and its commander Wu Faxian, fled the country and was killed in a plane crash—resulted in purges of PLAAF leadership and deep suspicion regarding the political reliability of PLAAF forces.[3]

After the reform and opening period began, Deng Xiaoping stated that "the Air Force will be first" as a force provider in future combat. However, PLA analysts described the PLAAF's main strategic missions during this period as homeland air defense and "supporting Army and Navy operations."[4] During this period, operationally the PLAAF's focus was described as territorial air defense, while China also continued to develop a more self-reliant aviation industry.[5] Through the end of the Cold War, the PLAAF's main missions consisted merely of territorial defense, interdiction, and close air support for the PLA Army (PLAA).[6] This set of roles was part of a PLA-wide mission that largely called for focusing northward on a potential ground-based, territorial incursion-style conflict with the Soviet Union.[7]

In the third period (from the 1990s onward), however, strategic concerns about a possible conflict with the Soviet Union were allayed after its collapse in 1991. The PLA also began observing changes in the types of major wars being fought globally, particularly the high-tech nature of wars such as the Kosovo War and both Gulf Wars, which emphasized air power over ground forces.[8] One study on the Second Gulf War argued that these wars led to "a new operational model" in which the application of air power could achieve the "strategic target," concluding: "localized warfare practice has... [revealed] the subduing function of the position of air warfare."[9] Overall, lessons-learned studies concluded that China "should take the requirements for winning future high-tech local wars as the basis" for "greatly strengthening national defense and modernization building" to improve the PLA's warfighting capabilities, with particular appreciation for the role that "high technology air strikes" play in modern warfare.[10] These concerns were echoed by senior CMC leadership, with Jiang Zemin calling on the PLAAF to convert from a homeland air defense force to a force "that is simultaneously prepared for offensive and defensive operations" (攻防兼备) in an important

1999 speech.[11]

The PLAAF Gains a Strategic Role

Observations regarding these changes to modern warfare affected both the PLA Air Force and the PLA Navy (PLAN). In the *Science of Military Strategy* 2001, PLA analysts noted a significant increase in both services' roles and responsibilities: "Opportunities for the Navy and Air force to independently accomplish strategic tasks are increasing more and more, and there are objective requirements at the strategic level to plan sea and air operations and construct the Navy and Air Force. Accordingly under the unified guidance of China's military strategy of active defense, China's... air force needs to establish the... strategy... of offensive air defense."[12] The concept of "offensive air defense" represented a step outward for the PLAAF in two important ways. First, it expanded the PLAAF's mission set from the Cold War-era missions of defending China's territory writ large and supporting PLAA operations. Second, it gave the PLAAF perhaps its first real opportunity to improve its status within the PLA since the Lin Biao incident had bequeathed the service with a legacy of suspicion and mistrust over two decades prior. Operationally, as the importance of aerial warfare grew within the PLA, the PLAAF's role in campaigns and operational concepts expanded. SMS 2001 describes important roles for the PLAAF in offensive and defensive operations, strategic maneuver, and strategic air raid (SAR) and defense against air raid (DAAR).[13]

SMS 2001 depicts the PLAAF as employing offensive air power in an expanding range of contexts in response to the changing demands of modern warfare.[14] The authors note that in past wars, air offensives were carried out primarily in "coordination" with strategic offensive actions by the other services, particularly the Army.[15] However, under the "high-tech conditions" that now dominate warfare, there are additional incentives for China to employ the PLAAF for "independent strategic offensive" operations without a corresponding ground campaign, akin to NATO's use of air power in the 1999 Kosovo War.[16] Other applications of air power are explored as well; when the PLA is already dominating and an adversary is forced to retreat, they argue, air power can compound that advantage through air-to-ground assault as well as air mobility and airborne assault.[17] The PLAAF is also expected to assist in the enforcement of strategic blockades by "cutting off the external connections of the enemy" such as communication and transportation hubs.[18] Finally, the authors envision that "vertical landing offensives" could be carried out simultaneously by the PLAAF and PLAN to "project strategic power and seize the land, shore, or large island of the opposing side," an allusion to PLAAF planning for operations during a Taiwan crisis scenario.[19]

Likewise, the PLAAF has an important role to play in defensive operations, particularly in countering enemy air raids.[20] To counter an air raid, air defense forces (which include SAM, AAA, radar, and ECM troops) from the PLAAF as well as other services conduct both air defense operations and air operations. While a main force defends key areas within the country, all services and branches would then launch counterattacks, particularly against C4ISR systems, airports, and missile launch sites.[21] If China were to face a blockade, SMS 2001 states that the PLAAF and other services should conduct coordinated operations to "win the local command of the air and... sea in important areas."[22] In the event that a retreat is required, the PLAAF would be called upon to provide air cover.[23] Finally, the PLAAF has additional roles that result from the unique structure of the PLA. Within the Chinese military system, airborne troops are subordinate to the PLAAF rather than the PLAA, giving the former a range of airlift missions beyond merely moving weapons, supplies, and personnel by aircraft.[24]

The PLAAF's role in strategic air raids (SAR) and defense against air raids (DAAR) is the most extensive coverage of the PLAAF's role in SMS 2001. These missions were particularly important for the threat environment envisioned by the authors, with "the success or failure of the SAR or DAAR directly influencing and constraining the course and outcome of war."[25] SAR is also the only operation described in SMS 2001 as conducted mainly by the Air Force in coordination with other services and arms.[26] As envisioned at the time, an idealized Chinese SAR operation featured the use of high-tech weaponry such as precision-strike missiles and stealth aircraft, with coordination among all services and arms as well as the employment of information and electronic warfare. Precision strike night-time operations would minimize enemy air defenses to "paralyze the adversary in one stroke."[27]

PLA forces engaged in SAR operations include both aviation and ground-based forces, most of whom come from the PLAAF. The air units "should be focused on the main direction of strike with the units in small formations (小编队) as the backbone of the strike forces," whereas ground units should be "quickly assembled for the convenience of command, support, and coordination of the strategic strike against scheduled targets."[28]

SMS 2001 characterizes strategic DAAR as requiring the ability to conduct sudden operations with only a short warning time, and thus readiness over a large operational space. Since the enemy will be seeking to knock out PLA air defense systems in "one blow," electronic warfare capabilities, an effective doctrine of joint operations, and the organizational and C4ISR systems necessary for coordination between units are all essential for successful DAAR.[29] The DAAR mission set incorporates early warning, command and control, strikes and counter-strikes, fortified defensive works, operational support, and civil defense.[30]

Modern Warfare Requires the PLAAF to Embrace Joint Operations

Given the requirements of high-tech warfare, SMS 2001 stresses that "the victory of war depends on the comprehensive confrontation capacity of the whole combat system," particularly the ability to integrate forces from multiple branches and services in order to improve overall combat effectiveness.[31] Therefore, the authors conclude, "Integrated Joint Operations (IJO) have become the basic pattern of high-tech local war.[32] Integrated Joint Operations is a PLA term of art that refers to joint operations as they are traditionally understood in the West; the PLA's previous concept of joint operations lacked genuine joint command and functioned more akin to combined arms.

A range of integrated joint operations directly involve the PLAAF, including offensive missions such as long-range strikes that can be carried out as a part of strategic offensive operations requiring stand-off strategic air raids or "surgical strikes."[33] The

PLAAF can also conduct air-to-sea and air-to-land maneuvering assaults against enemy forces, while protecting Chinese territory,[34] including counterattacks on China's land periphery in concert with the PLAA and coastal operations with the PLAN to contest regional air and sea control.[35] The PLAAF's previously mentioned airborne role is relevant for special operations as well.[36]

It is important to place these analyses of the PLAAF's role in historical context. At the end of the Jiang Zemin era, the PLAAF was emerging from decades during which its primary missions had been limited to territorial defense and support of the PLA Army. Recent developments in the role of air power in modern warfare had created a wider role for the PLAAF in offensive as well as defensive operations. As these theories of the employment of air power were developed, however, improvements in recruitment, education, training, and acquisition were also necessary if the PLAAF were to succeed in these expanded missions. In the early 2000s, the PLA as a whole assessed that it would not succeed in a conflict with technologically superior adversaries who were better trained and operating more modern systems.[37] Based on modern warfighting requirements, the PLAAF was one of the weak links in the chain.

The PLAAF's Evolution in the Hu Jintao and Xi Jinping Eras

The 15 years following the publication of the *Science of Military Strategy* in 2001 have brought many changes to the PLAAF, due to both broader recognition of the importance that air power plays in modern warfare and numerous PLA-wide reform and modernization efforts. The PLAAF's relative status within the

PLA has risen, exemplified by the arrival of its new service-specific strategy in 2004. Signs of this ascent can be seen in recent depictions of the PLAAF's missions and roles, and in the efforts China has made to acquire systems and capabilities the PLAAF needs to fulfill operational requirements in future conflicts.

New Status and a New Concept: The PLAAF as a "Strategic Air Force"

Two major changes affected the PLAAF in 2004. First, the PLAAF commander was granted a seat on the Central Military Commission (CMC) by dint of his position, along with the PLAN and PLASAF (now PLARF) commanders. This position gave the PLAAF an official voice on the senior-most body within the PLA, although in practice CMC membership has continued to be dominated by PLA Army officers. In November 2012, former PLAAF commander Xu Qiliang became the first PLAAF officer to serve as a Vice Chairman of the CMC.[38]

Second, the PLAAF received its first service-specific strategy in 2004. While the strategy itself has not been made publicly available, the most recent version of *Science of Military Strategy* published in 2013 describes the overarching theme as "air and space integration, with both attack and defense [capability]" (空天一体、攻防兼备) to carry out strategic- and campaign-level missions that reflect China's interests as a rapidly developing military power.[39] This concept has been referred to in official state media and other sources as constituting a "strategic air force."[40]

New Missions

In keeping with the themes of air and space integration and offensive and defensive capabilities, the PLAAF has shifted toward preparing to carry out a more focused but robust series of missions. It is important to note that the newest version of *Science of Military Strategy* 2013 is less tactically-focused than its predecessor, so it is difficult to directly compare the PLAAF's role in various campaigns from 2001 to 2013. However, SMS 2013 as well as other recent authoritative publications do discuss key themes in strategy and modernization tasks for the PLA, providing some basis for comparison.

SMS 2013 describes the basic objective of the PLAAF's strategy as realizing national reunification and safeguarding national territory (as well as China's "maritime rights and interests"), conducting active defense of Chinese territory, helping construct an integrated deterrence posture within the PLA, and honing the PLAAF's comparative advantages at conducting rapid and flexible response operations within the PLA. [41] Specifically, the PLAAF has five "strategic missions," which it notes have both peacetime and wartime components.

Figure 1: The PLAAF's Five "Strategic Missions"

1.	Participate in the primary "strategic direction"
2.	Conduct homeland air defense
3.	Safeguard China's border and maritime "rights and interests"
4.	Conduct emergency and disaster relief operations; assist with maintaining domestic stability
5.	Conduct foreign exchanges

First, the PLAAF will participate in the primary "strategic direction" by conducting operations such as warning strikes, contingency operations, joint fire strikes and other joint operations, blockade operations, island-landing operations, and organizing theater air defense operations. [42] This mission appears to incorporate elements of the PLAAF's already-defined concepts of strategic offensive and strategic air raid.

Second, the PLAAF is to engage in homeland air defense "organized with the capital as the center, [and] with the coastal areas as the key points."[43] SMS 2013 also notes that the PLAAF should "expand the scope of air monitoring and activities to effectively uphold the nation's territorial airspace security and sovereignty." [44] This responsibility has included conducting patrols within the Air Defense Identification Zone (ADIZ) established in the East China Sea in November 2013, and would likely include patrols in any future ADIZs if additional ones were established.[45]

The third mission noted is the PLAAF's role in safeguarding border and maritime "rights and interests," as well as coastal-defense operations. SMS 2013 does not elaborate on the PLAAF's role beyond coordinating operations with the Navy and Army. However, this still represents a step up in PLAAF's role compared to the 1980s, in which the PLAAF "supported" the other two services.

Fourth, the PLAAF has a role in conducting emergency and disaster relief.[46] The PLAAF has participated in emergency and disaster response both domestically and abroad, including after the Chengdu earthquake in 2008. More recently, after an earthquake struck Nepal on April 25, 2015, the PLAAF played a prominent role in China's response by transporting aid, equipment, and troops to conduct disaster relief in the country.[47] The PLAAF also has a role in maintaining domestic stability, including "striking at terrorism."[48] This may indicate a role for the PLAAF in conducting operations within China's borders, including drone operations, in addition to strikes abroad.[49]

Finally, the PLAAF participates in international military exchanges and cooperation activities. These are primarily conducted by aviation units at events such as the Russian Aviadarts international pilot competition, the Shanghai Cooperation Organization's combined military exercises, and performances by the PLAAF's "Bayi" (八一, a reference to the date of the PLA's founding) acrobatic team at home and abroad.

Operational Capabilities Under Development

In order to achieve these missions, SMS 2013 calls for the building of "one system" (系统), "five forces" (力量), and "seven operational capabilities" (作战能力).[50] This framework is a proposal rather than a description of current activities, but it provides a strong indication of likely focus areas for future PLAAF force building and modernization. In particular, assessing improvements to the seven operational capabilities, all but one of which appear linked to the "five forces," can provide further insights into the PLAAF's progress toward achieving air and space integration and attack and defense capability described in the concept.

Figure 2: PLAAF System, Forces and Capabilities

One System	Five Forces	Seven Operational Capabilities
Command information system	Air offensive forces	Medium- and long-range precision strike
	Air defensive/anti-missile forces	Air defense antimissile system-of-systems with "three-line control" structure
	Reconnaissance, early-warning, and surveillance forces	[Noted as essential for carrying out the PLAAF's various operational capabilities]
	Information operations forces	Information assistance support capability
		Electronic warfare and network warfare capability
	Strategic transport forces	Air strategic projection capability
		Airborne forces operational capability
		Comprehensive support capabilities

Informatization and Joint Operations: One System to Integrate Them All

Informatization and joint operations are integral to carrying out the PLAAF's "air and space integration" and "attack and defense capability" concepts. SMS 2013 explains the need for the PLAAF to focus on air and space integration through the contextual lens of worldwide trends in "air-space-network integration."[51] The "one system" described in SMS 2013 is a reference to the "command information systems" that "cover the Air Force's strategic activity space." It encompasses space-based information platforms that integrate the air, space, and land domains into a "three-level network" for the strategic, campaign, and tactical levels of warfare.[52] This system-of-systems includes Chinese-designated 4th generation aircraft (U.S.-designated 5th generation aircraft), aerial refueling, long-range reconnaissance aircraft, AEW&C aircraft, UAVs, and guided munitions (such as air-launched cruise missiles and anti-radiation missiles), including relevant operations and support components. Future systems to incorporate could include a stealth strategic bomber and "air and space integrated equipment."[53]

Offensive Strikes in Air and Space

The PLAAF should have an "air offensive force" that has been adapted to conduct both air offensive operations and offensive air defensive operations (under informatized conditions). This includes a better medium- and long-range air precision strike system for Chinese-designated 3rd and 4th generation aircraft. To do this, SMS 2013 calls for the PLAAF to streamline technical and other standards and focus on "remote combat capabilities." The term "remote" is defined in the text as 3,000 kilometers beyond China's borders, "so that the platform radius or the platform radius plus the firepower radius reaches the Second Island Chain" in support of larger air defense areas or zones (防空区域).[54] To improve its ability to conduct medium- and long-range precision strikes, the PLAAF has extended its area of operations by fielding new aircraft and missiles and increasing its use of aerial refueling.[55] The PLAAF is also conducting long-range training activities, particularly over water. For example, Chinese media reported that the PLAAF conducted four long-range exercises over the western Pacific in 2015.[56] These long range strike capabilities could potentially include a role for the PLAAF in China's nuclear strike capabilities, although authoritative Chinese sources do not discuss the matter.[57]

As its command information systems grow in reach and sophistication, the PLAAF is expected to expand its offensive and defensive operations to the air, "near-space," "outer-space," and "network-space."[58] This reflects the PLAAF's aspirations to play an increasingly important role in the space domain, as well as the stated importance of air and space integration (空天一体) to its continued development. However, the end state of the PLAAF's ongoing air and space integration efforts remains unclear beyond general trends toward incorporating C4ISR platforms ever more deeply into PLAAF operations. [59] The publicly-announced elements of the PLA's recently undertaken reorganization suggest that at the strategic level the PLAAF will likely have to continue sharing the space domain with other actors within the PLA, including not only the former PLA Second Artillery Force (now the Rocket Force) but also elements within the new Strategic Support Force.[60] SMS 2013 discusses the role of the PLAAF in air and space deterrence, exhorting the PLAAF to actively participate in "air and space military struggle" and "gradually develop the deterrent role of controlling space from the air" (逐步发挥以空制天的威慑作用).[61]

Defense of the Homeland

Also important is the development of an air defense antimissile force to "ensure the stability" of the national air defense system and resist air raids under informatized conditions. The PLAAF requires an air defense antimissile system-of-systems that balances the needs and requirements of territorial air defense and "multidirectional operations." Improvements required include filling gaps in coverage by building more ground stations and using airborne early warning and control (AEW&C) aircraft. SMS 2013 notes that "the resources invested in air defense will be much greater than those for offensive means." Compared to the early 2000s, the PLAAF today fields larger numbers of new and long-range surface-to-air missile (SAM) systems, including the HQ-9, SA-10, SA-20, and soon the SA-21 (S-400), of which China has purchased four to six battalions from Russia. [62] The PLAAF is also fielding more AEW&C aircraft, including the new KJ-500 system in addition to its older KJ-200 and KJ-2000 programs.

With these and future air defense systems, SMS 2013 states that the PLAAF should build a "three-line control" (三线控制) air defense structure to optimize its posture and "battlefield [force] construction." The three lines radiate outwards from China's borders: territorial airspace is the area of "reliable control," beyond China up to the First Island Chain and the main periphery countries is a "limited control and security cooperation area," and between the First and Second Island Chains is a "long-range surveillance and limited deterrence area." Scenario-based analysis by the RAND Corporation assesses that growing numbers of sophisticated SAM systems, combined with defense counter-air patrols by increasingly capable interceptor aircraft, could create a layered defense structure out to the First Island Chain by 2017.[63] SMS 2013 also states that other improvements needed to China's air defense system are "operations research-based planning" for using terminal antimissile systems as well as countering stealth combat aircraft and unmanned systems in the event that an adversary contests Chinese control over key areas of the mainland's airspace.

Eyes in the Sky

Third, a reconnaissance, early-warning, and surveillance force will bolster both attack and defense within the PLAAF's operational space by integrating air, space, and land assets, providing strategic warning, and "maintaining battlefield transparency." The PLAAF's strategic reconnaissance and early warning capability should evolve from air reconnaissance and early warning to air and space integrated early warning that is regularly employed for operations.[64] As mentioned previously, China has fielded increasingly capable AEW&C aircraft, including the KJ-200, KJ-2000, and the new KJ-500 program. Other components could include elements of China's satellite network, ground-based radar systems, maritime patrol aircraft to guard against enemy submarines, and unmanned aerial vehicles (UAVs).[65]

Strategic Airlift

A strategic air transport force will facilitate strategic projection and PLAAF maneuver and air landing operations. SMS 2013 notes that the need for the development of a strategic air transport system is "an important mark of a strategic air force," particularly the development of "medium and large-size, long-range, multifunctional transport planes" to move equipment and troops. Relevant capabilities include an air strategic projection capability and an air-landing operational capability to deploy airborne troops and special operations forces.[66] The Y-20 large military transport aircraft, which Chinese analysts have projected to enter service in the next few years,[67] will play an important role in bolstering the PLAAF's transport of equipment and forces to support PLA-wide contingency operations.

Cyber and Support Forces

Finally, SMS 2013 states that the PLAAF should have an information operations (IO) force capable of "effective suppression and destruction" via both soft-kill and hard-kill of an opponent's information systems, as well as an integrated "information protection capability." These include an information assistance support capability "covering the Air Force's operational space" and an electronic warfare and network warfare capability that combines both air and ground. Additionally, the PLAAF should have a comprehensive support capability that is "adapted to large-scale, high-intensity sustained operations."[68] Since the publication of SMS 2013, reforms announced as part of the PLA reorganization have included the establishment of a Strategic Support Force (战略支援部队) that appears to incorporate some of these functions, although it is unclear how the SSF will coordinate operations with PLAAF units.

Continuity Amid Distinctions: Treatment of the PLAAF in Other Recent Publications

How should we assess the relevance of the framework proposed in SMS 2013 for the PLAAF's development? A review of other recent documents discussing trends in the PLAAF's development reveals a broad overlap in key themes, though some topics or priorities are emphasized more heavily in some of the documents than others. The 2015 edition of the National Defense University's version of *Science of Military Strategy* (which is not related to the 2013 edition published by the Academy of Military Science and is generally considered less authoritative) examines operational requirements, trends, and key areas in PLAAF modernization. In addition to highlighting the importance of air and space integration, offensive and defensive capabilities, and informatization in the PLAAF, the NDU SMS describes five areas in which the PLAAF must become proficient. These areas largely track with the "five forces" discussed in SMS 2015 and include an air offensive force, an air defense antimissile force, an ISR force, and an information operations force. The NDU SMS also delves into the need for a robust "base protection force" to ensure the continuity of air operations under informatized conditions.[69] Also similarly to SMS 2013, a section on trends in Air Force force modernization focuses on offensive strikes, precision strike, and a system of systems to enable high-tech warfighting, but also discusses the importance of stealth and unmanned systems in modern warfighting.[70]

The limited discussion of the PLAAF in China's most recent white paper on military strategy released in 2015 likewise fits the picture of PLAAF strategy and building goals depicted in SMS 2013. Though the PLAAF is only mentioned specifically in three paragraphs, the white paper notes that the PLAAF will "endeavor to shift its focus from territorial air defense to both defense and offense, and build an air-space defense force structure that can meet the requirements of informatized operations" by strengthening "strategic early warning, air strike, air and missile defense, information countermeasures, airborne operations, strategic projection and comprehensive support" capabilities. [71] This list is almost identical to the seven operational capabilities targeted by SMS 2013 for strategic building of the PLAAF. The white paper also calls for increasing the proportion of PLAAF reserve and combat support forces vis-à-vis Army forces and indicates a role for the PLAAF in the preparation for military struggle, including "all-dimensional response and full territorial reach, and maintain[ing] vigilant and efficient combat readiness." The white paper indicates additional areas of modernization that have relevance for the PLAAF, including logistics, acquisition, and personnel recruitment and training.

In conclusion, the past fifteen years have seen many changes to the PLAAF's status, theory, and outlook. Now described as a "strategic service" that is working to achieve the requirements of having both offensive and defensive capabilities and integrating both air and space capabilities, ultimately, the PLAAF's progress toward those goals remains yet unclear. The recent reforms announced within the PLA raise additional questions. For example, as part of the PLA reorganization, the former seven military regions have been replaced by five "theater commands" that are tasked with leading military operations, while the service headquarters will be focused on manning, training and equipping their respective forces. It is not yet known how the PLAAF or other services will adjust to this latter role and manage the many new aspects of their relationships with the theater commands. Overall, however, the newest version of SMS 2013, along with other recent documents from the PLA and government sources, provide many indicators and benchmarks for assessing whether or not the PLAAF is successfully making progress toward reaching its goals. These documents should help PLA watchers and a broader audience alike better assess the

PLAAF's transformation as further information on the PLAAF's relationship with the theater commands and developments in PLAAF systems and equipment, personnel, training, and overall operational capability become available.

NOTES

---

[1] *China Air Force Encyclopedia* [中国空军百科全书], Aviation Engineering Press, vol. 1, 2005, p. 39.

[2] Shou Xiaosong [寿晓松] ed., *Science of Military Strategy* [战略学], Academy of Military Sciences Press, 2013, p. 219.

[3] After Wu Faxian was arrested, the PLAAF went 18 months without a commander. The collapse of the aviation industry also played an important role in the PLAAF's struggles during this period. For more information on this time period and the Lin Biao incident, see Kenneth W. Allen, Glenn Krumel, and Jonathan D. Pollack, *China's Air Force Enters the 21st Century*, Santa Monica, CA: RAND Corporation, 1995, pp. 71–74; John Wilson Lewis and Xue Litai, "China's Search for a Modern Air Force," *International Security*, Vol. 24, No. 1 (Summer 1999), pp. 64–94; and Kenneth W. Allen, "The PLA Air Force: 1949–2002: Overview and Lessons Learned," in Laurie Burkitt, Andrew Scobell, and Larry M. Wortzel, eds., *The Lessons of History: The Chinese People's Liberation Army at 75*, (Carlisle, PA: Army War College Press, July 2003), pp. 93–94.

[4] SMS 2013, pp. 219–220.

[5] SMS 2013, p. 220.

[6] The PLAAF has five branches: aviation, surface-to-air (SAM), anti-aircraft artillery (AAA), airborne, and radar, as well as other specialized units that include communications, electronic countermeasure (ECM) troops, chemical defense, and technical reconnaissance. People's Republic of China, Ministry of National Defense, "Structure and Organization of the Armed Forces." As of August 2, 2015: http://eng.mod.gov.cn/ArmedForces/index.htm. For more on these historical missions, see Mark Stokes, "The Chinese Joint Aerospace Campaign: Strategy, Doctrine, and Force Modernization," in James

Mulvenon and David M. Finkelstein, eds., *China's Revolution in Doctrinal Affairs*, pp. 245–246.

⁷ For more information, see M. Taylor Fravel, "The Evolution of China's Military Strategy: Comparing the 1987 and 1999 editions of *Zhanlüexue*," in *China's Revolution in Doctrinal Affairs*, pp. 79–99.

⁸ See Peng Guangqian and Yao Youzhi [彭光谦、姚有志], eds., *Science of Military Strategy* [战略学], Academy of Military Sciences Press, 2001, pp. 340–344.

⁹ Wang Yongming et al. eds., *Research into the Iraq War*, (Beijing: Liberation Army Publishing House, March 2003), p. 134.

¹⁰ Wang Yongming et al. eds., *Research into the Iraq War*, (Beijing: Liberation Army Publishing House, March 2003), preface. "High technology air strike" from The Military Training Department of the General Staff of the Chinese People's Liberation Army, *Research into the Kosovo War*, (Beijing: Liberation Army Publishing House, 2000).

¹¹ *China Air Force Encyclopedia* [中国空军百科全书], Aviation Engineering Press, vol. 1, 2005, p. 39. See also SMS 2013, p. 220.

¹² SMS 2001, p. 26. "Offensive air defense" is "攻势防空."

¹³ The terms SAR and DAAR are used within SMS 2005, although they do not appear in SMS 2001 (the 2005 version of SMS is an English translation of SMS 2001). See Peng Guangqian and Yao Youzhi, eds., *Science of Military Strategy*, (Beijing: Academy of Military Sciences Press, 2005).

¹⁴ The two "patterns" not mentioned in terms of specific air roles include strategic nuclear assault and a space offensive. SMS 2001, pp. 303–304.

¹⁵ SMS 2001, p. 299.

¹⁶ SMS 2001, pp. 302, 304.

¹⁷ SMS 2001, p. 301.

¹⁸ SMS 2001, p. 302.

¹⁹ SMS 2001, pp. 302–303.

²⁰ SMS 2001, p. 317.

[21] SMS 2001, p. 317. Aviation forces are not counted as part of the air defense forces, although they play a role in the air defense mission.

[22] SMS 2001, p. 318.

[23] SMS 2001, p. 320.

[24] SMS 2001, p. 334.

[25] SMS 2001, p. 340.

[26] SMS 2001, p. 342.

[27] SMS 2001, p. 343.

[28] SMS 2001, p. 344.

[29] SMS 2001, pp. 348–349.

[30] SMS 2001, pp. 349–352.

[31] SMS 2001, p. 447.

[32] SMS 2001, p. 447.

[33] SMS 2001, pp. 313; 461.

[34] SMS 2001, p. 460.

[35] SMS 2001, p. 479.

[36] SMS 2001, p. 479.

[37] See U.S. Department of Defense, "Annual Report on the Military Power of the People's Republic of China," Arlington, VA: DoD, 2002, p. 14. For more information on the combat capability of the PLAAF in the late 1990s and early 2000s, see Eric Heginbotham, Michael Nixon, Forrest E. Morgan, Jacob L. Heim, Jeff Hagen, Sheng Li, Jeffrey Engstrom, Martin C. Libicki, Paul DeLuca, David A. Shlapak, David R. Frelinger, Burgess Laird, Kyle Brady, and Lyle J. Morris, *The U.S.-China Military Scorecard: Forces, Geography, and the Evolving Balance of Power, 1996–2017,* Santa Monica, CA: RAND Corporation, 2015.

[38] He is also the first non-Army vice chairman to wear his branch's uniform on the CMC, as Admiral Liu Huaqing, who served as a Vice Chairman from 1989 to 1996, wore an Army uniform in that position.

[39] SMS 2013, p. 222.

[40] For more on the "strategic air force" concept, please see Michael S. Chase and Cristina L. Garafola, "China's Search for a 'Strategic Air Force,'" *Journal of Strategic Studies*, September 14, 2015.

[41] SMS 2013, p. 225.

[42] SMS 2013, p. 221.

[43] SMS 2013, p. 221.

[44] SMS 2013, pp. 221–222.

[45] However, SMS 2013 does not specifically mention the term ADIZ. See the following articles detailing one patrol by the PLAAF, for example: "Expert: China Capable of Defending East China Sea ADIZ," *China Military Online*, December 2, 2015. As of March 8, 2016: http://english.chinamil.com.cn/news-channels/china-military-news/2015-12/02/content_6796532.htm; "China Air Force Conducts West Pacific Drills, Patrols ADIZ," *Xinhua*, November 27, 2015. As of March 8, 2016: http://news.xinhuanet.com/english/2015-11/27/c_134862853.htm.

[46] SMS 2013 discusses some examples of using aviation troops to conduct MOOTW (p. 157) and the role of air assets in law enforcement operations and indirectly in aid operations (p. 163). It notes that MOOTW operations can cover a wide area, which may indicate a special role for the PLAAF given that SMS 2013 describes the advantages of the PLAAF as being able to operate over large territories and distances (p. 165). On coordination mechanisms, SMS 2013 states the CCP and CMC can empower relevant HQ command organs of the PLAAF or other services to coordinate and command MOOTW activities (p. 166).

[47] For example, see "China's Rescue Materials Arrive in Nepal," *Xinhua*, April 28, 2015. As of August 3, 2015: http://english.chinamil.com.cn/news-channels/2015-04/28/content_6466339.htm; People's Republic of China, Ministry of National Defense, "Defense Ministry's Regular Press Conference on April 30, 2015," April 30, 2015. As of August 3, 2015: http://english.chinamil.com.cn/news-channels/china-military-news/2015-04/30/content_6469486.htm.

[48] SMS 2013, p. 222.

[49] Drone operations beyond China's borders have been previously discussed by Chinese officials, including during a 2013 manhunt for a Burmese drug

lord who was wanted for the deaths of 11 Chinese sailors in 2011 an official from the Public Security Bureau said that "one plan was to use an unmanned aerial vehicle to carry 20kg of TNT to bomb the area, but the plan was rejected because we were ordered to catch him alive." See Ernest Kao, "China Considered Using Drone in Myanmar to Kill Wanted Drug Lord," *South China Morning Post*, February 20, 2013. As of August 2, 2015: http://www.scmp.com/news/china/article/1154217/china-considered-using-drone-myanmar-kill-wanted-drug-lord.

[50] This section is discussed in SMS 2013, pp. 222–224.

[51] SMS 2013, pp. 224–225.

[52] SMS 2013, pp. 222–223.

[53] SMS 2013, p. 224. For the latter, specific examples listed are "air and space operational aircraft, near-space strike weapons, and airborne laser weapons."

[54] Note that this term is not the same as the one used for an ADIZ (that term is 防空识别区).

[55] For some examples, see Zhao Lei, "Air Force Now Able to Launch Long-Range, Precision Strikes," *China Daily*, October 14, 2015. As of March 8, 2016:http://www.chinadaily.com.cn/china/2015-10/14/content_22178512.htm; "H-6U Aerial Refueling Tanker Improves PLA Air Force's Long-Range Raid Capability," *China Military Online*, September 8, 2015. As of March 8, 2016: http://english.chinamil.com.cn/news-channels/china-military-news/2015-09/08/content_6671974.htm.

[56] "China's Air Force Conducted Four Drills over the Western Pacific in 2015," *China Military Online*, January 4, 2016. As of March 8, 2016: http://english.chinamil.com.cn/news-channels/china-military-news/2016-01/04/content_6842698.htm.

[57] SMS 2001 notes that conventional weapons in the air and other domains are a component of overall strategic deterrence (p. 236). SMS 2013 includes historical examples of air power bringing about a deterrent effect (p. 139). Also, there is discussion about how deterrence plays a role in safeguarding maritime sovereignty rights and interests, facilitated by air strength projection, to create a sea-air strength system (p. 145).

[58] SMS 2013, p. 226.

[59] For example, SMS 2013 states that once war has broken out, "air strikes under space-based information support will be the primary manner of strategic application of the Air Force" (p. 227).

[60] Space is discussed in SMS 2001 on pp. 342; 350 and in SMS 2013 on pp. 222; 226.

[61] It is also unclear what this phrase refers to exactly. The literal translation of the phrase "controlling space from the air" is "using air to control space."

[62] For more information on the SA-21, please see: Timothy R. Heath, "How China's New Russian Air Defense System Could Change Asia," *War on the Rocks*, January 21, 2016. As of March 7, 2016: http://warontherocks.com/2016/01/how-chinas-new-russian-air-defense-system-could-change-asia/.

[63] Heginbotham et al., *The U.S.-China Military Scorecard*, pp. 101–109.

[64] SMS 2013, p. 227.

[65] For more information on ISR missions carried out by Chinese UAVs, see Kimberly Hsu with Craig Murray, Jeremy Cook, and Amalia Feld, "China's Military Unmanned Aerial Vehicle Industry," U.S.-China Economic and Security Review Commission Staff Research Backgrounder, June 13, 2013. As of March 7, 2016: http://origin.www.uscc.gov/sites/default/files/Research/China's%20Military%20UAV%20Industry_14%20June%202013.pdf.

[66] SMS 2013, p. 222. Unfortunately, no further details on these capabilities were provided in this section.

[67] Chen Hong, a professor at the PLAAF Staff Command College, has stated that the Y-20 will enter service as early as 2016. From "China's Y-20 to be Put into Military Use in 2016, Experts Say," People's Daily Online, March 1, 2016, http://www.china.org.cn/china/2016-03/01/content_37904239.htm.

[68] SMS 2013, p. 222. Unfortunately, no further details on this capability was provided in this section.

[69] Xiao Tianliang [肖天亮], ed., *Science of Military Strategy* [战略学], National Defense University Press, April 2015, pp. 356–357.

[70] SMS 2015, pp. 349–353.

[71] Information Office of the State Council, "China's Military Strategy," May 26, 2015, http://www.china.org.cn/china/2015-05/26/content_35661433_3.htm.

Chapter 4: Doctrinal Sea Change, Making Real Waves: Examining the Maritime Dimension of Strategy

Andrew S. Erickson[1]

Powered by the world's second largest economy and defense budget, beyond its shores China has been formulating and implementing a consistent, incremental strategy of prioritizing the upholding and ultimate resolution of its outstanding territorial and maritime claims in the Near Seas (Yellow, East, and South China Seas), while more gradually developing an outer layer of less-intensive capabilities to further its interests and influence farther afield.

Although with respect to specific military hardware capabilities China is often frustratingly opaque to outside analysts, when it comes to the military "software" of strategy that informs the organization and use of its forces the People's Liberation Army (PLA) is often far more transparent, at least in its broader objectives and dimensions. Demonstrably authoritative PLA texts, such as the Academy of Military Science's (AMS) multiple versions of *Science of Military Strategy* (战略学, or SMS), are increasingly joined by official Defense White Papers (DWP) as well as a wide range of other publications and data. Considering this material together offers a fairly clear picture of where China stands militarily and its intended course for the future.

Naval and broader maritime security development, the subject of this chapter, represents the forefront of Chinese military development geographically and operationally. In this sphere, the aforementioned sources portray the PLA Navy (PLAN) as undergoing a significant strategic transformation in recent years. Likewise transforming to support comprehensive efforts at sea are China's maritime law enforcement (MLE) forces, four of which are consolidating into a China Coast Guard (CCG), and its maritime militia. The PLAN thus retains a lead role in the Near Seas, although there the world's largest blue water coast guard and largest maritime militia share important responsibilities—typically in coordination with what will soon be the world's second largest blue water navy. Beijing is thus pursuing a clear hierarchy of priorities whose importance and realization diminishes sharply with their distance from mainland Chinese territorial and maritime claims, while engaging in a comprehensive modernization and outward geographic radiation of its forces.[2]

This ongoing sea change is encapsulated particularly clearly (if not always concisely or without repetition) in the 2013 and previous editions of SMS, as well as China's 2015 DWP. This first-ever defense white paper on strategy offers the latest high-level doctrinal and strategic expression of Beijing's military development efforts—and indicates more specifically how SMS (2013) is being refined, amplified, and implemented in practice. In particular, it suggests that China's leadership is embracing new realities and displaying new sophistication in prioritizing and envisioning maritime force development, integration, and utilization across a wide range of peacetime and wartime contingencies. It charges the PLA with safeguarding China's increasingly complex, far-ranging interests through an ideally seamless comprehensive approach combining peacetime presence and pressure with combat readiness. There is unprecedented emphasis on maritime interests and operations to uphold them—imposing new challenges and opportunities on China's maritime forces, with the PLAN at their core. The DWP goes so far as to state that the "traditional mentality that land outweighs sea must be abandoned... great importance has to be attached to managing the seas and oceans and protecting maritime rights and interests."[3] It underscores determination to strengthen Chinese "strategic management of the sea" and "build a combined, multi-functional and efficient marine combat force structure."

These official publications build logically on predecessor documents and are echoed rather consistently in other contemporary documents. They are not merely words on the page, but rather are reflective of China's increasing naval and maritime developments at home and growing interests and activities abroad. This reality is underscored by the unprecedentedly robust maritime content in the 13th Five Year Plan (FYP) (2016–20) passed by the National People's Congress and released on March 17, 2016. Operationalizing many of the concepts discussed in the aforementioned publications, this most authoritative and comprehensive of all national planning documents declares that China will:

1. Build itself into a "maritime power"

2. Strengthen the exploration and development of marine resources

3. Deepen historical and legal research on maritime issues

4. Create a highly effective system for protecting overseas interests and safeguard the legitimate overseas rights/interests of Chinese citizens and legal persons

5. Actively promote the construction of strategic strong points (战略支点) for the "21st Century Maritime Silk Road"

6. Strengthen construction of reserve forces, especially the construction of maritime mobilization forces[4]

"By any standard," as Ryan Martinson cogently contends, "China has already undergone a maritime transformation." Nevertheless, "Chinese policymakers believe that China's transformation is far from complete. There is much more wealth to be generated, power to be accreted, interests to be protected, and prestige to be enjoyed through adroit crafting of marine policy." China's top development plan thereby embodies "maritime aspirations that are increasingly global in scale and scope."[5]

Given the strong demonstrable link between China's official writings about military and naval strategy and its ongoing implementation of much of their content in practice,[6] it is time to examine those vital texts deeply for signs of Beijing's past, present, and future course and speed at sea—the purpose of the remainder of this chapter.

The Underpinnings of Modern Chinese Maritime Strategy: The PLA Navy in the Jiang Zemin Era

AMS published the modern era's first update to its seminal strategic work, the *Science of Military Strategy*, in 2001. Encapsulating numerous changes to China's approach to military modernization under Jiang Zemin in the aftermath of the U.S. defeat of Saddam Hussein's army in the first Gulf War and the birth of the "Revolution in Military Affairs," the 2001 Chinese-language version was used to educate senior PLA decision-makers, including those on the Central Military Commission (CMC), as well as the officers who would one day become China's future strategic planners. Leading foreign China scholars considered it along with a variety of other texts, such as the more operationally- and tactically-focused *Science of Campaigns* (战役学), published by China's National Defense University in 2000, to better understand actual PLA strategy and doctrine. The closest U.S. equivalent to these volumes collectively might be *Doctrine for Joint Operations* (JP 3-0).

In 2005, a version translated by a team of experts was published as China's first English-language volume on strategy, as part of an apparent effort to make PLA thinking accessible to an overseas audience. Its editors, Major Generals Peng Guangqian and Yao Youzhi, enjoyed significant ability to shape PLA strategy as advisors to the CMC and Politburo Standing Committee. SMS 2001 is worth considering carefully, even though it has now been superseded by the 2013 edition, as it represents an authoritative basis of comparison for examining the PLA Navy's subsequent strategic evolution.

SMS 2001 documents the beginning of what is today widely recognized as a significant transformation of China from a chiefly-land power to a hybrid land-and-sea power. The authors describe the current age as an "'era of sea'" in which maritime states, like their predecessors, will employ Mahanian and other strategies to "actively develop comprehensive sea power" and "expand strategic depth at sea." Throughout the volume, the continuing relevance of People's War was emphasized as a foundation of Chinese military strategy, including at sea. Although at the time this fixation seemed quaint or even obsolete to many non-PLA-specialists, it is today finding significant currency in the wide-ranging development and operations of China's maritime militia.

This irregular sea force dates to the early years of the People's Republic, and finds important missions in China's continuing doctrine of "People's War at Sea," yet even today it is insufficiently recognized or understood by most foreign observers, even those charged with military operations vis-à-vis the Asia-Pacific. This enormous force, charged in part with upholding Beijing's "maritime rights and interests," is unparalleled in virtually any other country save Vietnam, which cannot compete in either scale or capabilities. It played a meaningful role in one of China's last serious military conflicts; two maritime militia trawlers played a critical role in helping China win the 1974 Battle of the Paracels against Vietnam.[7] Today, China's most elite maritime militia units are playing an important role in such international maritime events as the 2009 Impeccable Incident between China and the United States and the 2014 HYSY-981 Oil Rig Standoff between China and Vietnam.[8] While copious open source information on China's maritime militia has been available in Chinese for multiple decades, SMS 2001 offered a compelling confirmation that China's "Little Blue Men" were a significant component of Chinese sea strategy on its periphery and a force to be reckoned with.

Now, China appears poised to take the development and deployment of its maritime militia to a yet-higher level. With regard to the sixth area of emphasis noted above in China's latest FYP—"maritime mobilization forces"—a recent *PLA Daily* article made the following point concerning earlier draft text: "Although this passage in the Plan is very brief, it has delighted Hainan provincial military district political commissar Liu Xin. In the past two years he has called for "vigorously promoting maritime militia construction." Liu Xin states that the fact that the construction of maritime mobilization forces was written into the Plan 'suggests that this has become national strategy.'"[9] As paramount leader and Commander-in-Chief Xi Jinping continues his thoroughgoing downsizing and reorganization of the PLA to make it leaner, meaner, and more capable of fighting and winning modern wars through integrated joint operations, the maritime militia may well strengthen its ranks with the addition of demobilized naval forces.[10]

SMS 2001's explanation of AMS's view of the evolving nature of warfare at the end of the Jiang Zemin era, and its strategic implications for Beijing, also remains highly relevant. AMS strategists argued that China, as both a land and a sea power, faces multi-faceted strategic opportunities and challenges. Despite its 18,000-kilometer coastline, China is geographically constrained by the world's longest island chain, centering on strategically-, politically-, and economically-vital Taiwan. Taiwan is far from the only territory that mainland China claims but does not control, however: "1,000,000 square kilometers," of maritime territory, "one ninth of China's national land territory," remains under contention. The authors also identify energy supply security in particular as critical to China's national development. Their statement that the South China Sea possesses "rich oil reserves equivalent to that of [the] Middle East" conflicts with Western assessments, however, leaving the reader wondering about the true strategic underpinnings of Beijing's claims there. In keeping with China's geographically informed hierarchy of strategic priorities, strategic analysis of Taiwan in SMS 2001 appeared clearer and more consistent than that concerning the South China Sea as a whole. Today, Beijing's doctrinal publications, official statements, and efforts vis-à-vis that vast body of water reflect somewhat clearer—if still more externally-unappealing—thinking.

Chinese strategists at the time foresaw possible threats to China's "sovereignty, maritime rights, and great cause of reunification" that, should all other measures fail, may necessitate defensive (and therefore inherently just) war on China's "borderlines, seacoasts, and air spaces." The resulting "high-tech local wars" may well require the PLA to confront a technologically-superior adversary. Accordingly, the authors of SMS 2001 suggested emphasizing preemption, fielding a broad spectrum of advanced military technologies, and integrating civilian and military forces in missions (e.g., "guerilla warfare on the sea"—again, a strong suggestion of the maritime militia and its role) that incorporate political, economic, and legal warfare. Its advocacy of emphasis on emerging technologies includes asymmetric platforms it collectively termed "trump cards" (杀手锏, sometimes poorly translated into English as "assassin's mace" [11]) that presaged China's rapid development and deployment of the world's largest force of advanced sub-strategic ballistic and cruise missiles.[12] In the decade and a half since SMS 2001, Beijing has pursued a maritime security development strategy that is massive in scale and scope and wide-ranging in its implications, but hardly mysterious overall; this foundational work remains relevant as a clear exposition of the goals and approaches that continue to inform China's ongoing turn to the sea.

Chinese Maritime Strategy at the Dawn of the Xi Jinping Era

As with so many areas of China's development in recent years, doctrinal publications and the "facts on the water" that they inform are noteworthy for both their strategic consistency and their rapidity of physical implementation (in terms of hardware and personnel development and deployment, as operational employment). Whereas SMS 2001 was a sweeping intellectual document outlining both the general rationale for things that China was starting to do and many apparently nebulous aspirations for further progress, the 2013 edition describes in more acute, compelling detail a significant step forward in maritime security development that is clearly unfolding in practice before the watchful eyes of foreign observers.

SMS 2013 argues that China must build geographically outward on its existing doctrine of "active defense" by "carrying out forward edge defense" and therefore extend the potential culminating point of any future conflict as far from the mainland as possible. In an era in which China's national interests have "surpassed the traditional territorial, territorial sea, and territorial airspace scope to continuously expand toward the periphery and the world, continuously extending toward the ocean, space, and electromagnetic space," and in which "the main war threat has switched from the traditional inland direction toward the ocean direction," the PLA "must expand its military strategic view and provide strong and powerful strategic support within a greater spatial scope to maintain [China's] national interests."[13] Under these conditions, Chinese strategists fear specifically that a "strong adversary" (a euphemistic reference to the United States, perhaps in concert with one or more allies such as Japan) will project "its comprehensive distant combat superiority in the oceanic direction" to threaten China's interests. Accordingly, "the difficulty of guarding the home territory from the home territory and guarding the near seas from the near seas will become greater and greater." Therefore, the PLA must "externally push the strategic forward edge from the home territory to the periphery, from land to sea, from air to space, and from tangible spaces to intangible spaces."[14]

The concept of "forward edge defense" articulated in SMS 2013 has clear maritime implications; it feeds the general call for strategic capabilities projection radiating coast-, sea-, and ocean-ward from China's continental core, and specifically for the establishment of a Chinese "arc-shaped strategic zone that covers the Western Pacific Ocean and Northern Indian Ocean."[15] Should China lose the strategic initiative, this "protruding" arc can become a "strategic outer line" whose deterrence, absorption, and control is enabled by "operations with the mainland and the coastal waters as the strategic inner line."[16] This relates to a formulation appearing increasingly in this and other Chinese sources: "using the land to control the sea, and using the seas to control the oceans" (以陆制海, 以海制洋).[17] In keeping with the outward expansion of Chinese defense parameters, the first half of this phrase (representing a continental approach to maritime security) has long been employed in Chinese writings, but the second half (befitting Beijing's emerging hybrid land-sea power posture) is newer in its emphasis.[18]

PLA strategists see the PLA Navy as now being in its third historical period, as defined by Chinese paramount leaders' progressively advanced visions for it; a period in which the previous period's strategy of "near-seas defense" has been joined by an additional outer layer of "far-seas protection" (远海护卫).[19] As the 2015 DWP elaborates, "The PLAN will continue to organize and perform regular combat readiness patrols and maintain a military presence in relevant sea areas" while also developing growing power projection capabilities as a limited blue water navy.

This is clear doctrinal enshrinement of the hierarchically prioritized, layered approach to Chinese maritime/military development and deployment that may be observed inductively from a plethora of data points and sources. It is precisely this current concept that the PLAN and its sister sea services are presently in the process of growing into and fulfilling.

Beginning in 2004 with Hu Jintao's assigning "New Historic Missions" to the PLA and a corresponding new strategy to the

PLAN, the third era in the service's development "gradually extends the strategic front lines from the near-seas outward into the far-seas, where national survival and development interests [are also at stake]." Answering this call is requiring the PLAN to "deal with multivariate maritime threats" and "accomplish diverse maritime missions."[20]

As part of "preparation for military struggle" in order to safeguard China's "expanding national interests," the PLAN must "deal with informatized maritime local war." The 2015 DWP further emphasizes "winning informatized local wars" (打 赢信息化局部战争) as the new "basic point" of China's latest "military strategic guideline." In an indication of growing emphasis on furthering outstanding island and maritime claims in the Near Seas, the document stresses that "basic point for [Preparation for Military Struggle] will be placed on winning informatized local wars, highlighting maritime military struggle and maritime PMS." Under these conditions, *Science of Military Strategy* (2013) assigns the PLAN eight "strategic missions":

1. *Participate in large-scale operations in the main strategic axis of operations.* Front-line operational responsibilities mean that the PLAN "must prepare for military struggle involving the most difficult and complex situations."

2. *Contain and resist sea-borne invasions.* During its Century of Humiliation, Chinese coastal areas suffered repeatedly from such incursions; today unprecedented wealth and infrastructure is concentrated there. The PLAN has a special responsibility to protect against such

contingencies, particularly involving the "large-scale
high-intensity medium-to-long-range strikes" thought
to be key to potential opponents' ways of war.

3. *Protect island sovereignty and maritime rights and
interests.* Chinese official statements and doctrinal
publications, including the 2001 SMS, have long
outlined and emphasized Beijing's claims, concerns, and
goals in this regard. The 2013 SMS asserts that "Around
1.5 million square km of [China's] jurisdictional waters
are under the actual control of other nations, and over
50 islands and reefs have been occupied by other states."
China's three major sea forces—the PLAN, CCG, and
maritime militia—all have important roles to play in this
regard.

4. *Protect maritime transportation security.* This reflects
an outer layer of Chinese maritime interests and effort
ranging far beyond the Near Seas. Sea lanes are regarded
as "the 'lifeline' of China's economic and social
development." Threats from non-state actors such as
pirates are already addressed effectively by the PLAN's
continuous Gulf of Aden escort task forces since
December 2008, but the additional concern that "once a
maritime crisis or war occurs, China's sea transport
lanes could be cut off" is much harder to address.
Accordingly, the authors predict, "the Navy's future
missions in protecting sea lines of communications
(SLOCs) and ensuring the safety of maritime
transportation will be very arduous."

5. *Engage in protecting overseas interests and the rights/interests of Chinese nationals.* The massive "going out" abroad of PRC passport holders in recent years to pursue resources and wealth on land and sea creates new interests and vulnerabilities, particularly in the form of growing risks to their life and property. Overseas PLAN rescue missions assumed "a new precedent" with the service's limited role in the 2010 Libya evacuation, and SMS 2013 holds that "protecting national overseas interests and the rights of citizens and expatriates will become a regular strategic mission of the Navy." The 2015 DWP places unprecedented emphasis on having the PLA "safeguard the security of China's overseas interests."

6. *Engage in carrying out nuclear deterrence and counterattack.* China is in the process of taking its nuclear deterrent to sea. The PLAN must thereby "leverage the advantages of concealment, strike capability and the operational range of sea-based nuclear forces, and collaborate with other strategic nuclear forces to actively carry out nuclear deterrence and nuclear counterattack missions."

7. *Coordinate with the military struggle on land.* Unlike in the Cold War, when Maoist thinking and dire technological limitations relegated the PLAN to at best a tripwire subordinate to the ground-force-centric focus on luring the enemy into a ruinous war of attrition deep in the mainland, the service is now capable and empowered in its own right as a front line force to ideally

help prevent conflict from ever approaching China's shores. On this basis, the PLAN "should play a strategic flank and containment role on the naval battlefield, as well as strongly coordinate with and support onshore operations."

8. *Protecting the security of international sea space.* In fulfilling the goal promulgated in a report from the 18th CPC National Congress to "build China into a maritime power," the PLAN is also charged with safeguarding "international sea security" in increasingly numerous and diverse ways under the rubric of "harmonious oceans." This will not only help China ensure its own specific security interests, but also further assert itself more generally as "a major power with global influence" that is credited with "fulfilling its international responsibilities." [21] On a related note, the PLAN is charged with multifarious military operations other than war (MOOTW), [22] whose missions must reflect the diversity of the threats they are designed to address.[23] "In particular," the authors close their navy-specific section by stressing, "China should fully use the international platform provided by the multinational far seas escort and joint rescue missions to continuously expand and deepen maritime security cooperation." Doing so "will gradually improve China's voice and influence in international maritime security affairs."[24] This relates to a larger emphasis in the 2015 DWP, in wording echoing repeated statements by Xi: "the national security issues facing China encompass far more subjects, extend over a greater range, and cover a longer time span that at any

time in the country's history." Accordingly, the PLA must embrace a "holistic view of national security" encompassing both traditional and nontraditional security, and to be prepared for full-spectrum operations including peacetime probing and pressure, as well as "comprehensively manag[ing] crises" in addition to fledged combat readiness.

In order to fulfill its eight "strategic missions," the PLAN must make the following specific efforts:

1. *Comprehensively strengthen the construction of maritime information systems.* The further strengthening and integration of such C4ISR capabilities is central to improving the PLA Navy's ability to fight and win modern wars, a key emphasis under Xi. "In comparison with developed countries' navies, there is still a large gap in the level of China's information systems, with some important areas in which the Navy is completely lacking." The PLAN must therefore transform "its model of generating combat power and build an informatized navy" by extending "key nodes" outward, improving and better networking information systems, and improving data fusion. American observers might term this a quest to prepare for "network-centric warfare with Chinese characteristics." Other PLA sources encapsulate the idea, using the tumid phrasing typical of PLA writing, as integrated "information systems-based system of systems operations" (ISSSO), a concept first endorsed by Hu in 2005, but "not fully

articulated and operationalized by PLA strategists until after early-2010."[25]

2. *Accelerate the navy's development of next-generation main battle armaments.* Herein lies a statement that reflects much discussion in leading PLA circles, but almost certainly remains debated in its specific prioritization and advisability by some Chinese strategists. In addition to ongoing emphasis on submarines, aircraft, and missiles, SMS 2013 states, "the Navy's developmental focus will be placed on large and medium surface combatants with aircraft carriers as the core." This reflects both an ambitious effort to pursue a U.S.-style gold standard, and a perhaps more measured and nuanced commitment to forming a "carrier development and usage model with Chinese characteristics" (有中国特色的航母发展和运用模式).[26] In any case, this deck aviation centrality is part of an effort, informed by "developmental trends of the world's great power navies," to "possess a three-dimensional strike capability that combines undersea, surface, and aerospace, and long, intermediate, and close ranges." While clearly inspired in part by efforts to promote China's "international standing" as a great power, this big bet on the biggest possible ships in an era of growing long-range anti-carrier weapons recognized explicitly in the 2015 DWP as entailing accelerated worldwide use of "long-range, precise, smart, stealthy and unmanned weapons" (an asymmetric physics-based capabilities competition on which China itself is working hard to capitalize) hinges on an assumption

that is debated intensely even in hidebound U.S. Navy circles: "In the foreseeable future, aircraft carriers will remain as the main platform for comprehensively projecting maritime firepower, troops, and information power."

3. *Strive to develop sea-based strategic nuclear forces.* Despite Chinese progress in this area, AMS strategists perceive "a large gap in comparison with developed countries," voicing particular concern regarding foreign ballistic missile defense systems. They therefore recommend applying a recently-established PLA Rocket Force approach to "developing and equipping of new types of strategic nuclear submarines" which will be "nuclear and conventionally capable, and able to conduct both types of operations." Such a course of action would raise potential foreign concerns regarding miscalculation, to put it mildly.

4. *Adjust maritime force deployment and battlefield layout.* At the heart of this mandate is "organically linking the three strategic areas of coastal mainland, near-seas and far-seas." This progressive radiating of capabilities outward, and particularly southward, from mainland China, together with their consolidation and integration, will be underpinned in at least two major ways. First, China will "gradually build a large area maritime defense system stretching forward [from] the mainland and relying on islands and reefs," an effort now clearly visible in industrial-scale feature construction, augmentation, and fortification in the Spratlys and Paracels. Second,

China will "strengthen construction of large and
medium sized ports and core airports focusing on
strategic home ports to fulfill the stationing, mooring,
and supply needs of carriers, strategic nuclear
submarines, and heavy destroyer-escort formations."
These efforts are clearly underway in the form of
Chinese port development in the greater Indian Ocean
region, particularly with China's establishment of its
first overseas naval supply facility in Djibouti.

5. *Concentrate on the features of future naval war to
optimize force structure.* The PLAN is charged with
improving the structure and efficiency of its commands
and forces alike. Organization must shift from service-
based to mission-based, with new combat and support
forces developed and special operations and amphibious
forces expanded. 'Carrier battle groups' are envisioned
to be at the core of the PLAN's future force structure, as
"a strategic 'fist' for mobile operations at sea."[27]

Finally, with respect to preparing for its potential strategic use
in war in accordance with China's overall maritime combat
capabilities under informatized conditions, AMS strategists
argue that the PLAN should "highlight" the following four
aspects in its preparations for future naval operations:

1. *Give prominence to operational depth.* In keeping with
the aforementioned imperative to coordinate fluidly
among geographically-defined operational areas
radiating out from China's mainland, "China must plan
overall for the two battlefields of the near seas and far

seas" in a unified, mutually-reinforcing fashion. Enemy efforts cannot be allowed to render PLAN operations "confined to or bottled up within the near seas"; rather, China's navy must be capable of "fighting out" to meet the enemy at a culminating point as far from China's homeland as possible and turning the tables by engaging in integrated multi-domain operations that "combine strikes against the enemy's front lines and rear areas." This is part of a larger pattern articulated in the 2015 DWP in which the PLA(N) as a whole and the Navy in particular are charged by the Party with safeguarding increasingly complex, far-ranging interests in "critical domains" involving "seas and oceans, outer space, cyberspace, and nuclear forces."

2. *Give prominence to offensive operations.* This is viewed as essential for "winning the initiative and striving for victory" in "future maritime local wars," in which PLA strategists believe the party being first to act will be at a distinct advantage. Relevant missions include "maritime joint sea and air strike mobile formations, blockades by submarine forces, air assault and air strikes, and special forces infiltration and sabotage." This appears to be precisely what the 2015 DWP is referencing in its injunction to "enrich the strategic concept of active defense."

3. *Give prominence to Integrated Joint Operations.* "Integrated Joint Operations" (一体化联合作战) is a PLA term of art referring to "truly joint" operations in the sense that jointness has long been conceived by

Western militaries, in contrast with earlier PLA efforts at joint operations that more resemble what the West knows as "combined arms". This is part of a larger effort articulated in the 2015 DWP to "establish an integrated joint operational system in which all elements are seamlessly linked and various operational platforms perform independently and in coordination." IJO is "the primary form of the Navy's operations in the near-seas" because it represents the "foundation for forming systemic advantages in maritime local wars." While the PLAN is unambiguously "the main combat force at sea," and the lead force by default in any joint maritime security activity and the coordination thereof, it is nevertheless part of still-coalescing "maritime combat system" that "integrates the three services as well as both civilian and military [elements] to serve the needs of the overall situation." In other words, China's MLE, particularly the four being consolidated into a unified CCG[28] as well as the maritime militia units, are an important part of this equation. These civil maritime and irregular forces may pursue peacetime and other discrete missions under their own purview, but in recent years their involvement in the most significant international maritime confrontations (such as the aforementioned Impeccable and HYSY-981 oil rig incidents) has occurred in close coordination with PLAN forces that appear to monitor them carefully, and perhaps even direct them, in a capacity that U.S. government terms "overwatch."[29]

4. *Give prominence to asymmetric warfare.* Here the PLAN is instructed to exploit particular features of "the near and far seas battlefields" to maximum effect against a potential adversary, wherein progress in each can relieve pressure on Chinese forces in the other. The near seas call for "a variety of simultaneous or alternating patterns of war fighting," whereas the far seas demand "relatively independent operations under conditions of joint operations, highlighting the use of submarines and long-range air assaults focused on striking the enemy's important nodes and high value targets." Such "pushing the battlefield toward the enemy's operational and strategic rear" can improve Chinese breathing room vis-à-vis "the near seas battlefield."[30]

These admonitions are somewhat abstract, and offer a wide range of potential interpretations. They are grounded conceptually in the continuous, progressive geographic and conceptual expansion of China's national security interests. In an operational sense, strategic space clearly helps create depth for the implementation of China's active defense strategy and the amorphous lines and areas at sea wherein it would wage maritime combat, including maritime people's war. However, a more complex question of interpretation remains concerning how precisely Xi is directing his military/maritime forces and related actors to address China's expanding interests.

In this vein, SMS 2013 calls for "relying on one's home territory while moderately expanding the strategic space" (依托本土适度拓展战略空间), a phrase with numerous possible interpretations.[31] The crux of the matter is the term "本土,"

which SMS 2013 employs frequently but does not define directly, and the physical locations to which it refers. Given China's emphasis officially on the "indisputable" nature of its sweeping claims in the South China Sea in this document and elsewhere, this ambiguous yet potentially broadly inclusive term may refer not only to mainland China, but also all South China Sea islands, reefs, and other features claimed by Beijing. The "favorable conditions" and "laying a solid foundation" to which the authors allude could thus refer to increasing presence in claimed areas to demonstrate administration and enforcement, all the better to solidify the territorial foundation for forward-supported strategic expansion.[32] China's aforementioned 'island building' and maritime fortification activities would follow directly from such an approach.

At a minimum, the authors envision a very significant further radiating-outward of China's interests, capabilities, and forces:

> Along with the continuous rise of our military's military capability, we will have higher strategic requirements and needs in the area of relying on one's own territory (本土) to expand the strategic space. We need to need to gradually push forward from the current strategic space mainly at the home territory and coastal seas toward the relevant sea regions, outer space, and the information network space... with the strategic thought of "reliance on the home territory, stabilize the peripheral, grasp and control the coastal seas, advance into space, focus on information," to form into a strategic space

that has key-points, divided into echelons, and is mutually supporting and linked, with home territory as reliance, Two Oceans as the key point, and network space as the crux.[33]

This brings us back to a Chinese maritime theater concept not widely discussed in previous authoritative Chinese documents: the idea of a dual Indo-Pacific focus for China's navy, as encapsulated in the aforementioned "arc-shaped strategic zone that covers the Western Pacific Ocean and Northern Indian Ocean."[34] This zone is now termed the "Two Oceans region/area" (两洋地区) in authoritative sources, and is described as "mainly" including "the Pacific Ocean, Indian Ocean, as well as the littoral regions of neighboring Asia, Africa, Oceania, North America, South America, and Antarctica, etc., with a total area occupying over 50 percent of the globe; within which the Two Oceans have a total area of 254.6 million square meters, occupying 71 percent of the global ocean area."[35]

The authors of SMS 2013 describe the Two Oceans region as being extremely important to China and its security interests. It represents "a crucial area in influencing" China's "strategic development and security in the future" as well as "the intermediate zone of our entrance into the Atlantic Ocean region, Mediterranean Sea region, and Arctic Ocean region." In accordance with the globalizing nature of China's activities, they declare, its "national interests will surpass in an extremely large manner the traditional territorial land, territorial sea, and territorial air scope, while the Two Oceans region will become the most important platform and medium." On this basis, Chinese actors "will create conditions to establish ourselves in the Two Oceans region, participate in resource extraction and space utilization of the oceans, and boost development in the two polar regions." To be sure, the authors allow, new challenges and "security threats" of both a traditional and a non-traditional nature should be expected to accompany this sweeping geostrategic expansion, "especially [from] the oceanic direction." These interrelated factors are likely to offer a continued rationale for concerted qualitative and quantitative development of the PLAN for years to come:

> Because our at-sea sovereignty and interests have frequently come under intrusions, while intensification in the crises may very possibly ignite conflicts or war, we need to form into a powerful and strong Two Oceans layout in order to face the crises that may possibly erupt. Therefore, we should focus on maintaining expansion in the national interests, defend the at-sea interests, and rely upon the home territory to reasonably and appropriately expand the strategic space toward the Two Oceans region.[36]

Even amid continued hierarchical prioritization, Chinese strategists appear to have left the PLAN considerable geographic "room to grow" for even its most important operations: literally half the globe!

Charting the Evolution of Chinese Naval Strategy

While the latest iteration of *Science of Military Strategy* arguably builds on its predecessors as part of a logical continuum, it is worth highlighting some specific differences, particularly between the 2001 and 2013 editions.

- *Change from "Local War under High Tech Conditions" to "Local War under Informatized Conditions".* Although the 2001 SMS introduced the growing importance of local war under high-tech conditions, and its gradual becoming the fundamental pattern in high-tech local war, the specific approach has evolved somewhat, reflecting both China's broader informatization policy and the PLA's focus on the sort of modern integrated, network-centric warfare for which the U.S. military is regarded as the gold standard.

- *Adoption of a two-layered strategy: "Near-Seas Defense, Far-Seas Operations"* (近海防御、远海防卫). The goal of China becoming a "Maritime Great Power" (海洋强国), which is emphasized as one of the key goals for the PLAN in the 2013 SMS, informs its new two-part naval strategy. There does not seem to be an equivalent strategic phrase to "far seas operations" in the 2001 SMS, but the idea of multi-layered operations in the near-seas and development of far-seas operational capabilities is not a new one. What makes this strategic phrase interesting is the difference in the choice of wording for defense: the term *fangwei* (防卫) rather than *fangyu* (防御) for the second part of the strategic formulation, logically suggesting a lower level of intensity for the latter, more geographically distant operations. Both terms could be translated as 'defense' and there is not always a clear distinction between the two, but they do have distinctly different implications. *Fangyu*, the more-narrowly-focused, higher-intensity, and more demanding of the two, refers to actively "resisting the operational missions of enemy attacks," and is "one of the fundamental types of warfighting." Examples might include using land-, ship-, and aircraft-based systems to defend PLAN surface vessels and submarines implementing a blockade of Taiwan. *Fangwei*, by contrast, refers to "defense and holding" across a broader range of more diverse, diffuse contingencies. Examples might include using the far-more-limited ship-based weapons systems on elements of a budding 'battle group' to create a protective envelope around a Chinese aircraft carrier transiting the Indian Ocean en route to showing the flag and assisting the evacuation of PRC citizens from a destabilizing Middle Eastern country. [37] To be sure, this strategic dichotomy is contextual rather than absolute, as SMS 2013 instructs the PLA(N), and in particular the PLA Navy, to blend and integrate the levels and areas of operations wherever and whenever it is required. [38]

- *Enhancing "active defense" to distance potential enemy operations from China's shores.* This new multi-layered PLAN strategy reflects broader efforts to "carry out forward defense" that represent a sea change from the concepts espoused in 2001 SMS. [39] Accordingly, SMS 2013 places unprecedented emphasis on strengthening forward presence: "Optimizing the strategic layout involves the handling of the needs of war threats, protecting expanding national interests, and the transformation of homeland defense toward forward operations...."[40] This entails moving from purely defense of the homeland into defense of strategic front lines, especially of sea areas, thereby pushing these operational frontiers far away from the Chinese homeland. It includes emphasis on the "strategic pursuit" (战略追击) of a routed enemy and the radiation of force projection into surrounding areas.[41] It requires giving prominence to "effective control" and engaging in joint, distant operations under informatized conditions.[42] Emphasis on asymmetric warfare—extensive but more theoretical in SMS 2001, considerably more focused on practical implementation in SMS 2013—is at the core of this sweeping effort to "transform the mode of generating combat power" (转变战斗力生成模式). Such "giving prominence to asymmetrical warfare" is intended in part to increase PLA ability to create "relative superiority."[43] New emphasis includes focusing on striking enemy important nodes and high-value targets, and pushing the battlefield toward the enemy's operational and strategic rear, thereby alleviating the pressure on battles in the near-seas.[44]

- *Expanding strategic space in keeping with national interests.* One of the key themes permeating SMS 2013 is the oft-invoked idea of expanding interests coinciding with the necessary expansion of strategic space past current front lines, namely eastward and southward into the Two Ocean region of the Pacific and Indian Oceans.[45] This builds on the far more elementary, less-extensive, and less-geographically specific discussion in

SMS 2001 of China's expansion of strategic space. Likewise, SMS 2001 introduces the concept of "strategic center of gravity" (战略重心), but it is the 2013 edition that stipulates that this is now moving southward toward the South China Sea. In evidence of a comparative consideration of key nations' military-strategic focus, SMS 2013 frequently describes the U.S. Asia-Pacific Rebalance as a shift in the American strategic center of gravity, using the term " '战略重心'的转移" to describe its interpretation of Washington's desire to "cast off" the Iraq and Afghanistan wars in order to focus more on the East Asian littoral. As for the similar locus of China's current military efforts, SMS 2013 discusses the importance of "battlefield construction" in the South China Sea, including efforts to pre-empt conflict through proper war preparation and battlefield construction, strategic prepositioning of troops, materials, and equipment. Such measures, it contends, will help to consolidate forward presence and expand strategic space, which will ultimately deepen the strategic defensive space. Observing Beijing's current activities in the South China Sea, it appears that some of these measures are indeed being implemented in practice.

- *Unprecedented stressing of the need to engage in "strategic prepositioning."* When considered in conjunction with such Chinese activities in the greater Indian Ocean Region as port development projects, port calls and naval drills with nations such as Pakistan, and recent establishment of a naval supply facility in Djibouti, the term "战略预置" (translated in the authoritative 2005 AMS translation of SMS 2001 as "preset," but perhaps more aptly-termed "strategic prepositioning"), may suggest integrated movement toward the implementation of a Two Ocean strategy. The related term 预储 was translated in the same work as "preposition," but regardless of the precise translation, strategic prepositioning is emphasized considerably more strongly in the 2013 SMS. There, the term is employed many times in various contexts to which much significance attached—in contrast to a single appearance in the 2001 SMS. [46] Importantly, in the author's note at the very end of SMS 2013, strategic preposition is listed as one of the items that was deliberately strengthened within the text per several experts' suggestion. [47]

- *Increased emphasis on MOOTW and international maritime contributions.* The 2013 SMS attaches much greater importance to the role of military operations other than war, and devotes a dedicated portion of its discussion of naval strategy to the Navy's role therein. There is also a stronger recognition, stated multiple times, of the Navy as an 'international service branch,' entailing greater responsibilities for protecting international seas. The related phrase "harmonious oceans" does not appear in the 2001 SMS, but is an important concept encapsulating one of the major strategic missions of the Navy in the 2013 SMS, having first been introduced in 2008 by Hu. [48] This emerging line of strategic thinking may not be prioritized equally by Xi, but is nevertheless continuing, with promising implications for Chinese and global security alike. In contrast to the aforementioned Chinese efforts to further Near Seas claims, which risk perpetuating a zero-sum mentality and ratcheting upward of regional geostrategic tensions, PLAN Far Seas operations can make a positive-sum contribution to international security. Provision of public goods in the form of UN Peacekeeping deployments, Gulf of Aden anti-piracy operations, overseas hospital ship visits, and perhaps even more robust efforts going forward can afford Beijing the recognition that it craves while creating true 'win-win' benefits and potential areas for future cooperation.[49]

Analyzed in juxtaposition over time, and compared against specific empirical manifestations of Beijing's burgeoning efforts in the maritime domain, China's major doctrinal publications and public statements reveal a sea change in strategic priorities and emerging capabilities to further them. China retains an incremental approach, in keeping with a disciplined hierarchy of national security priorities, but this layered development is already making major outward-radiating waves as the Middle Kingdom turns increasingly seaward as a hybrid land-sea great power.

Whether viewed deductively from strategic intentions, or inductively from development, operational, and tactical actions, China's increasingly-modernized and -integrated maritime forces—centered on the PLAN—are pursuing a two-fold effort: intensive "near seas active defense" of outstanding island and maritime claims on China's maritime periphery, coupled with "far seas protection" of more diffuse, diverse interests beyond.

Real-world developments, and particularly ongoing Chinese activities vis-à-vis the South China Sea, suggest that the strategic thinking embodied in the various iterations of SMS, the DWP, and related official publications and statements is not merely "words on a page" but rather is strongly indicative of actual PLA planning and action—both now and in the future. Analysts of China's armed forces in general, and its navy in particular, should therefore continue to consider in-depth what some of Beijing's latest conceptual thinking may mean when it is increasingly put into practice in the coming years. In that regard, three concepts in particular should enjoy top priority for further explication: Chinese "home territory" and its role in force projection, the nature and expansion of Chinese "strategic space," and activities and prioritization within the "Two Oceans" strategic zone envisioned for heightened naval operations.

NOTES

[1] The author thanks Conor Kennedy and Ryan Martinson for invaluable inputs.

[2] For articulation, empirical analysis, and specific substantiation of China's hierarchy of strategic priorities, see Andrew S. Erickson, "China's Near-Seas Challenges," *The National Interest* 129 (January-February 2014): pp. 60–66, http://nationalinterest.org/article/chinas-near-seas-challenges-9645; Andrew S. Erickson, "The Pentagon's 2016 China Military Report: What You Need to Know," *The National Interest*, May 14, 2016, http://nationalinterest.org/feature/the-pentagons-2016-china-military-report-what-you-need-know-16209; Office of the Secretary of Defense, *Military and Security Developments Involving the People's Republic of China 2016* (Arlington, VA: Department of Defense, May 13, 2016), http://www.defense.gov/Portals/1/Documents/pubs/2016%20China%20Mil itary%20Power%20Report.pdf; *The PLA Navy: New Capabilities and Missions for the 21st Century* (Suitland, MD: Office of Naval Intelligence, April 9, 2015), http://www.oni.navy.mil/Intelligence-Community/China.

[3] While the DWP's stress on this point suggests that debate concerning the optimal land-sea balance for China remains strongly debated, its inclusion is unprecedented historically and bureaucratically. For context, see Andrew S. Erickson, Lyle J. Goldstein, and Carnes Lord, eds., *China Goes to Sea: Maritime Transformation in Comparative Historical Perspective* (Annapolis, MD: Naval Institute Press, July 2009); Andrew S. Erickson and Joel Wuthnow, "Barriers, Springboards and Benchmarks: China Conceptualizes the Pacific 'Island Chains,'" *The China Quarterly* 225 (March 2016): pp. 1–22.

[4] Su Xiangdong [苏向东], Ed., China's Five Year Plan for Social and Economic Development (Full Text) [中国国民经济和社会发展第十三个五年规划纲要（全文）], Xinhua, March 17, 2016, http://www.china.com.cn/lianghui/news/2016-03/17/content_38053101.htm, http://www.china.com.cn/lianghui/news/2016-03/17/content_38053101_11.htm, http://www.china.com.cn/lianghui/news/2016-03/17/content_38053101_14.htm, http://www.china.com.cn/lianghui/news/2016-03/17/content_38053101_20.htm. The author thanks Ryan Martinson for bringing these documents to his attention.

[5] Ryan D. Martinson, "The 13th Five-Year Plan: A New Chapter in China's Maritime Transformation," Jamestown *China Brief*, January 12, 2016,

https://jamestown.org/program/the-13th-five-year-plan-a-new-chapter-in-chinas-maritime-transformation/.

[6] This correlation may be observed over time in Peter A. Dutton, "A Maritime or Continental Order for Southeast Asia and the South China Sea?" Presentation at Chatham House, 16 February 2016, https://www.chathamhouse.org/event/south-china-sea-and-future-maritime-east-asia; Bonnie S. Glaser and Peter A. Dutton, "The U.S. Navy's Freedom of Navigation Operation around Subi Reef: Deciphering U.S. Signaling," November 6, 2015, http://nationalinterest.org/feature/the-us-navy%E2%80%99s-freedom-navigation-operation-around-subi-reef-14272; Peter A. Dutton, Professor and Director, China Maritime Studies Institute, U.S. Naval War College, *Testimony before the U.S.-China Economic and Security Review Committee Hearing on China's Maritime Disputes in the East and South China Seas,* April 4, 2013, http://www.uscc.gov/sites/default/files/Dutton%20Testimony,%20April%204%202013.pdf; Peter Dutton, Associate Professor, China Maritime Studies Institute, U.S. Naval War College, *Testimony before the United States Senate Committee on Foreign Relations Hearing on Maritime Disputes and Sovereignty Issues in East Asia,* July 15, 2009, http://www.foreign.senate.gov/imo/media/doc/DuttonTestimony090715p.pdf; Peter A. Dutton, Associate Professor, U.S. Naval War College, *Testimony before the U.S.-China Economic and Security Review Committee Hearing on The Implications of China's Naval Modernization for the United States,* June 11, 2009, http://www.uscc.gov/sites/default/files/6.11.09Dutton.pdf; Peter A. Dutton, Associate Professor, China Maritime Studies Institute, U.S. Naval War College, *Testimony before the U.S.-China Economic and Security Review Commission on China's Views of Sovereignty and Methods of Access Control,* February 27, 2008, http://www.uscc.gov/sites/default/files/08_02_27_dutton_statement.pdf.

[7] Toshi Yoshihara, "The 1974 Paracels Sea Battle: A Campaign Appraisal," *Naval War College Review* 69.2 (Spring 2016): pp. 41–65, https://www.usnwc.edu/getattachment/7b5ec8a0-cc48-4d9b-b558-a4f1cf92e7b8/The1974ParacelsSeaBattle.aspx; Andrew S. Erickson and Conor M. Kennedy, "Trailblazers in Warfighting: The Maritime Militia of Danzhou," *Center for International Maritime Security,* February 1, 2016, http://cimsec.org/trailblazers-warfighting-maritime-militiadanzhou/21475.

[8] Conor M. Kennedy and Andrew S. Erickson, "From Frontier to Frontline: Tanmen Maritime Militia's Leading Role: Part 2," Center for International Maritime Security (CIMSEC), 17 May 2016, http://cimsec.org/frontier-frontline-tanmen-maritime-militias-leading-role-pt-2/25260; Conor M. Kennedy and Andrew S. Erickson, "Model Maritime Militia: Tanmen's Leading Role in the April 2012 Scarborough Shoal Incident," Center for International Maritime Security (CIMSEC), 21 April 2016, http://cimsec.org/model-maritime-militia-tanmens-leading-role-april-2012-scarborough-shoal-incident/24573; Andrew S. Erickson and Conor M. Kennedy, "China's Maritime Militia," CNA Corporation, March 7, 2016, https://www.cna.org/cna_files/pdf/Chinas-Maritime-Militia.pdf; Andrew S. Erickson and Conor M. Kennedy, "China's Daring Vanguard: Introducing Sanya City's Maritime Militia," *Center for International Maritime Security*, November 5, 2015, http://cimsec.org/chinas-daringvanguard-introducing-sanya-citys-maritime-militia/19753; Christopher P. Cavas, "China's 'Little Blue Men' Take Navy's Place in Disputes," *Defense News*, November 2, 2015, http://www.defensenews.com/story/defense/naval/2015/11/02/china-lassen-destroyer-spratly-islands-south-chinasea-andrew-erickson-naval-war-college-militia-coast-guard-navy-confrontation-territorial-dispute/75070058/; Andrew S. Erickson and Conor M. Kennedy, "Irregular Forces at Sea: 'Not Merely Fishermen—Shedding Light on China's Maritime Militia'," *Center for International Maritime Security*, November 2,2015, http://cimsec.org/newcimsec-series-on-irregular-forces-at-sea-not-merely-fishermen-shedding-light-on-chinas-maritime-militia/19624; Andrew S. Erickson, "Making Waves in the South China Sea," A ChinaFile Conversation, Asia Society, October 30, 2015, http://www.chinafile.com/conversation/making-waves-south-china-sea; Andrew S. Erickson and Conor M. Kennedy, "Directing China's 'Little Blue Men': Uncovering the Maritime Militia Command Structure," *Asia Maritime Transparency Initiative*, Center for Strategic and International Studies, September 9, 2015, http://www.andrewerickson.com/2015/11/chinas-daring-vanguard-introducing-sanya-citys-maritime-militia/; Andrew S. Erickson, "New U.S. Security Strategy Doesn't Go Far Enough on South China Sea," China Real Time Report [中国实时报], *Wall Street Journal*, August 24, 2015, http://blogs.wsj.com/chinarealtime/2015/08/24/newasia-pacific-maritime-security-strategy-necessary-but-insufficient/?mod=WSJBlog; Andrew S. Erickson and Conor M. Kennedy,

"Tanmen Militia: China's 'Maritime Rights Protection' Vanguard," *The National Interest*, May 6, 2015, http://www.nationalinterest.org/feature/tanmen-militia-china%E2%80%99s-maritime-rights-protection-vanguard-12816; Andrew S. Erickson and Conor M. Kennedy, "China's Island Builders: The People's War at Sea," *Foreign Affairs*, April 9, 2015, https://www.foreignaffairs.com/articles/east-asia/2015-04-09/china-s-island-builders; Andrew S. Erickson and Conor M. Kennedy, "Meet the Chinese Maritime Militia Waging a 'People's War at Sea'," China Real Time Report [中国实时报], *Wall Street Journal*, March 31, 2015, http://blogs.wsj.com/chinarealtime/2015/03/31/meet-the-chinese-maritime-militia-waging-a-peoples-war-at-sea/.

9 Yang Zurong [杨祖荣], "Military Representatives Discuss the 'Thirteenth Five Year Plan': Increase Manpower Efforts Concerning Economic and National Defense Construction," ["军队代表谈 '十三五': 加大经济建设和国防建设统筹力度"], *PLA Daily*, March 7, 2016, http://zb.81.cn/content/2016-03/07/content_6945906.htm.

10 Phillip C. Saunders and Joel Wuthnow, *China's Goldwater-Nichols? Assessing PLA Organizational Reforms* (Washington, DC: Institute for National Strategic Studies, National Defense University, April 2016), http://ndupress.ndu.edu/Portals/68/Documents/stratforum/SF-294.pdf

11 For background and explanation, see Andrew S. Erickson, *Chinese Anti-Ship Ballistic Missile Development: Drivers, Trajectories, and Strategic Implications* (Washington, DC: Jamestown Foundation, May 2013), especially p. 30, pp. 34–39; Andrew S. Erickson, "Raining Down: Assessing the Emergent ASBM Threat," *Jane's Navy International*, March 16, 2016.

12 See Andrew S. Erickson, "Academy of Military Science Researchers: 'Why We Had to Develop the Dongfeng-26 Ballistic Missile'—Bilingual Text, Analysis & Related Links," *China Analysis from Original Sources* 以第一手资料研究中国, December 5, 2015, http://www.andrewerickson.com/2015/12/academy-of-military-science-researchers-why-we-had-to-develop-the-dongfeng-26-ballistic-missile-bilingual-text-analysis-links/.

13 SMS 2013, pp. 105–106.

14 SMS 2013, p. 106.

15 SMS 2013, p. 106.

[16] SMS 2013, p. 108.

[17] SMS 2013, pp. 102, 109.

[18] For example, this concept was employed a decade ago to explain the rationale for Chinese anti-ship ballistic missile development. Wang Wei, [王伟], "The Effect of Tactical Ballistic Missiles on the Maritime Strategy System of China" ["战术导弹对中国海洋战略体系的影响"], *Shipborne Weapons* [舰载武器], 84 (August 2006): pp. 12–15.

[19] SMS 2013, p. 212.

[20] SMS 2013, p. 209.

[21] SMS 2013, pp. 209–12.

[22] SMS 2013 , p. 215.

[23] SMS 2013 , p. 217.

[24] SMS 2013 , p. 218.

[25] Nan Li, "China's Evolving Naval Strategy and Capabilities in the Hu Jintao Era," pp. 257–99; especially pp. 269–70, http://www.strategicstudiesinstitute.army.mil/pdffiles/PUB1201.pdf.

[26] SMS 2013 , p. 232.

[27] SMS 2013 , pp. 213–15.

[28] For leading analysis on China's civil maritime forces and consolidating CCG, see Ryan D. Martinson, "The Courage to Fight and Win: The PLA Cultivates Xuexing for the Wars of the Future," Jamestown Foundation *China Brief* 16.9, June 1, 2016, https://jamestown.org/program/the-courage-to-fight-and-win-the-pla-cultivates-xuexing-for-the-wars-of-the-future/; Ryan D. Martinson, "Shepherds of the South Seas," Survival 58.3 (2016): pp. 187–212, http://www.tandfonline.com/doi/abs/10.1080/00396338.2016.1186987?journalCode=tsur20;Ryan D. Martinson, "Deciphering China's Armed Intrusion Near the Senkaku Islands," *The Diplomat*, January 11, 2016, http://thediplomat.com/2016/01/deciphering-chinas-armed-intrusion-near-the-senkaku/; Ryan D. Martinson, "China's Great Balancing Act Unfolds: Enforcing Maritime Rights vs. Stability," *The National Interest*,

September 11, 2015, http://www.nationalinterest.org/feature/chinas-great-balancing-act-unfolds-enforcing-maritime-rights-13821; Ryan D. Martinson, "From Words to Actions: The Creation of the China Coast Guard," a paper for the China as a "Maritime Power" Conference, CNA Corporation, Arlington, VA, July 28–29, 2015, https://www.cna.org/cna_files/pdf/creation-china-coast-guard.pdf; Ryan D. Martinson, "East Asian Security in the Age of the Chinese Mega-Cutter," Center for International Maritime Security, July 3, 2015, http://cimsec.org/east-asian-security-age-chinese-mega-cutter/16974; Ryan D. Martinson, "China's Second Navy," U.S. Naval Institute *Proceedings* 141.4 (April 2015), http://www.usni.org/magazines/proceedings/2015-04-0/chinas-second-navy; Ryan D. Martinson, "Jinglue Haiyang: The Naval Implications of Xi Jinping's New Strategic Concept," *China Brief*, January 9, 2015, https://jamestown.org/program/jinglue-haiyang-the-naval-implications-of-xi-jinpings-new-strategic-concept/; Ryan D. Martinson, "Chinese Maritime Activism: Strategy Or Vagary?" *The Diplomat*, December 18, 2014, http://thediplomat.com/2014/12/chinese-maritime-activism-strategy-or-vagary/; Ryan D. Martinson, "The Militarization of China's Coast Guard," *The Diplomat*, November 21, 2014, http://thediplomat.com/2014/11/the-militarization-of-chinas-coast-guard/; Ryan Martinson, "Here Comes China's Great White Fleet," *The National Interest*, October 1, 2014, http://nationalinterest.org/feature/here-comes-china%E2%80%99s-great-white-fleet-11383; Ryan Martinson, "Power to the Provinces: The Devolution of China's Maritime Rights Protection," *China Brief*, September 10, 2014, https://jamestown.org/program/power-to-the-provinces-the-devolution-of-chinas-maritime-rights-protection/.

[29] See, for example, Office of the Secretary of Defense, *Military and Security Developments Involving the People's Republic of China 2015* (Arlington, VA: Department of Defense, May 8, 2015), http://www.defense.gov/Portals/1/Documents/pubs/2015_China_Military_Power_Report.pdf. pp. 7, 44.

[30] SMS 2013, pp. 216–17.

[31] SMS 2013, p. 244.

[32] SMS 2013, pp. 244–46.

[33] SMS 2013, p. 245.

---

[34] SMS 2013, p. 106.

[35] SMS 2013, p. 247.

[36] SMS 2013, pp. 246–47.

[37] Quotations are from Wang Bindang, Zhang Hao, and Ye Qinqing [王斌党, 张浩, 叶钦卿], Fangwei Does Not Equal Fangyu ["防卫不等于防御"], China Defense News [中国国防报], December 4, 2008; hypothetical examples were devised by the author.

[38] SMS 2013, p. 232.

[39] SMS 2013, Chapter 5, Section 1.

[40] SMS 2013, p. 265.

[41] SMS 2013, p. 122.

[42] SMS 2013, p. 121-27.

[43] SMS 2013, pp. 234 and 462.

[44] SMS 2013, p. 234.

[45] See, for example, SMS 2013 , pp. 121–123.

[46] SMS 2005, p. 320. This page, in Chapter 14, section IV, number 6, "Combining Preposition with Maneuver," describes how modern warfare is relatively short, with very high "war consumption." It explains that "the so-called prewar strategic preposition refers to the storing in advance, according to the strategic judgment, of the weapons, equipment and materials in organizational system in the vicinity of potential theater of operations, so that these weapons, equipment and materials can be quickly moved to the theater of operations at the advent of war."

[47] SMS 2013, p. 292.

[48] SMS 2013, pp. 229–230, 235.

[49] For in-depth consideration of these geographically-linked negative and positive implications, see Andrew S. Erickson, "China's Military Modernization: Many Improvements, Three Challenges, and One Opportunity," in Jacques deLisle and Avery Goldstein, eds., China's Challenges (Philadelphia, PA: University of Pennsylvania Press, 2014), pp. 178–203.

Chapter 5: PLA Rocket Force: Executors of China's Nuclear Strategy and Policy

Michael S. Chase

This chapter offers a detailed analysis of the evolution of Chinese thinking on nuclear and PLARF issues in the two most recent AMS editions of the Science of Military Strategy, as well as authoritative policy documents such as recent Defense White Papers. The first section of the chapter covers some organizational and topical similarities and differences between the two volumes. The second provides a summary of the PLA's foundational thinking on these topics, as conveyed in SMS 2001 as well as subsequent authoritative writings. The third addresses issues of nuclear policy, strategy, and force modernization, including the recent re-organization of the PLASAF into the PLARF. The fourth covers PLARF strategy and capabilities. The fifth and final section offers some concluding observations.

Although there have been a number of important developments in Chinese nuclear capabilities over the past decade, such as the deployment of road mobile ICBMs and nuclear-powered ballistic missile submarines (SSBNs), an analysis of authoritative Chinese sources reveals a high degree of continuity over time in PLA thinking on nuclear policy and strategy. At the same time, however, SMS 2013 does seem to suggest some evolution in Chinese thinking about nuclear issues, hinting at internal debates that are likely to emerge as China further develops its capabilities and embarks in 2016 on a major reorganization of the PLA's force structure. Analysts of Chinese nuclear policy will need to watch closely for these debates in the future, since China's growing capabilities will give Chinese leaders a broader range of policy options in their nuclear toolkit.

SMS 2013's coverage of PLARF strategy and missile force modernization underscores the priority Beijing attaches to further strengthening PLARF's nuclear and conventional missile capabilities. It also envisioned a growing role in space, and perhaps cyberspace, for China's strategic missile force, reflecting a degree of tension and uncertainty within the PLA regarding their future force structure (particularly for information warfare-related capabilities) that is only now being resolved with the major reorganization now underway.

Core Foundations of China's Approach to Nuclear Deterrence

SMS 1987 and SMS 2001 are important texts for scholars and analysts concerned with China's approach to nuclear deterrence because they provide a solid, authoritative baseline of Chinese thinking on nuclear issues and where they fit in the broader context of military strategy. As such, they allow for useful comparisons with later work, such as the portions of SMS 2013 that are relevant to nuclear policy and strategy.

SMS 1987 covers nuclear policy and strategy relatively briefly, but it is essential reading because it provides a starting point for examining Chinese thinking on these issues, illustrating the remarkable continuity in Chinese thinking over time. For example, SMS 1987 encapsulates China's nuclear no first use policy, stating that "China's nuclear strategy is defensive in nature, but if an enemy is first to use nuclear weapons, China will resolutely implement a nuclear counter-strike and carry out nuclear retaliation."[1] SMS 1987 also outlined the mission of the PLA's nuclear missile force as follows:

> "In peacetime, the mission of the Second Artillery is to bring nuclear deterrence into play, so as to deter enemies from launching a nuclear war against China, and to support China's peaceful foreign policy....in wartime, the strategic mission is to prevent conventional war from escalating into nuclear war, and to contain the escalation of nuclear war; and—if China suffers the enemy's nuclear attack—to conduct a nuclear counter-attack, striking the enemy's strategic targets and weakening its war potential and strategic attack forces."[2]

The general approach outlined in SMS 1987 carries forward to SMS 2001. Importantly, however, SMS 2001 identifies nuclear deterrence as one of four "main types of strategic deterrence," along with conventional, space, and information deterrence, with nuclear deterrence defined as "the deterrent action and posture of taking nuclear force as backup power to shock and contain the opponent by threatening to use nuclear weapons or determining to carry out nuclear counterattack." [3] Nuclear deterrence is seen as a psychological process that is closely linked to the achievement of policy objectives. According to the authors of SMS 2001, its essence is to influence the adversary's decision-making calculus by causing them to recognize that the "likely grave consequences" of their actions will outweigh any potential gains, thus forcing them to "obey the deterrer's volition or to give up his original attempts, thus enabling the deterrer to attain the political objective."[4]

According to SMS 2001, the deterrent potential of nuclear weapons brought about a transformation in international politics and military strategy. It states: "the advent of nuclear weapons breached the traditional model that weapons could be effective only within the scope of operations and combat, and that strategic objectives could only be attained gradually."[5]

One thing that nuclear weapons did not change, however, was the fact that real and concrete capabilities are required to deter an enemy. Nuclear deterrence is understood to be "based on the development level of [one's] nuclear strength." Importantly, the authors of SMS 2001 classify nuclear deterrence according to what they refer to as "three gradations" of nuclear strength: maximum, minimum and "moderate intensity" nuclear deterrence. In this rubric, "maximum nuclear deterrence" is "designed to threaten the opponent by disarming him using just a first massive nuclear strike to attain the aim of containing and coercing him, so long as the deterrer possesses quantitatively and qualitatively superior nuclear forces." In contrast, "minimum nuclear deterrence" has much lower requirements, as it "depends on a handful of nuclear weapons to threaten the opponent with strikes against his cities." Finally, there is "nuclear deterrence of moderate intensity," which the authors of SMS 2001 describe as occupying a place on the nuclear deterrence spectrum that falls in between the extremes of maximum and minimum deterrence. Specifically, they write that nuclear deterrence of moderate intensity relies on a "sufficient and effective" level of nuclear strike capability, such that one can threaten the opponent with "an unbearable destruction to an extent that achieves the objective of...deterrence."[6] The authors do not state explicitly which of these types of deterrence China practices, but their use of the words "sufficient and effective," which are often associated with descriptions of China's nuclear deterrent forces, implies that it is actually "nuclear deterrence of moderate intensity" rather than "minimum nuclear deterrence."

Although Chinese strategists frequently highlight the importance of nuclear deterrence, they also often acknowledge in SMS 2001 and elsewhere that nuclear deterrence "is not almighty, and it has many limitations." First, because nuclear weapons are so destructive, nuclear deterrence "can hardly be employed at will in warfighting, particularly in a local war." Moreover, because of the situation of mutual nuclear deterrence that exists between major nuclear powers, any nation making a nuclear threat will be "confronted with the danger of nuclear retaliation." As a result, "the credibility of nuclear deterrence is greatly reduced, and its effect in restraining a local war is clearly diminished."[7] In this view, the limitations of nuclear deterrence have become "increasingly exposed" in the decades since nuclear weapons were last used in combat. Conventional deterrence has become a more credible and controllable option, particularly with China's development of its long-range strike capabilities. Nuclear deterrence, however, continues to play an important role as the "backup power" of Chinese "integrated strategic deterrence."[8]

The Evolution of China's Nuclear Policy, Strategy, and Force Modernization

The essential elements of China's approach to nuclear deterrence outlined above have not been overwritten or fundamentally altered. Nonetheless, some subtle shifts in emphasis are visible over time.

A half-decade after SMS 2001 gave the foundational assessment described above, China's 2006 Defense White Paper summarized the key elements of China's nuclear policy and its general approach to nuclear weapons at the time. Although DWPs are diplomatic documents aimed at foreign audiences and must thus be taken with that caveat when they delve into sensitive matters, they do nevertheless carry considerable weight as fully vetted statements of official Chinese foreign and military policy, particularly in areas such as nuclear policy where China benefits from clearly communicating its intentions to neighbors and potential rivals.

The 2006 DWP, which was the first to address nuclear issues, states that China remains "firmly committed to the policy of No First Use of nuclear weapons at any time and under any circumstances," and contains an unconditional pledge not to "use or threaten to use nuclear weapons" against non-nuclear-weapon states or in "nuclear-weapon-free zones." At least in principle, it also voices support for the comprehensive prohibition and complete elimination of nuclear weapons." At the same time, however, China vows that it "upholds the principles of counterattack in self-defense and limited development of nuclear weapons," with the aim of "building a lean and effective nuclear force capable of meeting national security needs," including serving as a "credible nuclear deterrent force." Ultimately, China sees itself as to "exercis[ing] great restraint in developing its nuclear force," arguing that it "has never entered into and will never enter into a nuclear arms race with any other country."

In addition, multiple Defense White Papers have affirmed the basic structure of China's nuclear chain of command, including that its nuclear forces are "under the direct command of the Central Military Commission," placing ultimate control of China's nuclear decision-making within the highest echelon of the Party leadership rather than military careerists.[9] According to the DWPs, although "in peacetime [China's] nuclear missile weapons ... are not aimed at any country," if China were to "come under a nuclear threat" the country's nuclear forces would "go into a state of alert," readying to launch a counterattack in order to deter the enemy" from striking.[10]

Although they are official diplomatic documents with English translations provided directly by the Chinese Ministry of Defense, difficulties have nevertheless arisen at times in interpreting their meaning. China's 2013 defense white paper, *The Diversified Employment of China's Armed Forces*, did not explicitly mention the No First Use policy, unlike in previous editions. [11] Some PLA observers initially interpreted this omission as constituting at least an implicit departure from "No First Use" (NFU), if not an outright rejection of the policy.[12] However, PLA officers later explained that the more "thematic" approach of the 2013 DWP was meant as a departure from the "comprehensive" format of previous white papers, and hence a discussion of NFU was not required in this particular paper given its focus on other issues.[13] As a result of the confusion surrounding its publication, several Chinese officials and military officers came forward to reiterate and reassure their foreign counterparts that China's NFU policy had not changed.[14] China's most recent Defense White Paper was issued in 2015, and focuses specifically on Chinese military strategy. It highlights the role of the nuclear force as "a strategic cornerstone for safeguarding national sovereignty and security," and it reiterates NFU and other continuous aspects of Chinese nuclear policy.[15]

The most recent authoritative edition of the *Science of Military Strategy*, released in 2013, is consistent with statements on nuclear issues found in the Defense White Papers, while also going into greater detail on a number of key issues such as potential challenges to the credibility of China's nuclear deterrent. SMS 2013 is also much more direct in discussing Chinese force modernization and how Chinese responses are intended to ensure deterrence effectiveness, though it does not offer any details about specific systems China is developing. Notably, SMS 2013 also goes well beyond its own previous edition in certain key areas. In this aspect it reflects the emergence of policy and strategic debates that appear to have accompanied Chinese technological advances, suggesting that nuclear capabilities under development may open up new strategic options for Beijing.

At their cores there is a high degree of continuity between SMS 2001 and SMS 2013. Like SMS 2001, the new edition places nuclear deterrence within the broader context of a set of strategic deterrence capabilities that also includes conventional, space, and network warfare forces. And like the previous edition, SMS 2013 highlights the increasing importance of conventional deterrence, arguing that its power is growing along with the "informatization" of conventional strike capabilities. According to both SMS 2013 and other PLA publications, PLA strategists also believe space and information deterrence are also becoming more important, a trend that correlates with intensifying military competition in these domains. According to SMS 2013, "since entering the 21st century, along with the rapid development and widespread application of science and technology, especially information technology, networks and space are gradually developing into new strategic deterrence domains, allowing one to comprehensively utilize many types of deterrence methods."[16] It should be noted, however, that SMS 2013 does not go as far as to suggest that even the most powerful conventional, space, and cyber warfare forces can substitute for a nuclear deterrent.

With respect to nuclear policy, SMS 2013 reaffirms China's nuclear No First Use (NFU) policy and holds that China adheres to a "self-defensive" nuclear strategy. This characterization has remained consistent for decades.[17] As SMS 2013 puts it, the nature of nuclear weapons means they are primarily oriented toward a strategic deterrence role, and therefore "the deterrence application is the principal method of the application of nuclear forces."[18] As a corollary, nuclear deterrence, rather than the actual use of nuclear weapons, "is the primary form of military struggle in the nuclear domain."[19] SMS 2013 traces this assessment back to judgments Mao Zedong and Deng Xiaoping made about the utility of nuclear weapons in a deterrent role, noting that Deng described nuclear missiles as "deterrence forces" and "deterrence weapons."[20] According to SMS 2013, China's approach to nuclear counterattacks is based on the principle of "gaining mastery by striking only after the enemy has struck" (后发制人), and that, "the nuclear counterattack operation is the sole form for China's nuclear force to employ nuclear forces in actual war."

SMS 2013 also explains the roles nuclear weapons play in China's security strategy in a broader sense. First and foremost, according to SMS 2013, "nuclear weaponry acts as a strong 'shield' to protect national security."[21] More broadly than that, though, nuclear weapons also "centrally embody and reflect a country's comprehensive national power and its level of science and technology." Nuclear weapons are thus irreplaceable not only for the direct purpose of strategic deterrence, but also for the less concrete task of cementing a country's status as a major power. As the authors put it, "nuclear weapons have continuously served as an important mainstay supporting China's position as a major country, and in the future they will still be an important mark and symbol reflecting China's international position and image."[22]

As Dennis Blasko points out in his chapter on strategic deterrence in this volume, SMS 2013 underscores that despite the rise of soft power and the liberal international order since World War 2, Chinese strategists still see a nation's actual level of military capability as being an important determinant of the level of effectiveness of strategic deterrence in a broad sense, and the realm of nuclear deterrence is no exception. In the view of SMS 2013's authors, "the level of the nuclear counterstrike directly influences the efficacy of China's nuclear deterrence." Therefore, they argue, "increasing the quantity of guided missile weapons" for use in nuclear counterstrikes and raising the efficacy of those counterstrikes is a "fundamental target" of PLARF nuclear force construction, reflecting both "concrete plan and policy" as well as "guiding principle" for the PLARF's commanders.[23]

China's Increasingly Complex Nuclear Security Environment

However, recent PLA writings suggest that this achieving this 'fundamental target' is in fact becoming a more difficult problem for China. Both SMS 2013 and other authoritative sources indicate that China faces an increasingly challenging nuclear security environment, one in which it must contend with challenges posed by enemy missile defense, conventional prompt global strike (CPGS), and nuclear capabilities, a number of potential nuclear adversaries, and greater pressure to participate in arms control negotiations that could limit China's ability to achieve its force modernization goals.

According to SMS 2013, "Over the past few years, the nuclear security picture faced by our country has become increasingly complex." The authors offer four reasons for this pessimistic judgment. The first is that China's main potential adversary is the United States, which is increasing its missile defense capabilities. As they put it: "The main object faced by China in its nuclear struggle is the world's most powerful nuclear country. The U.S. sees China as its primary strategic adversary and is stepping up the building of a missile defense system for the East Asia region. The reliability and effectiveness of its ability to implement counterattacks against China are having an increasingly serious impact."

The second reason SMS 2013 cites is "an increase in the quantity of countries with nuclear weapons (or potential nuclear weapons) in China's neighborhood." Specifically, according to the authors: "In 1998, India and Pakistan both respectively carried out multiple nuclear tests, stepping into the world's nuclear club at one stroke. In particular, India's nuclear strength has grown rapidly. After entry into the 21st century, the problem of nuclear weapons on the Korean Peninsula has been constantly fermenting and the possibility of resolving it in the near future is very small."

The third reason is that "the world's principal countries are making great efforts to development new conventional military capabilities." Specifically, "the United States is in the process of implementing a conventional 'Prompt Global Strike' (PGS) plan. Once it has functional capabilities, it will be used to implement conventional strikes against our nuclear missile forces [in the event of a conflict], forcing us into a disadvantaged, passive position. This will greatly impact our nuclear counterstrike capabilities and weaken out nuclear deterrence outcomes."

The fourth is the likelihood that China will face greater pressure to engage in multilateral nuclear arms control discussions as the United States and Russia decrease the numbers of nuclear weapons in their arsenals. The authors state that "the external pressure on the development of China's nuclear forces has increased, and that even though "the quantitative scale of China's nuclear weapons is far from being on the same level as that of the U.S. and Russia," due to ongoing international efforts to reduce global stockpiles of nuclear weapons "the modernization of China's limited nuclear forces will experience increasing external pressure." The authors further elaborate on China's concerns about nuclear arms control issues, stating:

"Since the end of the Cold War, with the continuing progress of nuclear disarmament in the U.S. and Russia, the pressure China faces in terms of nuclear transparency and nuclear disarmament has increased. The struggle over nuclear arms control and disarmament has become more complicated by the day and the place of nuclear arms control and disarmament in the military struggle in the nuclear domain has become increasingly prominent."

To be fair, the authors of SMS 2013 do not look on these efforts with total hostility. They judge that arms control can play a positive role in areas such as safeguarding strategic stability, reducing the risk of nuclear war, and limiting unnecessary military expenditures. But this positive judgment is tempered with skepticism as to the true motives of more powerful countries, including the belief that nuclear superpowers are interested in nuclear arms control and disarmament in part as a means of "safeguarding their own nuclear and strategic advantages and limiting or weakening the capabilities of their strategic opponents."

SMS 2013 repeats the official Chinese mantra that the United States and Russia, as the countries with the world's largest nuclear arsenals, must bear a "special, primary responsibility for nuclear disarmament," and should continue to reduce their nuclear arsenals through "verifiable and irreversible methods." At some unspecified point in the future, "when conditions are ripe, other nuclear states should enter the process of multilateral nuclear disarmament negotiations." In the meantime, China must be on guard, and must handle pressure to participate in arms control negotiations very carefully to ensure that the timing and conditions of any future participation are conducive to protecting Chinese national security interests. SMS 2013 underscores that this is especially important not only because China's nuclear forces are much smaller than those of the United States and Russia, but also because there is still "a relatively large disparity" between China's nuclear capabilities and what it needs to meet its national security requirements. Thus China should continue to modernize and expand its nuclear forces, deflect pressure from the U.S. and other countries, and ensure it will be well prepared for future negotiations, so as to "gradually seize the initiative in the nuclear arms control and disarmament struggle."[24]

Another challenge that is not included in the list of four factors but is discussed elsewhere in SMS 2013 is inherent in the nuclear forces and doctrine of China's potential adversaries, particularly the United States. SMS 2013 notes that the United States is deemphasizing nuclear weapons in certain respects: "Given the sustained superiority of the U.S. in conventional military forces and the accelerated construction of a global missile defense system, reductions of nuclear weapons quantities and limits on the scope of nuclear weapons usage have further decreased dependence on nuclear weapons." Yet the United States remains a nuclear superpower. Moreover, like Russia, it has refused to adopt a NFU policy, and SMS 2013 indicates that U.S. nuclear deterrence strategy is based on the possibility of first use of nuclear weapons. Additionally, according to SMS 2013: "The nuclear weapons and nuclear forces of both countries have and continue to be in a state of high alert to be used whenever necessary for nuclear strikes. At the same time that the U.S. is reducing its quantity of nuclear weapons it has maintained and even strengthened the manpower, technological resources, and infrastructure to make it possible to rapidly expand and increase its nuclear forces and nuclear strength. Russia is currently stepping up arming itself with new nuclear weapon carrier vehicles and launch platforms and updating and replacing its guided missile nuclear weapons. There has been no substantive change in the nuclear strategies of the U.S. and Russia and competition in the nuclear domain is still being intensely carried out."[25] Furthermore, the authors write, "the United States and other western countries not only emphasize warfighting in conventional deterrence, but also have started placing an emphasis on nuclear warfighting deterrence. They have praised highly the possible advantages of such new nuclear weapons as nuclear earth penetrators and have attempted to make use of technical breakthroughs achieved in ultra-low-yield, high-precision tactical nuclear weapons to provide the means for implementing 'surgical' nuclear strikes and achieving the objectives of both deterrence and warfighting."[26]

Nuclear Force Modernization and Nuclear Deterrence

Against the backdrop of this increasingly complex nuclear security picture, SMS 2013 indicates that deterring nuclear attack against China is crucial for national security. It also underscores that this remains one of Second Artillery's core functions (other PLARF issues are discussed in greater detail below). Another is being prepared to carry out a nuclear counterattack if deterrence fails. According to SMS: "The implementation of nuclear counterstrikes is both PLARF's fundamental method of real war application (实战运用) and the foundation of implementing effective nuclear deterrence (有效核威慑). Only by truly possessing nuclear counterstrike capabilities can it be guaranteed that when suffering an enemy nuclear attack we will be able to organize an effective counterstrike, giving the enemy a certain degree of nuclear damage (一定程度的核毁伤), and only then truly achieving the goal of deterring (摄制) the outbreak of nuclear war. Consequently, successfully carrying out nuclear counterstrike operations is a crucial point and important responsibility of Second Artillery in fulfilling its historical mission." [27] Consequently, the main purpose of nuclear force modernization is enhancing the effectiveness of a nuclear counter-attack, which in turn makes nuclear deterrence more credible and effective. According to SMS: "Being able to carry out an effective nuclear counterstrike is the foundation of effective nuclear deterrence."[28]

SMS 2013 is more explicit on this point than the previous edition, particularly in its discussion of force modernization requirements needed to further improve the credibility of nuclear deterrence. Indeed, SMS 2013 indicates that a more modern nuclear force constitutes the mainstay of China's overall "deterrence system," which is also composed of informatized conventional forces, network attack and defense capabilities, and "flexible and diverse space forces," and an innovative approach to People's War based on mobilization capabilities. SMS 2013 indicates that China requires "lean and effective" nuclear strike forces to guarantee its status as a powerful country, ensure its core interests will not be violated, and sustain a stable environment for peaceful development. This in turn requires higher levels of informatization, improved command and control and strategic early warning capabilities, and enhanced survivability based on mobility, protective measures, and rapid reaction capabilities.

SMS 2013 also discusses nuclear deterrence in more detail than the previous volume. For example, it describes nuclear deterrence strategy that involves strengthening China's nuclear forces and "maintaining an appropriate degree of confusion" that ensures the opposing side will be uncertain about China's actual nuclear power, the timing and scale of nuclear counterstrikes, and so on. SMS 2013 indicates that such an approach "can increase the difficulty of decision-making by the opposing side and is beneficial to increasing the deterrence outcomes of China's limited nuclear forces." Furthermore, it suggests that some ambiguity about Chinese policy and intentions can be useful, notwithstanding the need for centralized decision-making in this extremely sensitive and strategic area. According to SMS 2013, "speaking with a unified voice from the highest levels of the government and military to the lowest levels can often enhance deterrence outcomes, but sometimes, when different things are said by different people, deterrence outcomes might be even better."[29]

"Real War" Employment of Nuclear Weapons

SMS 2013 again departs from the previous edition in its inclusion of a section describing nuclear issues in "real war."[30] This section explains that the possibility of nuclear war, especially large-scale nuclear war, is much lower today than it was during the Cold War, but warns that as long as nuclear weapons exist, the possibility they will be used in actual war cannot be ruled out. This is not only a function of the existence of nuclear weapons, according to the authors, but also of the fact that most nuclear powers have refused to commit to NFU policies and the possibility of first use remains "an important aspect of their nuclear strategies." Thus the issue of nuclear employment in real war cannot be dismissed, since there is still a possibility that future informatized conventional wars could escalate to the nuclear level.[31]

SMS 2013 thus discusses two possible types of nuclear employment in "actual war": preemptive nuclear strikes and retaliatory nuclear strikes. Here, SMS 2013 reiterates that China "insists on a policy of no first use of nuclear weapons and pursues a defensive nuclear strategy." Accordingly, any Chinese use of nuclear weapons in real war would be for "retaliatory nuclear counterstrikes." Within this context, SMS 2013 tracks with other publications that address nuclear counterattack campaigns in that it emphasizes centralized command and the concentration of decision-making authority at the very highest levels of China's leadership. It also highlights the importance of "tight defenses" to guarantee force survivability, which is the "basic prerequisite" for carrying out nuclear counterstrikes. In addition, like other publications, it emphasizes "key-point counterstrikes" to use China's limited nuclear forces against targets that would be likely "to have a major impact on the broader strategic picture."[32] Unlike the previous edition, SMS 2013 offers some guidance on how to attempt to manage escalation in the event a conventional conflict crosses the nuclear threshold. According to the authors: "In implementing nuclear counterstrikes, we need to be able to generate unsustainable destructive results against the other side, to shock and awe them, but, at the same time, we need to control the intensity, pacing, and target scope of the counterstrikes." Importantly, SMS 2013 appears to suggest that under such circumstances the purpose is not to "win" a nuclear war, but rather to deter further escalation or to resolve a conflict on acceptable terms.

One interesting area in which SMS 2013 goes beyond the previous edition, albeit only briefly, is in a discussion of the importance of unified planning. The authors explain that because PLARF and PLAN have nuclear capabilities, unified planning is required to ensure coordination of strike targets and timing. Moreover, the authors state that because PLARF and PLAN nuclear forces are at high risk of suffering heave losses in the event of an enemy nuclear first strike, it is essential that unified planning make the most effective use of surviving nuclear weapons in order to achieve the desired nuclear counterstrike objectives.[33]

Another new development in SMS 2013 is its discussion of the possibility of adopting a launch-on-warning or launch under attack posture, which the authors assert would be consistent with China's NFU policy. They write: "When conditions are met, and when necessary, one can rapidly launch a nuclear missile counterstrike when it has been clearly determined that the enemy has already launched nuclear missiles against us but said enemy nuclear warheads have yet to arrive at their targets and effectively explode or cause actual damage to us. This both conforms to our country's consistent policy of no first use of nuclear weapons and also effectively prevents our nuclear forces from suffering greater losses, improving the survivability of nuclear missile forces and their counterstrike capabilities."[34] Disturbingly, SMS 2013 does not address any of the risks associated with this approach. Indeed, as Gregory Kulacki has pointed out, "There is no discussion of the strategic challenges associated with a decision to launch on warning, particularly the risk of an accidental or erroneous launch either due to false or ambiguous warning, technical problems or damage to the early warning systems, or poor judgment."[35]

PLA Rocket Force (PLARF) Strategy and Capabilities

SMS 2013 also differs from SMS 2001 in that it provides much more detailed coverage of PLARF issues, which it treats in a chapter on service strategies. In particular, SMS 2013 indicates that the Rocket Forces—known as Second Artillery at the time of SMS 2013's publication prior to their recent elevation to a full service of the PLA—will play a major role in all of the main aspects of strategic deterrence critical to China's national security, including not only nuclear but also conventional, space, and information deterrence. Notably, this goes beyond the thinking about PLA rocket forces espoused in the previous edition, particularly with regard to the space domain. Indeed, looking to the future, authoritative writings by PLA strategists suggest the Rocket Forces will continue to serve as the core component of China's strategic deterrent, and will increase its role in this regard along with improvements in its nuclear and conventional missile capabilities.

The PLA Rocket Force's Role and Responsibilities

The PLARF was first established as the PLASAF in July 1966 as the arm of the Chinese military responsible for nuclear-armed ballistic missiles, and although its portfolio within the PLA has expanded dramatically since that time, its nuclear focus has not wavered. As the 2013 SMS puts it, nuclear deterrence "undoubtedly remains the core and foundation of China's strategic deterrence," and playing a central role in the containment of large-scale warfare and "effectively holding in check China's primary strategic opponents." Since the Rocket Forces are "the main part of China's nuclear force," they thus continue to be "the core force for China's strategic deterrence."[36]

This continuity is reflected in the fact that recent authoritative descriptions of the PLARF nuclear mission largely track with much earlier publications. Descriptions of the PLARF in writings such as SMS 2013 align closely with the first edition of SMS from nearly three decades ago.[37]

Importantly, though, the PLARF's roles and responsibilities expanded after the publication of that volume, with a conventional mission added in the early 1990s. As a result, by the publication of SMS 2013, launching conventional precision strikes with its conventional missiles was considered to constitute one of the PLARF's "main missions."[38] In the PLARF's view, its conventional precision strike weapons are the "crack troops and sharp weapons" of the PLA's conventional operations, and against China's most powerful adversaries they have a powerful deterrence role to play.[39] According to SMS 2013, for example, PLA strategists believe conventional ballistic and cruise missiles could serve as a powerful instrument of coercive diplomacy in addition to the important role they would play in any one of a number of PLA joint campaigns.

As a result, the PLARF now occupies a unique position among the world's military services due to its responsibility for nuclear deterrence and counter-attack as well as conventional long-range strike missions decoupled from any primary responsibility for air, sea, or land supremacy. As SMS 2013 puts it, the PLARF's nuclear and conventional long-range strike missile capabilities give it a "special position" among the instruments of Chinese military power and ensure that it "plays an extremely important role in defense of [China's] national security."[40] Indeed, like a number of other Chinese military publications, SMS 2013 describes the Rocket Force as "China's core force for strategic deterrence" (中国战略威慑的核心力量).[41]

Since the PLARF's conventional missiles are the "primary weapons" (*zhuzhan bingqi*, 主战兵器) and "principal component" of the PLA's long-range conventional strike forces, China has been focused since the 1990s on upgrading its conventional strike capability in terms of numbers of weapons, range, and accuracy.[42] Compared with other conventional weapons, land-based conventional missiles have advantages in terms of their ability to conduct long-range attacks, high precision, rapid response, and strong defense penetration capabilities. Even with the expected diversification of the Chinese military's long-range strike weaponry in the future, conventional missiles will continue to possess clear advantages, and will remain highly relevant in any future "confrontation with a powerful enemy," a Chinese military euphemism widely understood to refer to advanced military powers such as the United States. In short, the PLARF "possesses special functions for which there are no substitutes" (有不可替代的特殊作用).[43]

More generally, the PLARF's nuclear and conventional missile capabilities also serve to bolster China's international position, strengthening its image as a major country with a powerful military and protecting its national interests.[44] By deterring the outbreak of major war, the PLARF's capabilities are understood to have helped preserve a favorable external security environment, aiding in protecting and extending China's "period of strategic opportunity" (战略机遇期) during which China has (in the words of Deng Xiaoping) "bided its time" and focused on economic development.[45]

Finally, SMS 2013 reaffirms that as an important 'strategic force,' the Rocket Forces fall under the direct command of the Central Military Commission (CMC) and top-level leadership of the Chinese Communist Party (CCP).[46] It elaborates that the highest-level leaders of the CCP and the CMC must make all of the key decisions about the construction, development, and employment of China's strategic missile force, because of its strategic importance. In particular, "All significant nuclear deterrence actions and any scale of nuclear counterstrikes are undoubtedly categorized as significant strategic actions." Thus these decisions must be made at the highest level.[47]

PLARF Missile Force Modernization

SMS 2013 appeared to indicate that the PLARF's role was likely to become increasingly important in the future, as they continue to improve their nuclear and conventional missile capabilities in coordination with China's overall military modernization planning. To the extent that the recently announced reforms and the elevation of the former PLA Second Artillery Forces from an "independent branch" to full service status suggest increased prominence within China's military ecosystem, the AMS position now appears to have been prescient. SMS 2013 calls for quantitative and qualitative improvements in China's nuclear counter-attack capabilities, identifying nuclear missile force modernization as a "long-term and fundamental" responsibility for the PLARF, and describes maintaining those forces at "a certain scale" in order to "raise the efficacy of nuclear counterstrikes" as being "of the utmost importance."[48] One means of doing this mentioned in SMS is to increase the proportion of deployed missiles with intercontinental ranges, due to the geographic relationship between China and the counterstrike targets of what PLA authors often refer to euphemistically as China's "primary strategic opponent." In context, this can be seen as an implicit acknowledgement that preparing for the possibility of nuclear deterrence against the United States is a primary driver of PLA nuclear strategy and force modernization.

SMS 2013 states that the PLARF must "give prominence to the key points of nuclear capabilities development." It notes that, in the event of an opponent's nuclear attack, the survival of the nuclear missile force is a prerequisite for and the foundation of the implementation of a nuclear counterstrike. Additionally, SMS highlights the ability to effectively break through the opponent's missile defense system as a "necessary condition" for achieving required nuclear damage results against an opponent. Therefore, according to SMS, PLARF nuclear force capability development should prioritize enhancing survivability and defense penetration capabilities. SMS specifically calls for the PLARF to develop rapid mobile launch capabilities, hypersonic glide vehicles, and multiple warhead technologies, and to update and replace its missile weapons, because improving survivability and defense penetration capabilities is key to "increasing the efficacy of nuclear counterstrikes."[49]

SMS 2013 also calls for strengthening the PLARF's conventional missile force, which it identifies as a high priority given that China still faces a complex security environment and that "there is still a highly prominent contradiction" between the current state of the PLARF's conventional guided missile capabilities and "the requirements of dealing with actual security threats."[50] Furthermore, according to SMS, PLARF conventional modernization should focus on expanding the range of conventional guided missile firepower, placing emphasis on the development and deployment of "conventional guided missile weaponry with effective ranges exceeding 1500 km."[51] It should also focus on overcoming enemy defenses, improving rapid response capabilities, and enhancing accuracy.

PLARF capabilities displayed during China's September 2015 military parade in Beijing and news about capabilities under development confirm that this is the direction of Chinese nuclear and conventional missile force modernization. Among the nuclear and conventional missiles displayed during the September 2015 parade were several types of China's newest and most advanced strategic weapons, including DF-5B silo-based ICBMs,[52] which are capable of carrying MIRVs, DF-31A road-mobile ICBMs, DF-21D anti-ship ballistic missiles (ASBM), and DF-26 IRBMs, which Chinese commentators said have nuclear, conventional, and anti-ship variants.[53] As for future capabilities, China is developing the DF-41, a new mobile ICBM capable of carrying multiple independently targetable reentry vehicles (MIRVs).[54] China is also developing and testing hypersonic glide vehicles (HGVs), which it most likely intends to enhance the credibility of its strategic deterrent by demonstrating an advanced capability to counter missile defenses.[55]

In addition, SMS 2013 highlights the missile force's role in enabling the PLA to expand its operations into other domains, with space being the most notable. The volume suggests that the PLARF will focus on "developing new types of operations methods," and will thus play an increasingly important role in the space and information domains.[56] Specifically, the authors of SMS 2013 hold that expanded conceptions of national security interests and technology-driven changes in the conduct of modern warfare will cause military confrontations that utilize the network and space domains to become increasingly intense, raising "new requirements for military capability development."[57] They believe that this shifting context is crucial to the direction of the PLARF's "construction and development," requiring it to "developing new types of operations methods" and take PLARF operations capabilities "into space and other new domains."[58] With respect to space, this is in part because the PLARF's missile capabilities could be modified to carry out spacecraft launches, but also as a result of the development of ground-based missiles capable of carrying out attacks against satellites. In all, PLARF is considered an "important support" (重要依托) for the expansion of the PLA's operational capabilities into the space domain.[59]

Conclusion

In conclusion, Chinese nuclear strategy has remained largely consistent over time, though new capabilities are over time offering leaders a somewhat wider range of strategic options. Although recent authoritative writings on Chinese nuclear issues are largely consistent with the thinking of the Jiang Zemin era on critical points, they do offer a much more in depth consideration of a number of issues related to Chinese nuclear policy, strategy, and force modernization. SMS 2013, which offers in depth discussions of how China must prepare for growing pressures in the area of nuclear arms control, the PLARF's envisioned expansion into additional domains of warfare, and PLARF force modernization requirements, should be required reading for analysts who are interested in Chinese nuclear policy and strategy, Chinese arms control policy, and China's conventional rocket forces.

As valuable a source as it may be, however, analysts will have to bear in mind that the PLA's major reorganization announced in late 2015 and early 2016 will involve changes that could have important implications for China's nuclear policy and strategy as well as for its conventional military capabilities. Aspects of the organizational reforms that have already been unveiled highlight the importance China attaches to strengthening and integrate its most powerful strategic capabilities. Two parts of the PLA's organizational reforms in particular—the transformation of Second Artillery into the PLA Rocket Force, and the establishment of the PLA's Strategic Support Force to oversee space and cyber capabilities—will likely have important implications for China's approach to strategic deterrence. Up until December 31, 2015 PLA's Second Artillery Force was traditionally considered an "independent branch" of the military and was not technically a full service. Under Xi's reforms, PLA Rocket Force has now been formally elevated to service-level stature, inheriting Second Artillery's role as China's "core force for strategic deterrence." There has even been some speculation that PLA Rocket Force will eventually control all of China's nuclear-capable delivery systems, including PLAN SSBNs and PLAAF bombers, though this remains unconfirmed.[60] Even if PLARF does not ultimately take charge of these systems, however, it will still oversee the most impressive arsenal of strategic capabilities of any of the PLA's services and thus will serve a core role in any large-scale crisis or conflict between China and a major power.

NOTES

[1] *The Science of Military Strategy* [战略学], 3rd ed., Beijing: Academy of Military Sciences Press, 2013 (SMS 2013), pp. 228–229.

[2] *The Science of Strategy* [战略学], 1987, p. 115. Accordingly, the "basic guiding thought" of the Second Artillery includes principles such as "centralized command," "striking after the enemy has struck," "close protection," and "key-point counterstrikes."

[3] Peng Guangqian and Yao Youzhi, ed., The Science of Military Strategy, Beijing: Academy of Military Sciences Press, 2001 (SMS 2001), p. 217.

[4] SMS 2001, p. 217.

[5] SMS 2001, p. 218.

[6] SMS 2001, p. 218.

[7] SMS 2001, p. 218.

[8] SMS 2001, p. 222.

[9] China's National Defense in 2006, Beijing: State Council Information Office, 2006.

[10] *China's National Defense in 2008*, Beijing: State Council Information Office, 2009.

[11] Diversified Employment of China's Armed Forces, Beijing, State Council Information Office, 2013.

12 See James M. Acton, "Is China Changing Its Position on Nuclear Weapons?" *New York Times,* April 18, 2013.

13 See Yao Yunzhu, "China Will Not Change Its Nuclear Policy," *U.S.-China Focus,* April 22, 2013, http://www.chinausfocus.com/peace-security/china-will-not-change-its-no-first-use-policy; and M. Taylor Fravel, "China Has Not (Yet) Changed its Position on Nuclear Weapons," *The Diplomat,* April 22, 2013, http://thediplomat.com/2013/04/22/china-has-not-yet-changed-its-position-on-nuclear-weapons.

14 For example, responding to a question during a June 2013 press conference, Ministry of Foreign Affairs spokesperson Hong Lei restated China's longstanding nuclear policy, including that China "stands and calls for the complete prohibition and thorough destruction of nuclear weapons, firmly pursues a nuclear strategy solely for self-defense, adheres to the policy of no-first-use of nuclear weapons at any time and under any circumstance, and makes the unequivocal commitment that it will unconditionally not use or threaten to use nuclear weapons against non-nuclear weapons states and nuclear-weapon-free zones." See Ministry of Foreign Affairs of the People's Republic of China, "Foreign Ministry Spokesperson Hong Lei's Regular Press Conference on June 3, 2013," June 4, 2013, http://www.fmprc.gov.cn/eng/. PLA officers have made similar statements, such as when Lieutenant General Qi Jianguo reaffirmed the NFU policy at the Shangri-La Dialogue in Singapore in June 2013. "I want to make a solemn statement that the Chinese government will never discard our pledge of no first-use of nuclear arms," Qi said. "We have been sticking to this policy for half a century, and its facts have proven that it is not only in the interest of the Chinese people but also of the people of all the world." See "Shangri-La Dialogue: China Reiterates 'No First Use' Nuclear Pledge," *Straits Times,* June 2, 2013, http://www.straitstimes.com/breaking-news/asia/story/shangri-la-dialogue-china-reiterates-no-first-use-nuclear-pledge-20130602.

15 "China's Military Strategy," Beijing: State Council Information Office, 2015.

16 SMS 2013., pp. 228–229.

17 *The Science of Strategy* [战略学], 1987, p. 237.

18 SMS 2013., p. 235.

19 SMS 2013.

[20] SMS 2013.

[21] SMS 2013, p. 231.

[22] SMS 2013, pp. 230-231.

[23] SMS 2013, p. 233.

[24] SMS 2013.

[25] SMS 2013.

[26] SMS 2013.

[27] SMS 2013, pp. 231–232.

[28] SMS 2013, p. 235.

[29] SMS 2013.

[30] It is important to note that some readers might interpret the use of this term is as a discussion of "nuclear warfighting" in the sense of damage limiting or disarming strikes against an enemy's nuclear forces, but the content of the section and the way in which the term is often used in Chinese military writing suggests very strongly that "real war" or "actual war" is a more appropriate translation.

[31] SMS 2013

[32] SMS 2013

[33] SMS 2013

[34] SMS 2013

[35] Gregory Kulacki, "The Chinese Military Updates China's Nuclear Strategy," March 2015, UCS, p. 4, http://www.ucsusa.org/sites/default/files/attach/2015/03/chinese-nuclear-strategy-full-report.pdf

[36] SMS 2013, pp. 228–229.

[37] *The Science of Strategy* [战略学], 1987, p. 115. Accordingly, the "basic guiding thought" of the Second Artillery includes principles such as "centralized command," "striking after the enemy has struck," "close protection," and "key-point counterstrikes."

[38] See, for example, SMS 2013, pp. 231–232.

[39] SMS 2013, p. 231.

[40] SMS 2013, p. 228.

[41] SMS 2013, pp. 228–229.

[42] SMS 2013, p. 229.

[43] SMS 2013, p. 229.

[44] SMS 2013, pp. 230–231.

[45] SMS 2013, p. 231.

[46] SMS 2013, p. 228.

[47] SMS 2013, pp. 234–235.

[48] SMS 2013, p. 232.

[49] SMS 2013, pp. 233–234.

[50] SMS 2013, 2013, p. 233.

[51] SMS 2013, p. 234.

[52] Although China displayed its silo-based DF-5B ICBMs during the parade, it should be noted that unlike the various types of mobile missiles that were carried by transporter erector launchers (TELs), the DF-5Bs were divided into two parts and carried on separate trailers. Additionally, these trailers did not have the erector capability needed to launch a missile.

[53] Andrew S. Erickson, "Missile March: China Parade Projects Patriotism at Home, Aims for Awe Abroad," China Real Time Blog, Wall Street Journal, updated September 3, 2015. As of October 13, 2015: http://blogs.wsj.com/chinarealtime/2015/09/03/missile-march-china-parade-projects-patriotism-at-home-aims-for-awe-abroad/

[54] Office of the Secretary of Defense, *Military and Security Developments Involving the People's Republic of China 2013* (Washington, DC, May 2013), p. 30.

[55] Jason Sherman, "China Conducts Sixth 'Successful' Hypersonic Weapons Test, STRATCOM Chief Says," *Inside Defense*, January 29, 2016.

[56] SMS 2013, p. 233.

[57] SMS 2013, p. 233.

[58] SMS 2013, p. 233.

[59] SMS 2013, p. 229.

[60] "Expert: PLA Rocket Force May Have Strategic Nuclear Submarine, Bomber," *China Military Online*, January 8, 2016.

SECTION III: CHINA'S STRATEGY FOR INFORMATION WARFARE

Chapter 6: Electronic Warfare and the Renaissance of Chinese Information Operations

John Costello and Peter Mattis

Over the last decade and a half, Chinese information operations—and electronic warfare operations in particular—have evolved in scope and complexity to the point that they now play a central role in Chinese military strategy. The rapid development of information operations within the People's Liberation Army (PLA) is the result of several key factors, including the deep historical roots of information operations within the Chinese Communist Party (CCP) and the role of technological change in giving new relevance to old Maoist revolutionary concepts. As Mao wrote in the essay *On Protracted Warfare*, one must "as far as possible seal up the enemies' eyes and ears, and make them become blind and deaf ... confusing the minds of their commanders and turning them into madmen, using this to achieve our own victory." Information operations play a role in not only Chinese military strategy but also the generation of political power at home and abroad. Beyond the military applications of information operations, especially in the electromagnetic spectrum and to a lesser extent in cyberspace, they offer China a broad range of capabilities that reinforce existing CCP efforts to shape the international environment.

Information operations, broadly speaking, are those operations designed to deceive, disrupt, or otherwise manipulate an adversary's command, control, computers, communications, intelligence, surveillance, and reconnaissance (C4ISR) systems. Even conventional kinetic attempts to destroy critical nodes in an adversary's C4ISR system qualify as information operations—a distinction the Chinese military divides as 'hard' and 'soft' kills. For the past three decades, the PLA has broadly defined information warfare as "a war in which military groups seize information space and fight for information resources," and sometimes more narrowly as "confrontations in the information field between the two parties engaged in a war."[1] This language dovetails with the Chinese conception of warfare as confrontations of 'systems of systems' (体系对抗) that naturally incorporating political, diplomatic, and economic elements of state power and competition. However, the PLA has traditionally kept psychological and political warfare separate from electronic warfare. The conceptual integration of electromagnetic spectrum warfare with China's broader conception of information operations over the past decade and a half marks an important evolution in Chinese military strategy.

Control of the electromagnetic domain is central to information operations in the event of a conflict. The CCP believes it is entitled to an inherent "electromagnetic sovereignty" every bit as inviolable as the sovereignty of China's land and airspace, which the PLA may be tasked to defend with force if challenged. This sovereignty entails firm wartime and peacetime control of the airwaves and the frequencies that carry them. Even more so than the Internet and cyberspace, the political reliability of the electromagnetic spectrum is the first front in information warfare, constituting the main battlespace for information warfare preparations, strategy, and campaigns. Electronic warfare, psychological warfare, and political warfare are inextricably linked, with each of these spheres greatly influencing the conduct of PLA information operations in both peace and wartime.

Three insights on core characteristics of the modern informatized world have driven the recent evolution of the PLA's information operations. The first and most critical insight, with effects visible well beyond information operations, is the integration of peacetime and wartime. PLA information operations require continuous battlespace preparation activity during peacetime to either ensure the usefulness of these capabilities in wartime or to deter an adversary through a demonstration of PLA dominance at the outset. Second, the growing ubiquity of cyberspace and the electromagnetic spectrum, as well as the corresponding growth of information, has created 'international public spaces' (国际公共空间) that erode China's geographic isolation from various potential security threats. Third, as noted in the 2013 edition of the *Science of Military Strategy* (SMS 2013), non-nuclear deterrence has become increasingly important due to the increased likelihood of limited confrontations that would not escalate to nuclear threats.

Information operations have utility at all levels, from the political and strategic to the tactical. The CCP leadership has understood and appreciated this value since the Chinese Revolution, when the party and its subordinate military, intelligence, and propaganda organs waged an aggressive campaign to discredit the Kuomintang and transform battlefield successes into political victory. The PLA, however, lagged militarily as China's technological development failed to keep pace with other major powers. Only in the 2000s, with the greater emergence of cyberspace and the electromagnetic spectrum as military domains and the full maturation of the PLA's electronic warfare capabilities as tools in strategic information operations against space-based assets, could Beijing and the Chinese military begin to challenge the ways in which more modern militaries were exploiting the opportunities of the modern informatized world to enjoy advanced C4ISR capabilities. Although there are a number of angles by which C4ISR platforms can be attacked, the serious dependence of C4ISR platforms on the electromagnetic spectrum represents a potential Achilles heel that threatens modern militaries' ability to engage in rapid decision-making and precision strikes. As technology advances over time, this threat has only increased; electromagnetic suppression and spoofing, in particular, have become increasingly viable methods of disruption as electronic communications mediums become more complex.

Conducting information operations, especially in the PLA's operational context, brings its own set of challenges. Many of the capabilities that might be used once conflict begins (or once Beijing decides conflict is inevitable) have traditionally been spread across various PLA organizations. Nowhere has this problem been more evident than the PLA's cyber capabilities for intelligence and electronic warfare. Until the recent PLA reorganization, not only General Staff Department (GSD) organizations but also the military regions and services all possessed assets with these capabilities. The Central Military Commission (CMC) was ostensibly the central authority directing their use, but no subordinate operational element had the authority to coordinate operations during peacetime, an organizational gap that was keenly understood in internal PLA dialogue on the topic.[2] The PLA reorganization that began on

November 26, 2015 marks the beginning of the Chinese military's plan to resolve these problems.

The focus in the PLA reorganization on "new domains" of warfare such as the electromagnetic domain and outer space is telling. While cyber security and cyber sovereignty may be secured by diplomatic agreements and civilian information technology policy, space and electromagnetic sovereignty must be secured by military force. An artificial construct like the Internet is a fragile one, beholden to national participation that can be revoked physically, logically, or diplomatically. Outer space and the electromagnetic spectrum are not beholden to these standards, and remain open and vulnerable to attack both in and out of conflict.

This chapter first addresses three critical evolutions in Chinese information operations, including not only electronic warfare but also political and psychological warfare. It then examines Chinese views of the global trends that have made information operations particularly relevant to the PLA's core mission of 'preparing to fight and win local informatized wars'. Finally, it examines the bureaucratic implications of this argument for understanding the PLA reforms launched on November 26, 2015 and their future directions.

The Evolution of Chinese Information Operations

One of the most surprising aspects of Chinese information warfare strategy is how little it has changed over the last twenty years. Main themes first promulgated in Chinese information warfare writings in the late 1990s have remained remarkably consistent over time. What could be called the two pillars of

Chinese information warfare operational strategy, pre-emption and system-of-systems paralysis, are both present and consistent across the PLA's modern strategic literature.

Pre-emption is a fundamental component of Chinese information warfare. While the Chinese, with occasional exceptions, do not explicitly refer to this strategy as "pre-emption," that is what it amounts to in practice: the launching of a sudden, unexpected attack in order to gain the strategic initiative in a conflict. The 2001 edition of *The Science of Military Strategy* (SMS 2001) describes "large information offensives" as offering the potential for an "electronic Pearl Harbor."[3] The implication, unstated at the time, was that such attacks would be pre-emptive in nature; later strategic literature has made that characterization overt, although it is generally conveyed in less visceral terms. The 2013 edition of *Science of Military Strategy* (SMS 2013) states simply that information warfare should focus on "laying stress on preempting the enemy; emphasizing in the preliminary operations phase the careful selection of first-attack targets" and then striking.[4] The concept of pre-emption is particularly important in two respects. The idea ultimately derives from "active defense," a concept originating with Mao that prescribes offensive, asymmetrical attacks while maintaining a strategic defensive posture. Secondly, it upholds the ideas of both "defeating the superior with the inferior" and "each of us fighting in our own way," two asymmetric Maoist notions of warfare that canonize the questionable assertion that superior tactics and preparation can prevail even in the face of overwhelming technological dominance.

Electronic warfare is central to these preparations because of its relative consistency throughout the course of a war. While network warfare operations have long been held by Western analysts to be the most threatening to information systems, the growing dependence of all major powers on the electromagnetic spectrum for the unimpeded operation of their advanced C4ISR systems makes expeditionary military operations particularly vulnerable to electronic suppression. While most cyber weapons are nearly useless after first use, electromagnetic weapons remain effective as long as their intended targets, such as antenna receivers and sensors, lack the ability to fundamentally improve their defenses on while deployed, a notoriously difficult prospect for deployed military platforms and space-based relays.

Secondly, "system of systems paralysis" acts as both a strategy as well as an end-state for information operations. SMS 2001 suggests that a main way to attain victory in warfare is by "destroying the enemy's command and control system only," so that it will "paralyze the enemy's entire information system and drastically reduce the enemy's war capabilities."[5] Instead of the "step-by-step dismembering of the enemy's body," modern war calls for "destroying the enemy's brain and central nervous system," which is "more significant in expediting the process of war."[6] SMS 2013 maintains the concept, stating that one must "seize and control the battlefield initiative, paralyze and destroy the enemy's operational system of systems, and shock the enemy's will for war."[7] As James Mulvenon wrote in 2009, the PLA's information warfare operations, in particular their doctrine of carrying out computer network attacks on nonmilitary targets, "are designed to … shake war resoluteness, destroy war potential and win the upper hand in war," thus undermining the political will of the population for participation in military conflict."[8] The use of information operations—in any form—to paralyze enemy system of systems has Maoist antecedents in both the concept of protracted warfare and the aforementioned need to "blind and deafen the adversary."

The PLA struggled initially in the 1990s to draw these and other distinctions between informatized warfare and information warfare. Part of the confusion in PLA writings stemmed from their largely derivative analysis of modern warfare, which was based on U.S., German, French, and Russian texts examining information warfare and the impact of ubiquitous surveillance and precision strike capabilities. As Mulvenon observed in an early analysis of Chinese information warfare capabilities, the PLA had "a surprising grasp of U.S. [information warfare] doctrine, but borrow[ed] concepts inappropriate for the PLA's technological level."[9] By the time SMS 2001 was published, the Chinese military had started clarifying these distinctions. The results filtered down through subsequent publications, such as the 2004 Defense White Paper, which shifted from envisioning warfare "under high-tech conditions" to wars "under informatized conditions" in accordance with China's recently updated military strategic guidelines. Since then, information warfare has maintained three central components: electronic warfare, network warfare, and psychological warfare. This is best reflected by the definition given by the official reference work *Military Terminology of the People's Liberation Army*, which states that information warfare integrates "modes such as electronic warfare, cyber warfare, and psychological warfare to strike or counter an enemy ... interfer[ing] with and damag[ing] the enemy's information and information systems in cyberspace and electromagnetic space."[10]

Chinese Views on Warfare in the Electromagnetic Domain

Electronic warfare is in no uncertain terms at the center of PLA information warfare. This is not an artistic flourish or a dramatic prosaic concept, the PLA itself dates the creation of its information warfare forces to the creation of "specialized electronic warfare" forces in the 1970s. While network warfare has gained quite a reputation as a method of intelligence collection and (controversially) as an economic equalizer, electronic warfare remains the foremost *military* expression of information operations and is the central component of military information warfare. Network and psychological warfare certainly have military components, but are far more relevant to the intelligence and political dimensions of conflict.

Western countries should take note here. Network and psychological warfare each present a *strategic* problem in a prospective information war with China, and would primarily be used to delay mobilization, create chaos domestically, dissuade popular support for a war, and diplomatically isolate any country that might potentially start conflict with China. Electronic warfare, on the other hand, poses a distinct set of military challenges. Electromagnetic suppression of C4ISR via sea, land, air, and space-based platforms is a unilateral measure; it is hard to mitigate, hard to defend against, and is not easily remedied. Once present on the battlefield, electronic warfare, like artillery, becomes an irrevocable condition of full-scale war. The PLA not only acknowledges this, but has focused their frequent military exercises on learning how to operate successfully and win wars under these conditions. PLA exercises now often simulate war in a 'complex electromagnetic environment,' a term that encompasses mutual degradation or destruction of space-based C4ISR assets. A cornerstone component of China's anti-access/area denial capability (A2AD, though it should be noted that the Chinese do not describe their strategy with that term) is an iron blockade of the electromagnetic spectrum, and Western militaries planning for the possibility of direct conflict with the PLA must take note and contend with that possibility in their contingency planning.

Unlike network or space warfare, electronic warfare is not inherently strategic. In fact, it is only due to the now-ubiquitous military use of space-based information networks that electronic warfare has become a useful tool for strategic information operations. The PLA observes that the military use of satellite-based intelligence collection, navigation, and communications have strategically fused the space, network, and electromagnetic domains, which taken together constitute a new "strategic space" for international competition. This space is now a strategic 'high ground' offering substantial advantages to the military that controls it, a "commanding elevation for wars under informatized conditions."[11]

Electronic warfare, by virtue of its ability to effect 'soft-kill' against an adversary's satellites, has thus become an instrumental strategic weapon. However, the PLA did not come to this realization overnight. When examining strategic information operations, SMS 2001 held that "military satellites can become direct targets of electronic war" and that "space electronic war can become one of the new territories for electronic war," but the topic was treated almost as an afterthought. This stands in stark contrast to more recent Chinese strategic literature, which brings electronic warfare front-and-center as a primary means of satellite disruption. In

Lectures on Information Operations Studies, the influential
PLA strategist Ye Zheng writes "satellite countermeasures"
involve using electromagnetic attacks, among other methods, to
"cripple information support forces."[12]

Electronic warfare's primary role as an anti-satellite tool likely
comes as a result of two PLA lines of thinking. First, Chinese
strategic thinkers currently see the space domain as primarily
being used for "information support" and strategic intelligence,
surveillance, and reconnaissance. SMS 2013 states "space
information support is now, and for quite a long period to come
will be, the main mode for the application of space forces among
the various nations."[13] For many of China's strategic thinkers,
seizing space superiority and attaining strategic information
superiority often constitute the same task.

Secondly, although it is never addressed explicitly, it is uncertain
whether China would even consider anti-satellite jamming to be
a true 'act of war'. It seems more likely that China would
characterize it as a self-defense 'counter pre-emption' attack, or
perhaps an act of deterrence. This assumption stems from both
the ambiguities of soft-kill attacks like electronic warfare and the
PLA's habit of framing offensive attacks in defensive terms. SMS
2013 gives circumscribed guidance in use of electromagnetic
weapons against satellite targets, suggesting that an enemy may
use such weapons against China but never explicitly mentioning
them as a means of deterrence or attack against non-Chinese
space targets. Even so, China ominously advocates the use of
"certain space offensive means and capabilities" as space
deterrence against potential adversaries. The 2013 edition
makes an ambiguous distinction between these deterrence
measures and more aggressive "space attack and defense"

measures, which include hard-kill electronic methods like kinetic energy weapons (KEW), lasers, and particle beams.[14] Reading between the lines here, PLA strategists clearly think that using hard-kill methods of any kind against a foreign satellite would cross a line, potentially escalating a conflict or starting a war, but that soft-kill methods like electronic warfare would not, and should instead be treated as mere defensive countermeasures against enemy C4ISR.

Outside of strategic information operations, this ambiguity is also seen in authoritative writings on China's campaign level of warfare (equivalent to the United States operational level of war). In campaign-level information warfare, electronic warfare is expected to play a prime deterrence role as a regional 'stand-off' weapon. Ye Zheng gives the clearest explanation of this stand-off method in his description of "land-based high energy jamming," which calls for "short-wave [high frequency] interference capable of reaching the second island chain" and "capable of dealing with an enemy aircraft carrier's communications." [15] Potential enemies would be able to approach at the risk of losing C4ISR capabilities, rendering themselves blind, deaf, and dumb. Chinese strategic thinking may put anti-satellite jamming in a similar category, classifying the jamming of regional communications and intelligence satellites as a defensive measure rather than considering it to be an attack.

This type of extended standoff jamming reflects a much deeper development in Chinese strategic literature, one that extends Chinese views of sovereignty and 'strategic space' outward from traditional domains of warfare to incorporate virtual spaces like cyberspace and the electromagnetic spectrum. While Chinese views of "cyber sovereignty," the notion that cyberspace should be defined and ruled by state boundaries, are well known, the Chinese idea that the electromagnetic spectrum is subject to the state's will is less broadly understood by foreign observers. In SMS 2013, China makes the case that its national interests have transcended traditional physical dimensions and now "continuously expand toward the periphery and the world, continuously extending toward the ocean, outer space, and the electromagnetic space."[16] Noting China's need to assert itself in these "global public spaces," Academy of Military Science strategists advocate for China's armed forces to secure the electromagnetic domain and use it as a "brace-support" for the extension and protection of China's national interests.[17]

The electromagnetic domain does not exist in isolation from other non-traditional domains of warfare, and Chinese military theory has aimed over the past two decades to understand and master the complex interactions between them. The foundation of these efforts is China's theory of Integrated Network and Electronic Warfare (INEW). INEW is the much-ballyhooed brainchild of Dai Qingmin, the former head of the Fourth Department of the PLA General Staff Department, which was responsible for computer network attack and electronic warfare until the PLA's recent reorganization. INEW represents a certain maturity in PLA thinking on information warfare and reflects a growing, nuanced understanding of information technologies and weapons able to exploit them. The development of the concept marks a key point of departure in the evolution of Chinese strategic thought, moving from an earlier reliance on U.S.-derived doctrine toward a formulation of distinctly Chinese approach to information warfare.

In its most basic form, INEW seeks to integrate electronic warfare and network warfare on two levels. First, it seeks to merge electronic warfare and network warfare technologies together to create a hybrid capability. In this regard, INEW promises to make network warfare relevant to areas traditionally dominated by electronic warfare by enabling network attacks to 'bridge the air-gap' and enter relatively unprotected, isolated battlefield networks. This is possible as a result of the "developmental trend of networking in battlefield electronic devices" and their increasing prevalence in warfighting devices. [18] SMS 2013 envisions the use of such weapons by "transmitting information to the target computer via wired, wireless, or electromagnetic avenues ... exploiting loopholes in the adversary's computers to sneak into the adversary's network systems, and via spyware collecting and stealing the information stored and processed in those computers." [19]

INEW puts forward a view of information warfare that operates along a continuum in a combined electromagnetic-network space. Operationally, SMS 2013 states that "information operations with the integration of networks and the electromagnetic spectrum have become a kind of new operational pattern," one that is necessary for achieving battlefield dominance through information warfare. [20] Digital and analog technologies have converged to such a degree on the battlefield that electronic warfare and network warfare "cannot be mutually exclusive, with each [force] fighting their own battles." Because "carriers on which information relies are extending from disconnected electronic devices toward networks," so-called "one-dimensional electronic warfare" is unable to completely meet the needs of operational commanders; the integration of network warfare is necessary if one is to paralyze enemy information systems fully.[21] Essentially, the growing sophistication of communications has made it necessary to explore alternate means of disruption and denial outside of simple "communications countermeasures" that have traditionally relied upon jamming to prevent information transmission. The use of digital communications over wireless networks has presented new opportunities to attack enemy C4ISR ecosystems at their information-processing nodes, allowing for more damaging information operations.

Combining both network and electronic warfare forces under a single command is not a new concept, globally speaking, and neither is the integration of network and electronic warfare technologies. Both the U.S. and Israeli militaries are rumored to have not only developed these weapons but also used these them to suppress Iraqi and Syrian air defense networks in 2003 and 2007, respectively.[22] For China, however, INEW represents an attempt at merging their electronic-warfare strength at the campaign level with their network warfare strength at the strategic level to ensure dominance in all phases of conflict. INEW promises to bridge the gap between the strategic and campaign levels, allowing network warfare a greater role in campaigns that might ordinarily be dominated by electronic warfare. Network warfare relies on secrecy, preemption, and illicitly obtained network access to accomplish its objectives. Once the first salvo in conflict is launched, these access routes and exploits are revealed and thus compromised, severely limiting network warfare's ability to be used as an operational tool through the remaining stages of conflict.

Modernizing Psychological and Political Warfare for the 21st Century

The 1993 military strategic guidelines' exhortation for the PLA to prepare for "local wars under high-technology conditions" marked the beginning of China's decades-long process to adapt its armed forces to the realities of modern warfare. Just as the Persian Gulf War and NATO's operations in the former Yugoslavia demonstrated to the PLA the urgent need to develop informatized kinetic warfighting capabilities, it also highlighted the need for Beijing modernize the political and psychological warfare component of its information operations. Washington's international narrative about Iraq and Serbia's actions, which provided the *casus belli* for military action to uphold international law and humanitarian norms, highlighted for Chinese officials the power of setting the diplomatic context in successfully deterring an adversary or using force.[23] In a sense, modernized political warfare looks more like a return to the PLA's revolutionary tradition than a vision of future warfare, as it focuses on the role of information operations in the PLA's creation of political power for the CCP. Unlike political warfare during the Chinese Civil War, however, the PLA's targets are not other Chinese or the Kuomintang but rather a range of global actors, requiring the PLA to expand the scope of its political and psychological operations.

This challenge emerges from the changing nature of warfare under informatized conditions. As SMS 2013 explains, modern warfare is becoming a confrontation between 'systems of systems': "Informatized warfare is no longer the confrontation between individual operational elements, combat units, and combat power, and instead a confrontation between all elements of opposing systems is becoming the reality." Though it is tempting to read these words in terms of the competing C4ISR networks underpinning military operations, the driving force behind this concept is the increasingly close relationship between war and other features of political struggle, including economics, legal issues, and public opinion.[24]

Mao Zedong most famously elaborated the role of the PLA in creating and strengthening the CCP's political power in *Problems of War and Strategy* (1938): "political power grows out of the barrel of a gun." While the quote is most often invoked today with regard to the principle of party control over the PLA, the next sentences highlight what the PLA makes possible. Mao wrote "having guns, we can create Party organizations ... We can also create cadres, create schools, create culture, create mass movements. Everything in Yenan has been created by having guns. All things grow out of the barrel of a gun." These words offer further clarification of Mao's position adopted in the work report of the Gutian Conference in 1929 (later republished as *On Correcting Mistaken Ideas within the Party*). Mao used the conference to criticize the military- and warfighting-centric view of the party's military operations, arguing that those taking such a view failed to realize that China's political future, rather than any specific battle, was what was at stake for the army now known as the PLA:

> "They think that the task of the Red Army like that of the White army, is merely to fight. They do not understand that the Chinese Red Army is an armed body for carrying out the political tasks of the revolution. Especially at present, the Red Army should certainly not confine itself to

fighting; besides fighting to destroy the enemy's military strength, it should shoulder such important tasks as doing propaganda among the masses, organizing the masses, arming them, helping them to establish revolutionary political power and setting up Party organizations. The Red Army fights not merely for the sake of fighting but in order to conduct propaganda among the masses, organize them, arm them, and help them to establish revolutionary political power. Without these objectives, fighting loses its meaning and the Red Army loses the reason for its existence."

This particular passage later evolved into a set of directives enshrined in the Political Work Guidelines, which have changed very little in their core message between the available editions from 1964, 2003, and 2010. Political work in the PLA addresses eight key issues: (1) ensuring army units execute the programs, lines, and policies of the party; (2) organizing personnel for ideological education and preventing the encroachment of modern revisionist and capitalist ideology; (3) establishing and leading party committees at various levels; (4) conducting political work in time of war, to carry on propaganda and agitation incessantly; (5) raising and maintaining combat morale; (6) conducting security work and ensuring the political and organizational purity of PLA units; (7) developing cultural, recreational, and athletic activities of a mass nature; and (8) fostering close relationships between PLA units and local CCP and state organs.[25] Six of these eight mission areas relate directly to the challenges of offensive and defensive information operations.

SMS 2001 marked a transition point, as the volume contains a mix of forward-looking analysis and nearly-anachronistic combinations of emerging technology and traditional methods. PLA thinkers clearly understood that information operations stood on the cusp of significant changes ("the development of modern S&T has provided a rich base for psychological warfare to expand its methods and means"), but offered almost comical examples of what the changes might entail. For example, rather than observing the potential to target propaganda through personal electronic devices to enemy forces, the authors offer the possibility of using the emerging technology of unmanned aerial vehicles to deliver propaganda pamphlets.[26]

The critical point for information operations in SMS 2001 is its call to develop the PLA's political warfare capabilities. Though the authors foresee broadened information competition and new opportunities afforded by technology to expand the scope of information operations, they are reticent to address any specifics of what the future holds. They do, however, call upon the PLA to "explore a way to enhance the building of our psychological warfare forces and form a set of methods and forms of combat for psychological warfare with 'PLA characteristics'. It is an objective requirement to ensure that the PLA will win the strategic initiative in future high-tech wars."[27] SMS 2001 repeatedly makes the point that these operations will in part take place beyond the military battlefield, implying the PLA's role will need to expand.[28]

SMS 2001 outlines the scope and scale of modern information operations in a way that highlights the all-encompassing nature of information warfare. The distinctions between war and peace, domestic and foreign, civilian and soldier bear little on how and when the PLA should employ information operations:

> "The target of modern psychological warfare is not limited to the enemy forces as it also includes all people of the hostile country. Meanwhile, it assumes the mission of educating our own military and civilians, condensing their morale and keeping their mentality stable. Its key target, however, is the enemy's decision-making level, meaning it uses all kinds of means to attack that level's thinking, conviction, will, feeling, and identifying systems in order to cause wrong understandings, assessments, and decisions, and shake its thinking and conviction and will of resistance to achieve the objective of defeating the enemy without fighting. It is implemented not only in wartime but also in a massive and continued scale in peacetime."[29]

The implications of this expanded role are clearest in the PLA anachronism of "dis-integrating enemy forces" (瓦解敌方), which the 2001 edition describes as "one of the three PLA principles, which is its fine tradition as well as an important indispensable condition of supporting military attack to win victory." In the past, this was a battlefield mission, or at least requiring contact with the enemy. Examples include converting Kuomintang units to the Communist cause during the Civil War as well as captured foreign soldiers during the World War II and the Korean War. [30] Dis-integrating enemy forces primarily dealt with handling prisoners of war and other contacts with the adversary, according to the early Political

Work Guidelines. In the context of modern information warfare, however, this antiquated concept can potentially be applied on a much larger scale even prior to the point of conflict, with targets that extend far beyond enemy troops to include entire foreign societies.

SMS 2013 reflects the evolution of the PLA's efforts to conduct information operations against domestic and foreign targets. Rather than receiving separate treatment, political warfare is integrated where relevant to the book's analysis of strategy and warfare (with specific reference to the 'Three Warfares').[31] The need to shape perceptions appears in reference to two principal areas: maintaining the strategic initiative and deterrence. The core elements of "winning without fighting" and the integration of peacetime and wartime operations remain a consistent theme.

Information operations of all kinds influence deterrence operations in two important ways. First, according to SMS 2013, successful deterrence requires power, resolve, and the ability to convey that power and resolve to one's adversary.[32] Implicit in this argument is the necessity of the PLA building up channels to communicate the strength of its capabilities and China's direct interests. Deterrence is a concept rooted in both psychology and politics, and deterrence operations require manipulation of the target's decision-making. In attempts to deter escalation once hostilities have already broken out, deterrence is one of several possible goals of information operations aimed at disrupting adversaries' C4ISR networks.

As SMS 2001 predicted, information operations have become an important element in seizing and maintaining the strategic initiative according to the 2013 edition. Winning 'the right to speak' or possessing 'discursive/narrative power' (话语权) has become "another manifestation of seizing the initiative in local wars under informatized conditions." Achieving 'the right to speak' requires the "integrated application of public opinion warfare, legal warfare, and psychological warfare" to persuade the adversary and other international actors that one's own side is just, reasonable, and right. [33] In that broader context, discursive power refers to the ability to establish which events are important and how these events are understood.

The inclusion of discursive power in SMS 2013 is another sign of how information operations are closely linked to the CCP's priorities. By 2012, the party's concern with how China-related events were perceived abroad resulted in lengthy commentaries in the Central Committee and Central Party School journals critiquing Chinese shortcomings in this area, with years of effort to expand Xinhua and CCTV's reach and a $6.6 billion investment in overseas and external propaganda operations in 2009 not producing the desired effect on global public opinion. Despite their keen understanding of their shortcomings, however, CCP propaganda specialists have few meaningful suggestions for how to improve tangible outcomes and strengthen Chinese discursive power.[34]

The principal distinction between the treatments of information operations in the two editions is the degree to which operational military objectives are the focus. SMS 2001 offers a meditation on how information operations affect international politics, such as U.S. psychological warfare against the Soviet Bloc, and wars, such as Washington's effort to shape the context in which the world viewed the Persian Gulf War. At this time, the telecommunications and Internet revolution was just beginning to accelerate, and the only authors' only firm conclusion was that a potentially vast change about to occur in the international information environment. By contrast, the 2013 edition ties information operations together with specific political-military objectives like maintaining strategic initiative and deterring adversaries. Put another way, in 2001, the PLA tried to anticipate the future it would face; in 2013, the PLA outlined their solution to the challenges of modern warfare.

The operational focus of SMS 2013 reflects changes occurring within the PLA that have given the political commissars and the former General Political Department greater warfighting roles.[35] The most significant change occurred in 2003 with the revision to the Political Work Guidelines. The revised guidelines included the "Three Warfares" and designated the General Political Department and its subordinate personnel as the executors of these missions. Though still under the conceptual umbrella of "system-of-systems operations," PLA writings on modular force groupings include "Three Warfares" units as part of larger forces that might be put together for various campaigns, explicitly granting them a role throughout all phases of war.[36]

Unpacking the Increasing Centrality of Information Operations in PLA Strategy

Several central themes underpin the increasing importance of information operations to the PLA and the Chinese leadership. One of the most notable is the integration of peace and war; that is, the idea that in the present military environment wartime success depends ever more heavily on what preparatory activities take place in peacetime. As SMS 2001 noted, "The application of strategic material force includes the application of actual combat as well as the application of deterrence. Strategic guidance is evident in wartime as well as in peacetime. The function of strategy includes winning wars as well as preventing and limiting wars."[37] Initially, this idea applied most directly to preparing the PLA for warfare under high-tech conditions, but as information operations and deterrence became important tools for Chinese strategists, this integration became more operationally relevant. PLA activities in peacetime became vital to protecting the party-state and executing political-military objectives in wartime.

The connectivity of China to the outside world through global information networks is related to, but not wholly derivative of, the above insight into peace and war. Newly-contiguous information spaces narrow the distance China and potential adversaries, granting them greater access (albeit virtually) into China. Consequently, the warning time between the figurative 'strategic first shot' of a conflict and its literal first bullets has shrunk, requiring higher alerts during times of peace. With a narrowing of the spectrum between peace and war, deterrence naturally plays a more important role as part of national policy. Effective deterrence also buys time for information operations to reshape a context in which a potential adversary might otherwise instigate conflict to China's advantage.

Peacetime-Wartime Integration

China's concept of Peace-War Integration（平战结合）developed out of the conviction that the reality of warfare under informatized conditions has unalterable implications for how a country should prepare for war. This view of the importance of peacetime preparation evolved out of Deng Xiaoping's policy

choices that privileged the civilian economy over the needs of
the defense industries. Throughout the 1980s, military budgets
stagnated and much of China's defense industrial capacity was
converted for civilian usage. Choice, rather than necessity, made
the PLA dependent on the civilian economy.[38] However, the
technology requirements of the revised 1993 military strategic
guidelines, "local wars under high-tech conditions," turned
Deng's choice into a necessity. As SMS 2001 put it, "The forms
of wars are being moved from mechanized wars to informatized
wars. The entire military system and society are increasingly
connected closely together, and the sources of fighting capacity
are increasingly coming from the integrated national strength."
For an informatized force, the technological component of
national strength received emphasis and became the "core of
war preparation."[39] Although military reliance on the civilian
economy was a policy choice to support Deng's broad
modernization agenda, the new situation required
manufacturing goods suitable for peacetime and wartime use as
well as for military and civilian use.

The PLA's evaluation of warfare under informatized conditions,
however, soon pushed its approach to the integration of
peacetime and wartime from general long-term preparation for
war closer to operational readiness for immediate warfighting.
SMS 2001 observed "wars are becoming more unexpected and
short, initial actions are usually provided with the characteristics
of decisive battles that require quick transition from peacetime
to wartime," and subsequent documents, such as SMS 2013 and
the 2015 Defense White Paper entitled China's Military Strategy,
have also emphasized peacetime-wartime integration.[40] The
2015 white paper comments that only by "observing the
principles of combining peacetime and wartime demands,

maintaining all time vigilance and being action-ready" will the PLA be able to have an effective operational duty system.

As the PLA writ large embraced peacetime-wartime integration, the line between the two has blurred entirely for information operations as a result of their ability to cross domains and spaces and the need for continuous preparatory activity. However, this unique place for information operations within PLA warfighting and war preparations has a long history. SMS 2001 described information operations as "ambiguous, straddling the divide between a clear-cut attack and a deterrence strike and therefore straddles the divide between peace and war."[41]

Several other features of information operations ensure that they are different than conventional military operations. First, to be effective, information operations units across the spectrum of non-traditional domains—political/psychological warfare, network, and electronic warfare—must be constantly preparing the groundwork for wartime operations. In the realm of political warfare, for example, both SMS 2001 and SMS 2013 highlight the need for propaganda to fortify the Chinese people to support a war as well as educating external audiences of the Chinese government's basic peacefulness and the justice of any cause for which Beijing would use force. Electronic warfare is even more invasive in operational terms during peacetime. Extensive reconnaissance must precede any effort to jam, manipulate, or otherwise disrupt the informational linkages that make up an adversary's system of systems. When reconnoitering computer networks, accessing the networks themselves is a small step away from being able to manipulate or destroy data. Without constant probing, the ability to use electronic warfare tools in

space, the network domain, and the electromagnetic spectrum
cannot be assured.

Second, the covert nature of many information operations and
the difficulty in attributing soft kills against one's C4ISR systems
create an ambiguity as to the state of war or peace between
countries engaged a struggle for information dominance. SMS
2001 observes that soft-kill capabilities make it "harder to define
the difference between wartime, war, and peace," because they
can be used during peacetime "without destroying personnel
and equipment, and without betraying an air of warfare during
their implementation." [42] This belief seems premised on the
questionable notion that attack attribution can never resolved to
the point of satisfying cautious policymakers in an adversary
nation.[43] Whether the PLA continues to believe this after the U.S.
Department of Justice issued economic espionage indictments
for five PLA officers in May 2014 is unknown, even if the PLA's
behavior in cyberspace may have changed as a result.[44]

The Conventionalization of Deterrence

The PLA's understanding of deterrence also creates an impetus
behind information operations, because conventional
deterrence has supplanted nuclear deterrence in practical terms.
When attempting conventional deterrence, information
operations are key to creating the conditions to deter an
adversary. After the Cold War, the advent of precision-guided,
high-performance munitions has offered a destructive
capability that is more flexible to use than nuclear weapons and
offers greater credibility in most situations that countries are
likely to find themselves in.[45] This point of view is consistent
across the 2001 and 2013 editions of *The Science of Military*

Strategy. The former noted that although post-Cold War crises "will not endanger the survival of the country, they can still endanger the dignity of a country and people, endanger the country's legitimate position in international political life, and endanger favorable military strategic situations." [46] When survival is not at stake, nuclear weapons simply cannot be credibly used for deterrence. As noted above, the soft-kill elements of electronic warfare offer another set of widely usable tools, because damage to data, networks, and sensors is very different from dead soldiers.

Information operations also underpin the three factors—power, resolve, and information transmission—that make deterrence effective. According to SMS 2013, the foundation of deterrence is convincing an adversary of the possibility of violence, so that they change their behavior. [47] Power is self-explanatory, but information operations either convey the impression of power by drawing attention to specific capabilities (e.g. asymmetrical "assassins' mace" or "trump card" capabilities) or creating uncertainty about what damage might result from an attack. Resolve is a function of interests and willpower, both of which can be demonstrated and amplified through domestic propaganda and other measures to prepare the public for war. Two of the more notable forms related to information warfare are the rise of hawkish Chinese defense intellectuals, who are quoted regularly in Chinese and Western media, and the military-civil integration program for national defense education. The former broadcasts Chinese concerns to a wide audience without tying authoritative media, like the *People's Daily* and *PLA Daily*, to direct threats to use force. [48] The latter provides students entering universities with basic information about military affairs and encourages a supportive attitude

toward the PLA. [49] Finally, without effective information
channels, power and resolve will not be understood by the target
of deterrence operations. These channels can be direct or
indirect, such as messages conveyed through a third-party
country, but they have to be cultivated and information
operators need to be able to confirm that their target understood
the signals.[50]

Recent strategic literature has described the United States
moving toward a "new triad" composed of nuclear, space, and
cyber forces to replace the old nuclear "triad" of long-range
intercontinental ballistic missiles, nuclear submarines, and
long-range strategic bombers. China clearly envisions its own
strategic guiding principles shifting away from a sole focus on
nuclear deterrence toward a hybrid posture, concentrating
primarily on long-range information strikes with nuclear
weapons as a backstop. SMS 2013 argues that this triad would
include a "conventional 'prompt global strike' system in the next
decade so as to have the capability to implement conventional
strikes anywhere within one hour," replete with abilities to strike
through the network domain. Unmistakably present but
unmentioned in these descriptions is the role of electronic
warfare in this triad; the electromagnetic spectrum is the
invisible backbone between space-based communications and
cyberspace, acting as the carrier of targeting information,
intelligence, and command and control for many of these
platforms. [51]

A Globalized, Networked World Creates Contiguous Spaces

One of the fundamental changes identified by Chinese military
thinkers affecting information operations was how the

Information Age has changed the physical proximity of threats. Many information operations, especially psychological warfare and soft-kill capabilities, do not have the same geographic limitations of kinetic weapons. Even seemingly mundane developments, such as the spread of media reports, have evolved beyond recognition. The physical distribution of newspapers and radio broadcasts offered only a trickle of information compared to the flow of information that has opened up between China's hundreds of millions of Internet users and the rest of the world.[52] The widespread adoption of space-based telecommunications has led to the growth of an international electromagnetic space with entirely new avenues for information to flow in and out of China.

An Academy of Military Science study of information operations published in 2009 offers perhaps the single best analysis of how information technologies reshaped national security. It is worth quoting at some length:

> "Entering the Information Age, the rapid development of Internet, satellite television, and wireless communication information technology created great changes to the connotations and implications of traditional national security. National security has gone beyond the traditional four-dimensional geopolitical boundaries—land, sea, air, and space—to increasingly include information frontiers as a fifth dimension to secure. Hostile forces relying upon modern information technology are able to leap across geographic boundaries of the target country, and through

> various forms of information dissemination
> influence the thinking and the behavior of the
> target country's people, threatening the
> psychological security of the target country."[53]

The connections opened up by the Information Revolution help explain the revival of traditional Chinese views of information operations. During the Chinese Revolution and Civil War, the political and military battlefield occurred within the geographically contiguous space of China. The contained space and the need of the CCP to operate in contested areas made the PLA more than just a military fighting force, as Mao Zedong highlighted at the Gutian Conference. The PLA needed to take on many different political tasks, because only armed soldiers or those marching with them could operate while opposing armies were still present in the field. The PLA's role in the network domain is not dissimilar to that of the Eighth Route Army from that earlier era. The PLA possesses capabilities to secure Chinese networks, broadcast messages intended to boost public support for Beijing's policies, and reconnoiter and attack adversaries. While other elements of the Chinese party-state can carry out some of these tasks, the PLA possesses unique capabilities across the entire spectrum of information operations.

Reshaping the PLA's Information Warfare Bureaucracy

On November 26, 2015, Xi Jinping announced a far-reaching set of reforms that dissolved the basic organizational structure that had served the PLA since the early 1950s. Unlike Xi's reforms, previous rounds of organizational reform under Deng Xiaoping, Jiang Zemin, and Hu Jintao merely tinkered around the edges of the Central Military Commission (CMC), the four General

Departments, and the services. Nor did previous reforms do nearly as much to undermine the dominance of the PLA's ground forces, which has been an entrenched interest impeding the PLA from becoming a truly joint fighting force. Xi's proposals, which began being implemented in the weeks following their announcement, replaced the Military Regions with theater commands, created the Strategic Support Force and upgraded the Second Artillery to a service, created a new ground forces headquarters to allow for genuinely joint top-level departments, and placed a number of key offices directly under the CMC.[54] The sum of these organizational changes was encapsulated with a simple phrase: "The CMC has supreme command; theater commands lead on warfighting; the services lead on force development."[55]

This round of structural reforms comes closest to providing the organizational cohesion for information operations that began emerging conceptually in the 2000s. The full details of the PLA's restructuring remain unknown; however, Chinese reporting and analysis strongly suggests that a desire to integrate and centralize information operations drove the creation of the Strategic Support Force.

Although there are still questions as to which specific units will comprise the Strategic Support Force, there is widespread expert consensus that the force will at a minimum centralize China's space, cyber, and electronic warfare forces under a single command as an "information warfare service." Song Zhongping, former PLA Second Artillery Force officer, suggests that the network warfare force will focus on network attack and defense, space forces will focus on ISR and navigation, and the electronic warfare force will focus on jamming and disruption of communication and sensors. Admiral Yin Zhuo's support for Song's interpretation reinforces the suggestion that the Strategic Support Force is an information warfare service, because of the admiral's position as member of the PLA Navy Expert Advisory Committee for Network Security and Informatization and the All-Military Network Security and Informatization Expert Advisory Committee. Based on other comments, it is also likely that these forces eventually will include China's strategic information management and intelligence support forces.[56] This reformation of China's information warfare forces is aimed at optimizing its institutions toward wartime mobilization and readiness by merging wartime constructs—such as "information operations groups"—with current peacetime institutions. China's wartime information warfare strategy calls for its information warfare forces—cyber, electronic warfare, and space cadre all—to form into ad-hoc "information operations groups" at the strategic, campaign, and tactical levels. The Strategic Support Force would save much-needed time and energy by creating such a construct in peacetime, even if not named at such, and priming these forces toward intelligence preparation of the battlespace, war readiness, and comprehensive planning for information dominance.

Although the reorganization looks to centralize aspects of electronic warfare in the electro-magnetic spectrum and the network domain in the Strategic Support Force, the biggest question is whether political and psychological warfare will be integrated or will remain segregated off. As noted above with reference to SMS 2001, in the PLA's organizational structures psychological warfare has traditionally fallen under political work rather than military operations and information warfare. However, the revised Political Work Guidelines and SMS 2013 indicate recognition that psychological warfare should be more closely aligned with operational concerns. Official press on the Political Work Department—the successor to the General Political Department—states that the department will focus primarily on personnel issues, but since the PLA has never been completely transparent about information operations the question remains unanswered until more information is available.

Now largely disposed of the primary mission of modernization, the PLA can focus its main energies on strategic operations, readiness, and, perhaps most importantly, reforming its institutions to best meet the requirements of Chinese national security policy and grand strategy (rather than institutional inertia constraining policy, as has been the case for much of the PLA's history). The grand realignment of China's information operations forces under the Strategic Support Force and the re-subordination of information operations to political power is a necessary next step.

Conclusion

Taken as a whole, China's approach to information operations is a continuous plan of action that extends from peacetime and international crises to open warfare. Any would-be adversary first will need to consider how Beijing might attempt to shape international perceptions of a conflict using political and psychological warfare, as well as the extent to which the CCP has prepared the Chinese population to resist such efforts from abroad. If a crisis developed, the would-be adversary could expect steadily escalating pressure across not only the political but also the electromagnetic and network domains. This could include deal-making and persuasion in international political bodies, 'spontaneous' demonstrations against the adversary's diplomatic facilities, and mobilizing friends of China within the adversary's country to speak out against their government's actions. As a situation intensifies, the would-be adversary would need to be careful of triggering an escalatory Chinese response. The PLA's theoretical and doctrinal comfort with soft-kill capabilities, particularly electronic warfare, may result in a low threshold for their use, especially against purely military targets. As the authors of SMS 2001 opined, the "first shot" at the political or strategic level is not the same as the first shot fired in anger.[57] Information operations may constitute a first line of deterrence designed to raise the costs an adversary might face and to mobilize the Chinese population to demonstrate resolve and rally around their government.

This layering of information warfare capabilities, tantamount to a sort of information "defense in depth," is made possible by the steady informatization of both the PLA and Chinese society as a whole. The growth of this infrastructure has led to a dramatic increase in China's vulnerable 'border areas' in both physical and non-traditional domains, increasing the strategic space necessary to defend China's national interests. The pervasive Chinese use of network technologies and space-based communications platforms has caused the domestic Internet and the global electromagnetic domain to become military battlegrounds, constituting potential "commanding high points" in the event of strategic information warfare. Just as China used to regard its deep hinterlands and massive population as strategic assets, informatization has led to a much different kind of "defense in depth," one with overlapping measures of electronic, psychological, and political deterrents.

The enduring relevance of Marxist-Leninist-Mao Zedong warfare principles to information warfare demonstrates the creativity of Chinese political scholars in adapting well-worn communist tropes to new forms of warfighting and evolving technology. Western militaries must confront the possibility that China's approach to warfare, with its emphasis on maximizing surprise, concealment, irregular tactics, and "defense in depth," may be better suited to information warfare than Western equivalents. China's authoritarian control over domestic information systems and the electromagnetic spectrum also may provide some advantage in electronic warfare, network warfare, and psychological warfare. In much the same way that the United States military has been a global exemplar in its adoption of precision-guided munitions and network-centric warfare, the PLA may very well become a model force in modern information warfare, capable of heavily employing electronic warfare to overcome more conventionally powerful adversaries.

NOTES

---

[1] Shen Weiguang [沈伟光], Information Warfare [信息作战] (Hangzhou: Zhejiang University Press, 1990), p. 9.

² See, for example, "JFJB on Adjustment, Reform of PRC Armed Forces Structure, Staffing," OSC Summary, April 1, 2008, CPP20080401088001.

³ SMS 2001, p. 189.

⁴ SMS 2013, p. 13.

⁵ SMS 2001, p. 305.

⁶ SMS 2001, p. 417.

⁷ SMS 2013, p. 116.

⁸ James Mulvenon, "PLA Computer Network Operations: Scenarios, Doctrine, Organizations, and Capability," in Roy Kamphausen, David Lai, and Andrew Scobell, eds., *Beyond the Strait: PLA Missions Beyond Taiwan* (Carlisle, PA: Army War College Press, 2009), p. 258.

⁹ James Mulvenon, "The PLA and Information Warfare," in James Mulvenon and Andrew N.D. Yang, eds., *The People's Liberation Army in the Information Age* (Santa Monica, CA: RAND, 1999), p. 177.

¹⁰ Military Terminology of the PLA, [中国解放军军语], (2011), p. 259.

¹¹ SMS 2013, p. 145–146.

¹² Ye Zheng [叶征], *Lectures on Information Operations Studies* [信息作战学教程] (Beijing: Academy of Military Sciences Press, 2013), p. 125.

¹³ SMS 2013, p. 181.

¹⁴ SMS 2013, p. 183.

¹⁵ Ye, *Lectures on Information Operations Studies*, p. 125.

¹⁶ SMS 2013, p. 105.

¹⁷ SMS 2013, pp. 84–85.

¹⁸ Ye, *Lectures on Information Operations Studies*, p. 44.

¹⁹ SMS 2013, p. 192.

²⁰ SMS 2013, p. 268.

²¹ Ye, *Lectures on Information Operations Studies*, p. 44.

²² John Costello, "Chinese Views on the Information 'Center of Gravity': Space, Cyber, and Electronic Warfare," *Jamestown Foundation China Brief*,

April 16, 2015. https://jamestown.org/program/chinese-views-on-the-information-center-of-gravity-space-cyber-and-electronic-warfare/.

[23] For a lengthier treatment, see, Dean Cheng, "Chinese Lessons from the Gulf Wars," in Andrew Scobell, David Lai, and Roy Kamphausen, eds., *Chinese Lessons from Other Peoples' War* (Carlisle, PA: Army War College Press, 2011), 153–200.

[24] SMS 2013, p. 93.

[25] "Political Work Regulations for the Chinese People's Liberation Army," in Ying-mao Kau, Paul M. Chancellor, Philip E. Ginsburg, and Pierre M. Perrolle, *The Political Work System of the Chinese Communist Military: Analysis and Documents* (Providence, RI: Brown University East Asia Language and Area Center, 1971), pp. 221–224.

[26] SMS 2001, p. 328.

[27] SMS 2001, p. 330.

[28] SMS 2001, pp. 327, 328.

[29] SMS 2001, p. 327.

[30] SMS 2001, p. 323.

[31] The "Three Warfares" are the PLA's current moniker for three strands of political warfare: "psychological warfare" (心理战), public opinion or media warfare (舆论战), and legal warfare (法律战).

[32] SMS 2013, pp. 135–137.

[33] SMS 2013, p. 129.

[34] "Beijing in 45b Yuan Global Media Drive," *South China Morning Post*, January 13, 2009; Peter Mattis, "China's International Right to Speak," *China Brief*, October 19, 2012. https://jamestown.org/program/chinas-international-right-to-speak/.

[35] The former General Political Department—rather than the Political Work Department—is used, because the structural reorganization of the PLA beginning November 26, 2015 may have changed the location of the units involved in political warfare, like the Liaison Department.

[36] Kevin McCauley, "System of Systems Operational Capability: Operational Units and Elements," *Jamestown Foundation China Brief*, March 15, 2013.

https://jamestown.org/program/system-of-systems-operational-capability-operational-units-and-elements/.
[37] SMS 2001, p. 10.

[38] Adam P. Liff and Andrew S. Erickson, "Demystifying China's Defence Spending: Less Mysterious in the Aggregate," *The China Quarterly*, No. 216 (December 2013), pp. 805–830; Tai Ming Cheung, *Fortifying China: The Struggle to Build a Modern Defense Economy* (Ithaca, NY: Cornell University Press, 2009).

[39] SMS 2001, p. 151.

[40] SMS 2001, p. 152.

[41] SMS 2001, p. 188.

[42] SMS 2001, pp. 62, 69.

[43] For example, SMS 2013, p. 131.

[44] Ellen Nakashima, "Following U.S. Indictments, China Shifts Commercial Hacking Away from Military to Civilian Agency," *Washington Post*, November 30, 2015.

[45] SMS 2013, pp. 137–138.

[46] SMS 2001, p. 28.

[47] SMS 2013, p. 135.

[48] Andrew Chubb, "Propaganda, Not Policy: Explaining the PLA's 'Hawkish Faction' (Part One)," *China Brief*, July 25, 2013. https://jamestown.org/program/propaganda-not-policy-explaining-the-plas-hawkish-faction-part-one/. ; "Propaganda as Policy? Explaining the PLA's 'Hawkish Faction' (Part Two)," *Jamestown Foundation China Brief*, August 9, 2013. https://jamestown.org/program/propaganda-as-policy-explaining-the-plas-hawkish-faction-part-two/.

[49] SMS 2001, p. 154.

[50] SMS 2013, pp. 136–137.

[51] SMS 2013, pp. 72.

[52] Jiang Jie, Li Wusheng, Lu Zhengtao, Wang Wentian, and Zhang Tingshen, chief eds. [蒋杰,李武胜,吕正韬,王雯田,张廷慎], *The Planning and*

Implementation of Strategic Psychological Warfare under Informatized Conditions [信息条件下战略心理战策划与实施], (Beijing: Academy of Military Sciences Press, 2009).

53 Jiang et al, *The Planning and Implementation of Strategic Psychological Warfare*, p. 38.

54 Kenneth Allen, Dennis Blasko, and John Corbett, "The PLA's New Organizational Structure: What is Known, Unknown and Speculation (Part 1)," *China Brief*, February 4, 2016, https://jamestown.org/program/the-plas-new-organizational-structure-what-is-known-unknown-and-speculation-part-1/.

55 "CMC Opinion Regarding the Deepening of National Defense and Military Reform [中央军委关于深化国防和军队改革的意见]," *People's Daily* [人民日报], January 2, 2016.

56 John Costello, "The Strategic Support Force: China's Information Warfare Service," *China Brief*, February 8, 2016, https://jamestown.org/program/the-strategic-support-force-chinas-information-warfare-service/.

57 SMS 2001, p. 373.

Chapter 7: China's Military Strategy for Network Warfare

Joe McReynolds

Over the past two decades, Chinese political and military leaders have come to recognize the necessity of information collection, processing, analysis, and dissemination to the successful use of military power. As a result, improving the PLA's utilization of information, a process the Chinese refer to as "military informatization," has become a crucial aspect of China's military modernization planning.[1] There is a general consensus within the PLA that the widespread military and civilian use of information technologies across the globe has led to new domains in which states may interact, compete, and even wage war.

In this context, the global agglomeration of networked and network-capable digital devices popularly known in the West as "cyberspace" or "the cyber domain" has increasingly taken center stage in PLA strategic thinking. PLA strategists and academicians have come to understand the "network domain" (网络领域) as a non-traditional but central battlefield in the informatized wars they seek to be capable of fighting and winning. Exerting dominance in the network domain, they believe, is an essential requirement if China is to prevail against or deter a 'high-technology adversary' such as the United States in a future military conflict.

Thoroughly understanding China's strategic perspective in the network domain is an important but difficult challenge, in part due to the secrecy and political sensitivities that have historically surrounded China's network warfare forces and capabilities. Furthermore, there is no single unified perspective on the topic; the PLA is not a monolith, and when examining various topics central to network warfare one finds significant divergences in viewpoint between different camps of PLA theoreticians. However, a survey of relatively authoritative strategic texts such as the Academy of Military Sciences' (AMS) recently updated *Science of Military Strategy* (SMS) and PLA officer Ye Zheng's influential *Lectures on the Science of Information Operations* (LSIO) enables us to paint a fairly robust portrait of the current state of PLA strategic thinking.

This chapter engages with both authoritative sources and the consensus of the field to explore PLA thinking on network warfare strategy, both in the abstract sense of network warfare's fundamental characteristics and in the more concrete sense of determining when and how the PLA might choose to initiate or escalate network warfare operations against an adversary. Since network warfare capabilities are by necessity shrouded in some degree of secrecy and the thinking of PLA strategists on these issues is by no means monolithic, an attempt has been made to convey not only areas of consensus, but also topics where ambiguity and major points of contention remain.

Conceptualizations of Network Warfare in Authoritative PLA Writings

In order to understand the PLA's strategic thinking on network warfare, some context regarding sources of information and foundational conceptions of the topic is essential. Authoritative PLA writings from as far back as the Jiang Zemin era, such as the 2001 edition of the *Science of Military Strategy*, hold that modern information operations—and by extension, network warfare—are a fundamentally novel concept rather than a mere extension of conventional warfare into an intangible domain, with some influential PLA theoreticians even going so far as to argue that the importance of the new battlefield of "intangible spaces" to modern warfare now surpasses that of traditional "tangible" battlefields.[2] SMS, which was written for an audience of both senior Chinese policymakers involved in military affairs and officers in training, has endured as one of the key foundational texts of modern PLA strategic studies up to the release of the newly updated 2013 edition, and remains relevant as a description of the enduring core tenets of PLA strategic thought. The 2001 edition of the *Science of Military Strategy* speaks of the "information domain" and "information warfare" as encompassing computer networks, the electromagnetic spectrum, spaces of psychology and perception, and intelligence operations; over time these have come to be understood as component domains of the overall information domain, rather than merely forms of information operations.

The theoretical work done at that time forms a foundation upon which increasingly sophisticated studies of network warfare have subsequently been conducted. Over time, finer distinctions have been drawn as to how PLA strategy should differentiate between those subdomains, with electronic warfare, network warfare, psychological warfare, and intelligence operations each having different considerations even as they interconnect with one another and with 'traditional' domains of warfare. Technological progress has also played an important role in pushing the PLA to evolve its thinking over time. PLA analysts note that critical infrastructure such as electrical power networks, electronic communications networks, the Internet, computer systems, embedded systems, space-based precision timing networks, and ad hoc networks such as Internet-of-Things and "ubiquitous computing" technologies all exist at the intersection of the physical, network and electromagnetic spaces.[3]

PLA strategists now generally conceive of network attack and defense operations as having four layers: the physical layer, the energy layer, the logic layer, and the non-technological layer.[4] In the physical layer of computer network warfare, conventional physical methods are used to directly damage and/or destroy computer network systems. The energy layer refers to use of the electromagnetic spectrum to penetrate computer systems one does not have network access to. The information layer involves attempting to subvert or destroy an adversary's computer networks and protect one's own networks via methods reliant on computational logic, such as viruses or software vulnerability exploitation. Finally, attack and defense aimed at the non-technological layer encompasses efforts to deceive, circumvent, or penetrate networks through the human beings that control and access them, such as through human intelligence collection, social engineering, or psychological warfare. This schema gives maximal breadth to the concept of network warfare, going beyond mere 'hacker versus hacker' contests to encompass full spectrum information operations in the network domain.

The 2013 edition of the *Science of Military Strategy* is a particularly valuable resource for understanding this evolving strategic approach to network warfare. Despite the sensitivity and secrecy surrounding network warfare within the PLA and in the Chinese media, a study that aims to be as comprehensive as SMS cannot afford to ignore network warfare due to the centrality of information warfare to modern war-fighting. Furthermore, the fact that each AMS-authored edition of SMS is the result of a rigorous, years-long drafting process involving dozens of authors, and is then published as a rare official product of an institution with significant influence on Chinese military strategy, ensures that the information these volumes contain on network warfare represents something approaching a consensus position within the PLA.

Looking beyond the consensus-based writings of the *Science of Military Strategy*, PLA academicians and analysts have produced numerous studies of network warfare in recent years. However, Ye Zheng's *Lectures on the Science of Information Operations*, issued as part of the Academy of Military Sciences' influential series of officer teaching materials, stands out from the crowd for both its comprehensiveness and the high degree of influence its author appears to have on PLA strategic thinking. Ye has been at the vanguard of PLA network warfare theory for at least a decade, arguing that information warfare demands originality in one's thinking just as the advent of nuclear warfare once did.[5] As the head of the Academy of Military Sciences' Informatized Warfare Research Office (信息化作战研究室), he leverages the Academy of Military Sciences' authority and imprimatur to take strong positions on a number of contested topics. His work advocated that China should not differentiate between network operations conducted in wartime and those carried out in peacetime, with constant preparation to execute network warfare operations and a perpetual state of mobilization for network warfare forces, a position that aligns closely with the modus operandi of the newly created Strategic Support Force.[6]

In his writings, Ye also reflects current Chinese strategy in his rejection of any separation between military and civilian considerations in the network domain, espousing a comprehensive national network security strategy that appears to reflect the current position of the Chinese leadership.[7] In Ye's view, the necessity of peacetime maintenance of one's ability to covertly infiltrate an adversary's networks, the importance of civilian human capital to military capabilities, the continual evolution of relevant technologies, and the way in which computer network operations are characterized by a perpetual cat-and-mouse game of vulnerability discovery and attack prevention all argue in favor of this intermingling. Ye also argues that the network domain can give rise to internal as well as external security threats as a result of the freedom it grants citizens to exchange information and organize, with the Arab Spring serving as a prime example of how this type of openness can facilitate revolution and regime change.

Schools of Thought within the PLA on Network Warfare

Although the PLA has reached a degree of consensus on foundational network warfare theory, the PLA's increasing recognition of the power of network warfare in modern informatized conflicts and the importance of network warfare theory for PLA strategic planning has encouraged vigorous debate on the topic by PLA academicians, and they are far from monolithic in their conclusions and prescriptions. They weigh their common theoretical foundation against perceived trends in both the network warfare capabilities of other countries and global information technology development, attempting to strike a balance between theory and practice that "places equal emphasis on [strategic] goals and [real-world] mechanisms" (道器并重).[8]

Most PLA academics who discuss network warfare strategy on a theoretical level can be broadly grouped into one of two camps: those who primarily take a realist stance emphasizing the role of concrete capabilities development (现实主义功能派), and those who focus primarily on the potential for network powers to bind one another via institutional norms (制度主义规约派).[9] This division should not be taken as defining these two camps in direct opposition to one another; in fact, the majority of PLA writings on network warfare integrate aspects of both perspectives to varying degrees. As network warfare has progressed from the realm of abstract theory to an operational reality, Chinese thinking on the topic has been increasingly driven by real-world events, with theory providing supporting context that helps determine how those events are interpreted.

Network Realists

The "network realist" school of thought emphasizes the role of computer network attack (CNA) and computer network defense (CND) capabilities in conflict, exploring a number of ways in which they may pose a sufficient threat to deter or defeat an enemy. One such method is "unrestricted network warfare" (网络超限战), an extension of the general "unrestricted warfare" concept popularized by Qiao Liang and Wang Xiangsui in their volume of the same name, wherein attacks in the network domain against critical infrastructure are used to paralyze an opponent's conventional warfare capabilities.[10] Such attacks would be directed not only at military command, control, communications, computers, intelligence, surveillance and reconnaissance (C4ISR) but also against civilian telecommunications networks, financial systems, and public utilities. Another method is "asymmetric network warfare" (网络非对称战争), wherein a military invests heavily in information warfare capabilities that allow it to deter an adversary which holds an advantage in conventional warfare, achieving what one analyst refers to as "twice the deterrent effect with half the effort."[11] Strains of network realist thinking can be observed in both the 2013 SMS (to a greater degree than is found in the 2001 edition) and Ye Zheng's LSIO.

These theoreticians approach preparation for deterrence and compellence from a perspective focused on the development of network security infrastructure and military capabilities. Many embrace the notion that due to the offense-dominant nature of the network domain, it is only through the development of offensive technologies that an underdog can overcome the deterrent capabilities of a country with superior information technology.[12] In the words of several PLA academicians taking this view, "the targets of network warfare are unrestricted; they not only include traditional military targets, but also span government, financial, social, and other realms of non-traditional targets, extending to all manner of the adversary's military and civilian frequency-transmission equipment, information networks, and information infrastructure base that would be relevant to civilian life and a nation's potential warfighting capacity."[13] In the view of these authors, by striking not only military but also civilian targets one can "cause great destruction, bringing about a rapid change in the overall situation of a conflict." However, Ye and some others argue in favor of caution with regard to using network warfare to create physical destruction in the civilian sphere. Ye, for example, states that even when physical destruction is possible, it may not be prudent due to "moral, legal, and diplomatic issues" that would result.

Network Institutionalists

The PLA's "network institutionalists" seek to achieve network domain supremacy (and thus, they argue, a strategic deterrent capability) primarily through institutional arrangements and the establishment of systemic norms of state behavior in the network domain. In this perspective, a domain posture that focuses overwhelmingly on the development of one's own military capabilities is potentially counterproductive due to the lack of clearly understood, mutually agreed-upon norms between countries on key questions such as which actions constitute a "network attack" or "network warfare," making it likely that translating traditional military deterrence and compellence principles directly to the network domain will create an environment ripe for miscalculation, escalation, and unnecessary conflict—what one Chinese author terms a "dangerous game."[14]

Both realists and institutionalists agree that the network domain will remain offense-dominant in its character for the foreseeable future, since both attack attribution and the development of effective defense capabilities are extremely difficult tasks, and offensive threat vectors capable of penetrating current best known network defenses are regularly discovered. In the institutionalists' view, while investment in network defense can help partially mitigate the damage an adversary can inflict, a country that is strategically reliant on the strength and impermeability of its network defenses is inadvertently constructing what one author terms a "network Maginot Line," creating a false sense of security and increasing the odds that one's defenses will be breached without warning at a strategically inopportune moment. [15] Development of international norms and legal regimes, while difficult and by no means a panacea, might in theory offer an alternate means of establishing strength and security that avoids the pitfalls of a deterrence strategy centered primarily on the direct use of force.

Strategic Implications of the Network Domain's Core Characteristics

Both the *Science of Military Strategy* and other foundational PLA academic works on network warfare theory describe the network domain as having several unique characteristics that distinguish it from the conventional, space, and nuclear domains. Authoritative descriptions of these characteristics reflect a consensus within the PLA that directly shapes Chinese military strategic decision-making, as these characteristics carry a number of significant strategic implications.

Permeable and Expansive

First, the PLA understands the network domain to be highly permeable and expansive; as a battlespace, it is interconnected in many ways with the civilian network domain, allowing network warfare to simultaneously take on not only military but also political, cultural, scientific, and economic dimensions, sometimes even in ways that may not be immediately observable or obvious. Furthermore, computer networks naturally lend themselves to cross-domain operations for both deterrence and aggression. The 2001 edition of SMS raises the possibility of an "electronic Pearl Harbor," envisioning a scenario in which network and electromagnetic strikes disable an adversary's ability to engage in conventional warfare.[16] Network warfare thus effectively "expand[s] the scope of deterrence and compellence targets," with "both soft kill and hard destruction" as possible effects.[17] PLA authors write that information warfare is a type of warfare that involves all people, in which individuals, enterprises, society, and national communications networks form integrated entities. These cross-space and cross-border characteristics mean that there is no clear divide between the "front" and "rear" areas of the network battlespace.[18]

As a result, when preparing to engage in modern network warfare, the military and civilian spheres are not distinct; in fact, they constantly intersect. Civilians and other actors not belonging to the military are in many senses capable of participating in the conflict, and in many cases civilian and military actors must work together, unlike in most other domains and modes of warfare. In response to this reality, many PLA analysts now affirmatively argue in favor of network operations that not only strike at military targets but are also aimed at causing calculated psychological effects and influencing public opinion amongst an adversary's populace.[19] Such operations are in keeping with the Chinese view of the network and psychological domains as constituent sub-domains of the broader information domain.

The network domain has both physical and intangible dimensions, including both a global space within the information environment and also dispersed physical nodes across land, sea, air, and outer space that form an organic whole through expansive information networks. If any segment suffers an attack or is damaged, a country's overall security in the domain can be affected if information is not rerouted around the damage. As a result, the leap from conducting "network operations" to carrying out "cross-domain operations" is relatively small. By the 2013 edition of SMS, recognition of this duality had permeated authoritative conceptions of network warfare and deterrence, with the concepts expanding to explicitly accommodate not only "pure" network attack and defense operations and methods but also traditional military strikes as part of cross-domain operations.[20]

The increased networking of combat systems has also caused the domain's military applications to expand. Electronic information systems that were once isolated and independent are now bound together through military and battlefield networks, including communications networks, command and control networks, sensor networks, and other computing platforms. However, as these military systems become increasingly networked, the potential for "chain reactions, cascading effects, and overall system fragility" may also increase. This understanding of the network domain's expansiveness and centrality is reflected in statements by China's high-level military and civilian leadership, most notably President Xi Jinping's recent statements that "without network security there is no national security."[21] Similarly, the authors of the 2013 SMS break from the previous edition's general regarding information warfare objectives to concretely assert the centrality of network power to China's overall ability to project national power, engage in strategic deterrence, and defend itself in a conflict.[22] Ye concurs with this thinking in LSIO, adding as a historical note that Chinese scholars were initially too narrow in their conceptions of the network domain (for example, first defining it as the more narrow "computer network domain"), and that the definition has expanded in response to observing in practice how the domain could in fact be broader than initially theorized.[23]

Ambiguity of Intentions and Attribution

Second, authoritative Chinese military authors assert that in the network domain an adversary's intentions and identity may often appear ambiguous prior to the onset of full-spectrum warfare. Computer network attack, defense, and exploitation activities are "more often than not" carried out simultaneously, without clear dividing lines between them.[24] Network reconnaissance and penetration activities during peacetime offer not only the usual rewards of espionage but can also serve as battlespace preparation, obtaining information about a target network's structure and defenses and thereby improving one's ability to inflict damage on an adversary's networks in the event of a later conflict.[25] Regarding this fluidity, the 2013 edition of the *Science of Military Strategy* states:[26]

> "From a technical point of view, the working principles of network reconnaissance and network attack are basically the same, and the means and methods of network reconnaissance are usually also those for network attack. According to the desires and intentions of the actor, one may just press a button or issue a program command, and in doing so completely switch between network reconnaissance and network attack. There is therefore a continuous

relationship between network reconnaissance
and offensive and defensive network operations."

In LSIO, Ye describes this ambiguity between wartime and
peacetime in network warfare in perhaps the starkest possible
terms, arguing that absolutely no distinction should be made
between the two in order to "preserve a high degree of war
preparedness and defense status."[27] This preparedness refers not
only to troop training and readiness, but also to maintaining a
constant presence in the adversary's networks in order to
reconnoiter and find vulnerabilities that will enable further
access and/or destruction. Network domain operations rely on
valid information, processing nodes, and transmission links.
When compared with conventional warfare, these operations
are often less about targeting an opponent's assets and damaging
or destroying them, and more about exerting influence and
control over those assets through dominance of the information
environment. Control of cyberspace is thus a prerequisite
condition for success in a wide range of strategic and tactical
operations, and network reconnaissance is an essential
prerequisite for obtaining that control.[28]

Despite this ambiguity of intent, since network reconnaissance
is both non-destructive (at least initially) and widely engaged in
by all nations for the purposes of espionage, the authors of the
2013 SMS believe it has been clearly demonstrated that the act
of network reconnaissance alone is unlikely to lead to escalation
or the outbreak of war. As a result, PLA strategists appear to
have arrived at a strategic understanding of peacetime network
operations that is in some sense similar to China's approach to
asserting increasing control of disputed islands in the South
China Sea, taking actions during peacetime that incrementally

put China into a superior tactical position should conflict ever break out but that are unlikely to lead to direct conflict in and of themselves, despite being provocative and unwelcomed by China's neighbors. If conflict eventually does break out, China is in a better initial position than it otherwise would be; if conflict does not occur, China has gained its preferred outcome without a fight.

Network warfare is also ambiguous with regard to attribution, as judging the origin of network attacks is understood to be significantly more difficult than in the conventional and nuclear domains, particularly if attribution must be established in a short period of time during a political or military crisis. Even if the country of origin of an attack is conclusively established, it could be difficult to determine whether that attack was carried out with government approval or was the result of spontaneous action by passionate civilian nationalists, hacktivists, or other non-state actors.

Diverse and Evolving Capabilities

Third, network warfare takes place through an incredibly wide range of capabilities and sub-domains. Compared with war in the traditional sense, network operations forces and methods are more diverse, as are their potential uses.[29] These forces and methods include not only traditional electronic warfare and network warfare units, but also new types of network operations units and the cross-domain interactions they enable, such as network warfare units and methods that carry out joint warfare with land, sea, air, and space forces through interconnected networks.

The network domain itself is also constantly evolving, with both conceptual groupings and concrete capabilities likely to vary by country and over time as a result of ongoing technological and theoretical progress. Network offensive and defensive methods are being updated and replaced continuously due to rapid technological change. Network deterrence based on 'bluffs' as opposed to concrete capabilities is thus seen as being an unreliable and unwise approach, due to both the ambiguous nature of escalation signaling in network warfare and the difficulty of reliably assessing one's own strength in the network domain relative to one's adversaries.[30] The vast majority of network attack capabilities are unobservable or are subject to a low level of visibility, and this limited observability means that attacks can often break out in unpredictable ways and at unexpected times. The unpredictability of network warfare may also frustrate efforts to plan high-level strategic or campaign operations integrating network warfare capabilities, since despite their potentially powerful effects they cannot be faithfully relied upon to function as intended when a critical moment arrives.

The advent of what the Chinese term "system-of-systems" warfare (体系作战) has increased this uncertainty, since under this arrangement military information networks serve as the connecting tissue for an increasingly diverse range of military end-users and weapons systems. Furthermore, the topology of the global network domain is constantly changing; some targets may be visible or vulnerable for only a short time period, and both sides in a conflict can adjust or change their network infrastructure without warning.

Offense Dominance

Fourth, PLA sources almost uniformly agree that offense is fundamentally dominant in network warfare, since as Ye puts it in LSIO, attacks often rely on a single vulnerability or point of failure in an adversary's systems, whereas mounting a successful defense requires that one must be constantly aware of *all* possible vulnerabilities in one's own systems and networks.[31] Ye and some others further believe that the offense-dominant nature of the domain dictates that being first to strike with a "surprise attack" is essential, since information warfare is won by quickly seizing "information superiority."[32] In this view, the act of seizing information superiority is a self-reinforcing cycle, allowing a proactive force to quickly compound any initial advantages gained through its first strike.

Compared with traditional warfare, network warfare operations also operate under unusually loose time and space constraints.[33] Such operations can be implemented in a moment, and at least in theory network warfare can break out at any time, with targets being attacked at the speed of light and missions completed in the span of moments without regard for geography or other spatial restrictions. Some PLA authors argue that achieving victory in modern warfare depends heavily on acting more quickly than one's enemy, and that achieving dominance in the network domain can more broadly enable a military to get inside their adversary's "OODA" (Observe, Orient, Decide, Act) Loop and successfully execute an offensive action.[34]

Capabilities Can Be Double-edged Swords

Fifth, capabilities in the network domain can sometimes be a 'double-edged sword' of sorts. There is a danger (though not as severe as is seen in nuclear deterrence) that launching attacks can damage the attacker's own interests, and particularly the interests of the attacker's civilian population, rather than merely damaging the enemy. The 2013 edition of SMS goes so far as to argue that "the difficulty of effectively controlling the consequences of a network confrontation" is "an important factor restricting the outbreak of large-scale network war."[35] Furthermore, since a state's ability to conduct computer network operations (CNO) generally increases in tandem with its overall informatization level and thus its reliance on information technology, the countries with the most offensive capabilities in the network domain may find themselves to also be the most vulnerable. As discussed below, this may allow an "underdog" to upset a dominant power that has more to lose, either via conventional and electromagnetic attacks on their physical network infrastructure or through an offensively-oriented network attack strategy.

Asymmetric Potential

Finally, there is a range of opinion within PLA analyses on the key question of whether the network domain's asymmetrical structural advantages that favor "underdogs" who launch swift and decisive strikes necessarily outweigh the practical advantages enjoyed by "network superpowers" who have made extensive investments in concrete network warfare capabilities and have worked during peacetime to establish "network dominance" over their adversaries. Across the whole of PLA writings on the topic, the consensus among theoreticians appears to be that a country in China's position—a rising power with considerable resources and a rapidly developing civilian economy—could benefit by tilting its military modernization toward the development of network warfare capabilities, particularly in the near-to-medium term while there is not yet hope of matching or surpassing the United States' full spectrum of conventional warfare capabilities.[36]

Ye and others argue that this means network warfare can potentially serve as both a strike measure and a strategic deterrent.[37] Such a deterrent can be advertised to adversaries through peacetime drills and simulations that demonstrate one's cyber operations capabilities, including battlefield simulations and political, economic, and cultural initiatives. Network deterrence can also be used in wartime to influencing an adversary's willingness to escalate a conflict or expand its selection of targets.

Ongoing Debates Relevant to PLA Network Warfare Strategy

Despite a broad consensus among the PLA's strategic thinkers on many aspects of network warfare as outlined above, a number of debates persist as to how China should structure and task its network warfare forces. These debates take place primarily at a relatively granular level, below the broad strategic division between network "realists" and "institutionalists" outlined above, but they have significant implications for the PLA's network warfare strategy.

Network Warfare and Cross Domain Operations

Chinese writings on network warfare have always referenced the idea of coordinated operations and deterrent capabilities across domains (albeit with different nomenclature than that employed by Western scholars), and there is a general consensus among PLA analysts that in informatized warfare the network domain is inextricably linked to operations in the land, air, and sea domains. In this view, network operations are both a component of China's overall war strategy used to realize specific strategic operational objectives and also a supporting element employed to protect or aid tactical operations in other domains of warfare.

When the 2001 edition of the *Science of Military Strategy* talks of an "electronic Pearl Harbor," for example, it envisions a scenario where a network-electromagnetic strike disables an adversary's ability to engage in conventional warfare. Information warfare is described in this account as "expanding the scope of deterrence targets," with "both soft kill and hard destruction" as possible means of "disrupting the opponent's information flow process."[38] For the purposes of resisting the enemy's attacks, similarly, "networks and electronics are integrated, software and hardware are integrated."[39] In the 2013 edition, the topic is directly addressed within the narrower context of network warfare, with the authors stating that the concept of network deterrence force "includes not only the typical network attack and defense operations forces and methods, but also includes traditional military strike forces and methods."[40] Throughout LSIO, Ye also repeatedly stresses the importance of integrating soft-kill and hard-kill measures together. [41] The physical layer of the network and electromagnetic space, which includes critical infrastructure such as electrical power networks, electronic communications networks, the Internet, embedded systems, space-based precision timing networks, and informatized systems-of-systems, exists at the intersection of the network and electromagnetic spaces and the conventional military domains. These entities in the network and electromagnetic space can simultaneously become both targets and areas of operation for military forces. Chinese writings frequently discuss types of physical locations that are vulnerable to network attack, such as industrial production networks, electrical networks, and transportation networks.[42]

In both the 2013 SMS and other works authored by PLA officers that examine the potential of network warfare capabilities to serve as a strategic deterrent, one sees a recognition that the inherent fluidity of boundaries between virtual networks and physical information infrastructure is crucial to understanding possibilities for network deterrence, including a consensus that the coordinated, simultaneous employment of multiple forms of deterrence will produce a net deterrent effect greater than the sum of its parts.[43] These writings also reflect an understanding that cross-domain network deterrence is often bi-directional—that is, it can cross either from conventional domains into the network domain, or from the network domain into conventional domains. Network deterrence activities thus encompass not only the threatened physical destruction of information infrastructure but also network attacks aimed at degrading conventional warfare capabilities.

However, as PLA analysts have begun examining the specific circumstances under which certain objectives may or may not be best attained via cross-domain methods, significant variations in opinion are evident. Because the nature of combat strength in the network domain is so different from in traditional warfare domains is so, fusing the two types requires planning around the unique characteristics of these spaces and presents new difficulties for military planners in the realms of both operational timing and attack assessments.

Some of the PLA's more pessimistic analysts argue it is unrealistic to coordinate network and conventional attacks because of the large difference in operations timing and tempo between the two spheres.[44] And although reliable assessments of attack effectiveness are essential for the ongoing implementation of war plans and the adjustment of troop deployments by wartime commanders, great uncertainty exists regarding the PLA's ability to predict the real-world effectiveness of their planned network operations. For example, in any given coordinated plan involving both network and conventional strikes, a single failed or delayed intrusion of an adversary's network, detection of an attack by the adversary's 'honeypots' or sensors, or the adversary's unexpectedly early recovery from the effects of an attack can all impact assessments of cyberspace operations. This stands in direct contrast to assessments of the effects of possible attacks in the land, sea, air, and space domains, all of which are believed to be more objective and reliable.

Despite the above difficulties, most PLA analysts and academicians agree that there are still numerous opportunities for integration between network and physical operations, and that the particular characteristics of any given military objective will determine the extent to which cyber operations should be employed in a cross-domain fashion. As weapons in the network domain become increasingly sophisticated and powerful, it is likely that cross-domain operations will continue to be a prominent topic of discussion in PLA theoretical circles. Chinese military analysts have argued that although the successful deployment of Stuxnet embodies a gradual, long-term shift toward 'pure' network weapons that cause 'hard' rather than 'soft' damage, in practice coordinated cross-domain operations are the surest way to achieve a given result.[45] Israel's 2007 strike on Syria's nuclear facilities using a combination of air power and network warfare using what is alleged to be 'Suter' technology has been cited by Ye and others as a prime example, with Ye arguing that information operations will continue to complement rather than stand apart from conventional elements of warfare.[46]

Aerospace network and electronic warfare is depicted in many PLA sources as just such a complementary arrangement, to an extent that they are arguably 'inseparable' from the PLA's conception of offensive and defensive space operations.[47] Since space-based communications relay systems provide highly effective battlefield communications and network support for integrated operations among air and naval forces, attacks on these systems can render an adversary 'myopic'. As a result, space control has been described as informatized warfare's "winning hand," and whoever controls space will ultimately achieve victory.[48]

The recent creation of the Strategic Support Force, which brings space, electronic, and network warfare capabilities under a single unified command, suggests that this view is currently dominant at the highest levels of PLA strategy. Ye and other

PLA analysts have long advocated that the PLA should increase preparations for warfare under an environment in which both sides proactively take 'soft' actions to degrade the other's C4ISR capabilities across domains. Ye argues in LSIO that:[49]

In operations under informatized conditions, the two opponents will widely utilize soft-kill information operation measures, jamming, suppressing, and damaging their opponent's information systems, making the opponent unable to obtain true, valuable information or unable to promptly, accurately acquire information, causing the opponent to make errors in judgment and causing command failures.

Throughout LSIO, Ye also repeatedly stresses the importance of integrating soft-kill and hard-kill measures together in the early stages of war rather than relying on either in isolation.[50] He conceives of "Integrated Information and Firepower Warfare" (IIFW) as a practical model for the real-world integration of this concept. By pairing network and electromagnetic warfare with conventional arms and targeting links in the enemy's communications chain with both 'hard' and 'soft' strikes in the beginning stages of a major conflict, he argues, one can "vastly increase the operational effectiveness" of those weapons systems.[51] Ye believes that if long-range precision strikes are properly employed in this fashion, it would have an inherent 'shock value' that would pay dividends in the realms of psychological and political warfare beyond its impact on the enemy's armed forces.

However, Ye does not portray IIFW as a one-size-fits-all prescription for the beginning stages of a conflict; instead, IIFW is presented as a potential tool in the PLA's toolkit, one of a number of possible approaches that could be employed as the situation warrants. According to Ye, the precision strike component of IIFW is only viable when two conditions are met: first, an all-out confrontation must be inevitable, and second, China must believe it has the decisive upper-hand in the information domain. Ye and others believe that strikes along the lines of IIFW can only work if it has the full breadth of information support behind it, ranging from technical reconnaissance to information processing, sensing, and other C4ISR-related tasks. When taken together with the persistent theme in Ye's writing that there exists a first-mover advantage in information confrontations and his recognition that mutual degradation of C4ISR capabilities is likely in the event that rival powers commit militarily to a major conflict, Ye's writings give the strong impression that he believes IIFW is more suited to the early stages of a conflict rather than in the midst of full-scale information warfare.

The Relationship Between Civilian and Military Network Warfare Forces

In a departure from the vague, hypothetical descriptions of what network warfare forces a country might construct found in many other writings on the topic, the 2013 SMS explicitly divided China's network warfare forces into three types.[52] The first group is the PLA's "specialized military network warfare forces," (军队专业网络战力量) which are military operational units specially employed for carrying out network attack and defense. The second are "PLA-authorized forces," (授权力量) which are teams of network warfare specialists in civilian organizations such as the Ministry of State Security (MSS), the Ministry of Public Security (MPS) and others that have been authorized by the military to carry out network warfare operations. Finally, there are also "non- governmental forces," (民间力量) which are external entities that spontaneously engage in network attack and defense, but can be organized and mobilized for network warfare operations.

The 2013 SMS's mention of these forces was unusual in that it openly acknowledged the existence of both China's military and civilian network warfare forces, a rarity prior to the creation of the Strategic Support Force. It is extremely uncommon for China's civilian intelligence services to be referenced in a high-level PLA document, much less for the hierarchy of authority governing their sensitive network warfare operations to be discussed. The fact that the 2013 SMS was a highly vetted consensus document that received input from dozens of authors and is published under the name of the responsible AMS *danwei* rather than the names of its project leads suggests that this decision likely underwent careful consideration, further adding to the mystery. One possible interpretation is that the statement that China's civilian network attack forces operate under the PLA's "authorization" (授权) may reflect an ongoing power struggle within the Chinese system between the PLA's leadership and the aforementioned civilian government organs to determine who truly controls Chinese actions in cyberspace; such an unusual and unprecedented move may have represented an attempt to "plant the flag," organizationally speaking, for the PLA.

If this interpretation is accurate, then the existence of the Strategic Support Force has likely decided this battle of organizational prerogatives decisively in the PLA's favor. Prior to the creation of the SSF, the PLA's network warfare forces were spread widely throughout the services, the military regions, and multiple General Staff Department entities. Now that they have for the most part coalesced into a single centralized institution reporting directly to the Central Military Commission, the already-formidable clout of the PLA within China's network warfare ecosystem is likely to grow considerably.

Network Warfare and the Concept of "People's War"

PLA network warfare theoreticians have not yet reached a consensus on the extent to which the traditional Chinese military concept of "people's war" extends to the network domain, and a wide range of opinion can be found among influential PLA writings on the topic.

In LSIO, for example, Ye argues that to successfully wage information warfare, civil- military integration must be fully brought to bear to carry out people's war, citing the People's Armed Police (PAP) and China's militia forces as being at the center of this idea.[53] Ye further argues for a total mobilization of China's network warfare capabilities in the event of a conflict, including not only military forces but also "cyber supervision institutions, network security enterprises, nongovernmental hacker groups, and the like." In Ye's view, these organizations can not only "support and coordinate military actions on the front line battles of network warfare," but also "have the possibility of being network warfare's principal force when it is not a convenient time or place for the military to appear."

Others, however, express far greater caution about civilian involvement in network warfare. The authors of the 2013 SMS state that despite the relatively high ability of civilians to participate in network warfare relative to other forms of combat, the bulk of network warfare in a major conflict would nevertheless be conducted by specialist forces within the PLA, with hacktivism, denial-of-service (DDoS) attacks against civilian sites, and other outside attacks ultimately amounting to little more than cyber graffiti.[54] Even Ye is somewhat equivocal, acknowledging that despite his advocating that the PAP and militia units have a supporting role in wartime, the PLA will necessarily be the 'main force' in any network conflict.[55]

Outside the context of a full conflict, some PLA writings raise the possibility that during peacetime China may choose to encourage non-military network warfare forces, ranging from militia units to hacktivists, to play a meaningful role in the conduct of low-level network operations.[56] In the event of geopolitical hostilities that have not yet risen to the level of a full conflict, this would be fairly easy to accomplish. Since Chinese civilian hackers have repeatedly shown themselves willing to proactively attack foreign adversaries, it appears likely that an active command from the PLA to attack would not be required, only the absence of any action to prevent or punish patriotic hackers.

The Essence of Decision: When Will the PLA Initiate Network Warfare Operations?

In the event of a conflict, there are a number of factors that PLA analysts believe must be weighed in determining whether or not to initiate network warfare operations against an adversary and what form those operations should take. None of these factors, in and of themselves, weighs decisively for or against launching such a strike; rather, PLA analysts generally believe that commanders will have to consider them in concert with one another.

China's Strength Relative to Global Adversaries

In order to understand China's incentive structure and preparations for network warfare, one must first understand China's perception of its own capabilities. Although it is difficult to accurately assess the PLA's overall opinion of its own network warfare capabilities due to a lack of candid and public writings by knowledgeable sources, China's overall view of its defensive capabilities is clear: the PLA views itself as being pervasively vulnerable to computer network attack by an adversary such as the United States.[57] Due to a combination of China's recognition that the network domain is offense-dominant and the widespread Chinese perception of the United States as the global leader in network attack research (rendering it, in the words of one Chinese researcher, "the world's only network superpower" or 唯一的网络超强), Chinese analysts do not view this vulnerability as temporary or likely to be substantially rectified in the foreseeable future, but rather as a fundamental reality that must be fully accounted for in Chinese strategic planning.[58] The authors of SMS 2013 argue that since China's "main strategic opponent" (a euphemistic way of referring to the United States) has superior network warfare capabilities, the strict balance of power in a hypothetical network-domain conflict would not necessarily tilt in China's favor.

This perceived vulnerability is not only relevant in wartime in a hypothetical future conflict; in the PLA's view, China's networks are currently being constantly penetrated by its adversaries through network reconnaissance operations, a perception that has been hardened by the allegations made in 2013 by Edward Snowden regarding the activities of U.S. intelligence agencies.[59] Although comments by Chinese military and political leaders to this effect are often treated dismissively by Western analysts as an attempt to deflect attention from China's robust CNO activities, this perception extends beyond public speeches and into PLA writings on military theory restricted to internal distribution (军内发行), representing a broad consensus among PLA academicians tasked with proposing strategy and doctrine for the network domain.

First-Mover Advantage

As Ye and most other PLA network warfare theorists have noted, information warfare in general and network warfare in particular display an enduring offense dominance.[60] Part and parcel of this offense dominance is an understanding that attacking with an unexpected "first strike" is essential if one is to act at all, since information warfare is won by quickly seizing "information superiority." In the view of Ye and others, the act of seizing information superiority is a self-reinforcing cycle, allowing a proactive force to quickly compound any initial advantages gained through its first strike. In Ye's discussion of the importance of first strikes in network warfare, he takes as a given that launching such an attack would require a strong understanding of foreign surveillance and monitoring assets aimed at one's own information systems. If China's C4ISR systems have been compromised to a greater degree than previously realized, for example, it would enable a foreign adversary to not only anticipate and defend against a Chinese first strike, but potentially pre-empt it with a first strike of the adversary's own. This follows in part from the nature of network warfare discussed above, wherein one's attack capacity hinges on the discovery of unanticipated attack vectors. As SMS 2013 put it, a country that has successfully penetrated its adversaries for network reconnaissance can transition to network attack "with the press of a button."[61]

This operational requirement creates opportunities for Chinese aggression to pay large dividends against a more defensively oriented adversary, but it also provides an avenue for China's adversaries to deter that first strike in the network domain. If an adversary successfully demonstrates somehow to Chinese military decision-makers that the PLA's foreign penetrations are not as secure as they believe, their confidence in their own ability to successfully carry out information warfare operations will be greatly diminished. The PLA's organizational culture of micromanagement, mistrust of subordinates, and over-reliance on information and information systems poses additional challenges to taking effective action

Uncertainty of Timing and Network Attack Effects

Although PLA network warfare theoreticians like Ye Zheng often propose using network attacks and electronic interference in concert with conventional warfare capabilities to launch a "bolt out of the blue" attack, in practice catching an adversary unaware may prove difficult. Any geopolitical crisis leading to a military confrontation would likely also spur a mutual rise in tensions and preparedness. Furthermore, China's conventional forces require time to mobilize, and the activation of China's defense mobilization apparatus would most likely be visible to the adversary in various ways. The success of a combined "hard/soft" first strike therefore relies on not only extensive preparation but also well-chosen timing within a narrow window of optimal opportunity.[62] Although network warfare operations can be carried out at nearly any time regardless of external considerations, any accompanying conventional warfare—particularly a heavily involved operation such as an amphibious landing in a Taiwan contingency—would be much more vulnerable to factors outside of the PLA's control such as unfavorable weather. [63] Once a network attack has been launched, the speed and non-geographic nature of network warfare means it cannot generally be recalled or cancelled in response to subsequent unwelcome events.[64]

Furthermore, the extent to which a network warfare attack will achieve its desired effect against a sophisticated foreign adversary such as the United States is highly uncertain. Even if PLA commanders were somehow able to guarantee that a debilitating network warfare strike would be successful, those commanders have no reliable way of predicting whether it will take minutes, hours, or days for the United States to stand up backup systems and networks and return to full operating strength. If the PLA were to attempt to maximize the element of surprise by initiating a debilitating strike with obfuscated attribution prior to any signs of conventional Chinese defense mobilization, that would in turn greatly lengthen the amount of time the network attack's effects would have to be felt in order to offer a military benefit, further heightening the challenge for the attacker.

This is not to say that these challenges are insurmountable; if properly timed and executed, such a first strike could successfully establish information dominance in the conflict's critical early stage, stymieing the adversary's mobilization procedures to such an extent that it compels their capitulation or acquiescence and secures Chinese objectives before the conventional dimension of the conflict can escalate further.

Moreover, even without the element of surprise, once open warfare commences a campaign of coordinated network and kinetic strikes still offers great value to the PLA. For a first strike, however, the degree of uncertainty inherent in network warfare cannot be easily discounted and may cause the PLA to be hesitant about 'pulling the trigger' on initiating the conflict despite the offense-dominant nature of network warfare.

Opportunities Are Lost Once They Are Used

PLA analysts have also noted that one of cyberspace warfare's most important characteristics is that using a sophisticated cyber weapon will often quickly degrade or even nullify its effectiveness entirely. [65] According to this thinking many cyberspace weapons should be understood as "single-use resources" (一次性资源) that will effectively cease to exist once used, since a competent adversary is likely to quickly discover the source of their own vulnerability and then patch or close it. Countries with advanced network warfare capabilities, including China, are likely to retain their most innovative weapons until it is necessary to use them as a "trump card" to attain a major strategic objective.

This thinking has been further reinforced by the 2013 revelation of the "Stuxnet" attack on Iran's nuclear program, which relied heavily on the at the time under-appreciated attack vectors of USB thumb drives and industrial system vulnerability analysis in order to penetrate and attack Iran's hidden, air-gapped nuclear facilities. After Stuxnet, the odds of an attack against a nation-state succeeding by utilizing similar attack vectors has likely gone down considerably, due to the success of an earlier attack highlighting the existence of the vulnerability. The result is that in a warfighting scenario short of a major conflict where network warfare operations might offer the PLA a significant military benefit, such as in a South China Sea territorial conflict with a militarily inferior Southeast Asian adversary, the PLA might be tempted to 'keep its powder dry' and fight primarily or fully with conventional forces in order to avoid revealing the workings of its most advanced network warfare techniques to more formidable geopolitical adversaries such as the United States.

This One's For All the Marbles: Network Warfare in a Major Conflict Scenario

The primary goalpost driving the PLA's long-term informatization and modernization efforts is to become capable of fighting and winning a high-stakes regional war against a "high tech adversary" (高技术对手) such as the United States, including in scenarios such as a war against Taiwan that would hypothetically trigger the United States' direct military involvement. If this scenario were to occur, the global consequences of victory or defeat for all parties would be tremendous, with regime stability in China being gravely threatened by a loss. In the event of such a crisis, China's most likely course of action in the network domain would be to preemptively deploy a wide variety of CNO and CNA capabilities as part of a broader attempt to both compel Taiwan's surrender and deter the United States from intervening militarily, or failing that, to deter the United States from escalating its military response as the situation progresses.

PLA theorists emphasize the idea that a successful 'first strike' in network warfare relies on comprehensive information support and battlespace awareness, including robust and ongoing sensing, processing, and information collection capabilities. A significant "first- mover advantage" thus accrues to the side that first initiates offensive operations if they are able to degrade or destroy the adversary's information support infrastructure and lessen their ability to retaliate, resulting in a strong incentive for aggressive behavior in the network domain immediately prior to the formal onset of hostilities. Such operations would most likely be targeted primarily at the United States' terrestrial and space-based C4ISR networks and early-warning systems, and could encompass both 'hard' and 'soft' kill operations.[66]

Authoritative PLA writings such as LSIO stress the value of coordinating CNO and other forms of offensive information operations with conventional firepower, particularly "long-range precision strikes" (远程、精确的火力打击), to produce "real-time hard- and soft-kill operations" (实时的软硬一体打击作战).[67] As previously mentioned, two important preconditions must be met for carrying out such a strike: first, an all-out confrontation must appear inevitable, and second, China must have already established information superiority. If launched at the outset of a conflict, the CNO component of such a strike would be timed to coincide with or slightly precede planned conventional operations, occurring while the adversary has not yet had time to seize information-domain superiority or to prepare itself for a full confrontation.

Peacetime Operations Prior to Conflict

Prior to the onset of open hostilities, the main mode of network warfare for both China and its adversaries will consist of reconnaissance activities. Just as tactical maneuvers in the traditional land, sea, air, and space domains are focused on obtaining an advantageous geographical location, reconnaissance operations in the network domain focus on obtaining advantageous information and access to produce a military advantage in the event of conflict. [68] Similar to a geographical advantage, obtaining an intelligence information advantage in network warfare prior to the onset of a conflict can have a decisive influence on a war's result. The goal of these reconnaissance operations is thus to attain a superior position in the network domain, such as acquiring access to an adversary's network, in order to carry out operations as part of a future strategic or tactical military campaign.

Ye and other PLA theoreticians argue that an upsurge in patriotic hacking activity during peacetime tensions would allow China to benefit from the network domain's ambiguity between peacetime and wartime and the difficulty of definitively establishing attack attribution in a timely fashion.[69] According to this thinking, if it is opportune for the PLA to move beyond standard network reconnaissance operations to attacks on enemy assets, soft-kill attacks that would most likely provoke an escalation of hostilities if launched in other domains can be prudently employed in times of peace via network warfare, so long as they do not "betray an air of warfare during their implementation." As Ye puts it, "attribution is difficult, so secrecy can be maintained during peacetime operations," and the fact that "network warfare and information reconnaissance actions in particular can be launched without the participation of a military entity" dictates that adversaries must respond cautiously to attacks for fear of erroneously escalating a conflict over a misattributed action.

Network Warfare and Conflict Escalation

Ye and other influential PLA authors highlight aspects of network warfare in their writings that when taken together strongly indicate a prescription for a "first strike" strategy if network warfare begins to escalate, such as the importance of "proactively" attaining information superiority, the self-reinforcing nature of "seizing the information high ground," and the difficulty of distinguishing between an adversary's peacetime and wartime conduct in network operations.

The impulse toward a first strike is heightened by Chinese perceptions of what the consequences of that strike will be on an adversary's decision-making calculations. Many influential writings on network warfare by PLA analysts and academics, including LSIO and the 2013 SMS, convey a belief that even some forms of overt soft-kill network operations against an adversary's assets may not result in the adversary retaliating with a full- spectrum response that includes escalating the conflict into the conventional domain of warfare. This reticence on the part of one's adversary can occur either because a successful first strike renders the adversary incapable of retaliation, or because non-lethal attacks on information networks do not carry the same political/psychological imperative for escalation as a lethal attack might. As Ye concludes in LSIO, "it is possible to damage the enemy's command, control, intelligence, information, and air defense military network systems without bloodshed, and it is possible to silently damage, paralyze, and control the enemy's commercial, governmental, and other civil network systems, achieving the goal of winning a battle without coming to blows."

This concept is central to understanding the PLA's thinking on network warfare as it pertains to a Taiwan scenario. The authors of the 2013 SMS, for example, state their belief that civilian infrastructure controlled by or located within foreign countries can be targeted more freely with network warfare than with conventional weapons without necessarily provoking the degree of conflict escalation that a conventional attack on civilian targets would.[70] This line of thinking is not new; the authors of the 2013 SMS are in fact echoing a school of thought known as "unrestricted network warfare" (网络超限战) that has long been advocated by some of the PLA's more hawkish network warfare theorists. This goes well beyond the prescriptions of the 2001 edition, and its presence in an authoritative work suggests that more aggressive voices may be gaining ground in the PLA's internal deliberations on network warfare strategy. In its simplest form, this thinking takes the old adage "no blood, no foul" and applies it to network warfare. Even if these thinkers are ultimately mistaken in their understanding of the likely responses of the United States or other potential Chinese adversaries, proactive demonstrations of the United States' commitment to escalatory retaliation may be required in order to persuade Chinese leaders to reassess this assumption and refrain from behaving in an aggressive and escalatory fashion.

An additional factor that may dispose PLA commanders toward escalation is that there is an emerging consensus among PLA strategists and academics that China should prepare for warfare under an environment in which both sides proactively take 'soft' actions to degrade the other's C4ISR capabilities. As Ye predicts, "in operations under informatized conditions, the two opponents will widely utilize soft-kill information operation measures, jamming, suppressing, and damaging their opponent's information systems."[71] The 2013 SMS similarly emphasizes that the PLA must plan for a future of network warfare in which its defenses will inevitably be breached, its military networks will at times be taken down by adversaries and its modern C4ISR systems cannot be fully relied upon.[72] Although they do call for a major effort to strengthen China's network defenses, this is undertaken in the hope that those defenses will not catastrophically fail, not with any expectation that they will fully withstand outside attacks.

If influential voices within the PLA are convinced that China is better prepared for such an eventuality than the United States, a Chinese decision to proactively target C4ISR assets with network and information attacks to prevent the United States from intervening on behalf of Taiwan or other allies becomes far more likely. Note that this does not necessarily extend to U.S. domestic targets such as power grids and other infrastructure that would primarily harm civilians if damaged; such targeting appears to be properly understood as a highly escalatory measure that would more likely draw the United States fully into a China-Taiwan conflict rather than deterring participation.

China's "red lines" with regard to network attacks against its own assets remain unknown. Although the active defense doctrine specifies that China will "surely counterattack if attacked" in any sense, few specific details of what sort of attacks on Chinese systems might provoke specific responses are unknown. As is standard for nuclear powers, the PLA Rocket Force would most likely treat any network attack on China's nuclear systems as a grave threat (and potentially as an equivalent with a similarly-targeted conventional strike). In order to ensure that its nuclear deterrent remains credible,

China might respond to such a provocation with immediate and massive retaliation. Beyond that extreme case, however, little informed supposition is possible.

Finally, PLA analysts acknowledge that the potential for network attacks to cause unintentional escalation can pose a command and control challenge for the PLA's own forces. Network forces by their nature demand greater autonomy and freedom to take initiative than conventional forces; network attack and defense can change unpredictably and operations are conducted rapidly, making it important that soldiers are entrusted to "grasp opportunities on the network warfare battlefield."[73] However, this also presents significant potential pitfalls for the PLA. Since it is possible for network attacks launched by individuals to "exert a direct and powerful influence over an adversary's integrated systems in various spaces, including not only the realm of military conflict but also politics, defense, economics, and foreign diplomacy," PLA analysts argue that soldiers cannot simply do as they wish or follow their individual desires; the behavior of a member of any network operation can directly affect the success or failure of the entire operation, and thus of China's military strategy. The real risk for the PLA of undesired escalation or other strategic failures brought on by overly aggressive or ambitious individual network forces is likely one of multiple considerations that has led to the centralization of Chinese network warfare forces under the recently created Strategic Support Force.

Conclusions

Over the past decade since China's foundational thinking on network warfare was first promulgated, the Chinese approach to the topic has continued to evolve in response to both external circumstances and the PLA's improving capabilities. In examining the various major strains of this approach, one common element is a sense that China's network warfare capabilities are presently inadequate to the task of deterring or defeating a "high-technology adversary" such as the United States. Even though the PLA's current network warfare capabilities would likely be sufficient to deter a weaker enemy in the most plausible conflict scenarios that China may encounter in the near future, the PLA's material and strategic modernization effort centers on developing armed forces that can win hypothetical conflicts against adversaries with superior conventional forces using asymmetric means. Major Chinese efforts on a number of fronts, from an aggressive push to break the military's reliance on foreign hardware and software to attempts to build a diplomatic coalition challenging the United States' perceived dominance of the Internet's core infrastructure, all suggest that China's self-perception of structural vulnerability in the network domain is genuine and keenly felt.

Western analysts of the PLA often frame discussions of China's expanding network warfare capabilities as a question of whether the Chinese will one day become a "status quo" power in cyberspace. Implicit in this thinking is the notion that cyberspace has a natural equilibrium, which China will one day have a material interest in protecting despite their current aggressive use of computer network operations against military and commercial targets. The emergence of China as a truly status quo power in the network domain appears unlikely; the benefits China accrues from asymmetric information warfare are vast, their perception of the status quo is that it leaves them intolerably vulnerable in a critical offense-dominant domain of warfare.

Instead, the key question that remains to be answered is whether China's military and civilian leadership will ever feel they've resolved enough of their asymmetrical vulnerability in the network domain vis-à-vis the United States to wield a strong capability in the event of a major conflict, one capable of exploiting what they perceive as ongoing American weaknesses such as over-reliance on space-based C4ISR systems. If such a milestone ever comes to pass, this appraisal of Chinese strategic thinking on network warfare suggests the result would be an emboldened and possibly more aggressive China posing a greater threat to the core interests of the United States and its allies.

NOTES

[1] For more information on the "informatization" concept, see Joe McReynolds and James Mulvenon, "The Role of Informatization in the People's Liberation Army under Hu Jintao," in *Assessing the People's Liberation Army in the Hu Jintao Era*, Roy Kamphausen, et al, eds., (Carlisle, PA: Army War College Press, April 2014).

[2] "A Summary of Information Operations" [信息作战学综述] in *Lectures on the Science of Information Operations* [信息作战学教程] ed. Ye Zheng [叶征] (Beijing: Academy of Military Sciences Press, 2013), pp. 1–20.

[3] Ye Zheng [叶征] and Zhao Baoxian [赵宝献], "What Kind of Warfare is Network Warfare?" [网络战, 怎么战？] *China Youth Daily* [中国青年报], June 03, 2011. Zeng Wei [曾炜] (PLA Wuhan National Defense Information Academy), and Zou Jianjin [邹剑金] (PLA Wuhan National Defense Information Academy), "Research on Developments in Military Information Warfare Technology and Equipment" [军事信息对抗技术与装备的发展研究], Science and Technology Information [科技信息] No. 15 (2014).

[4] See, for example, Zeng Yanwu [曾燕舞] (Air Force Radar Academy) and Guo Wei [郭伟] (Air Force Radar Academy), "Survey of on the Security of Military Information Network" [军事信息网络安全综述], Fire Control and Command Control [火力与指挥控制] 33.7 (2008).

[5] "A Summary of Information Operations" [信息作战学综述] in *Lectures on the Science of Information Operations* [信息作战学教程] ed. Ye Zheng [叶征] (Beijing: Academy of Military Sciences Press, 2013), pp. 1–20.

[6] *Lectures on the Science of Information Operations* [信息作战学教程] ed. Ye Zheng [叶征] (Beijing: Academy of Military Sciences Press, 2013). Ye Zheng [叶征] and Zhao Baoxian [赵宝献], "A Matter of National Survival: Looking at the Five Forms of Combat in Cyber Warfare" [关乎国家存亡: 看网络战 的五种作战样式], China Youth Daily [中国青年报], June 3, 2011, and others.

[7] Ye Zheng [叶征] and Zhao Baoxian [赵宝献], "Concerning Reflections on Cyber Sovereignty, Cyber Borders, and Cyber National Defense" [关于网络主权、网络边疆、网络国防的思考], Renmin Network [人民网], July 22, 2014

[8] Zhang Yongfu, [张永福] "The Global network Arms Race Intensifies" [全球网络军备竞赛激烈], February 3, 2012. See also Liu Jifeng [刘戟锋], "Information Warfare and Placing Equal Emphasis on Goals and Mechanisms" [信息作战与"道器并重"], *Guangming Daily* [光明日报], November 14, 2011.

[9] Dong Qinglin [董青岭] and Dai Changzheng [戴长征], "Deterrence in the Network Space: Is Retaliation Feasible?" [网络空间威慑: 报复是否可行?], World Economics and Politics [世界经济与政治], No. 7, 2012.

[10] Qiao Liang [乔良] and Wang Xiangsui [王湘穗], *Unrestricted Warfare* [超限战], (Beijing: PLA Literature and Arts Publishing House, 1999 / 2010). The revised 2010 edition is more relevant for this discussion.

[11] Li Guoting [李国亭], "New Proposition in Military Strategy—Information Deterrence" [军事战略新命题—信 息威慑], *Studies in International Technology and Economy* [国际技术经济研究], No. 3, 2006. Dong Qinglin [董青岭] and Dai Changzheng [戴长征], "Deterrence in the Network Space: Is Retaliation Feasible?" [网络空间威慑：报复是否可行?], World Economics and Politics [世界经济与政治], No. 7, 2012.

[12] Luan Dalong [栾大龙], "Pulling Back the Curtain on the New Network Warfare" [全新的网络战已经拉开帷 幕], *Network and Computer Security* [计算机安全], No. 25, 2003.

[13] Zhao Ming [赵明] (Electronic Engineering Institute), Dai Lichao [代立超] (Electronic Engineering Institute), and Wang Jinsong [王劲松] (Electronic Engineering Institute), "A Research on ECM in Cyberspace" [应对网络 空间电子战对策研究], National Defense Science and Technology [国防科技] 34.2 (2013). See also: Zhu Li [祝 利] (PLA Electronic Engineering Institute) and Lin Yuezheng [林岳峥] (PLA Electronic Engineering Institute), "Research on Electronic Warfare Targets in Cyberspace" [赛博空间电子战目标分析], Aerospace Electronic Warfare [航天电子对抗] No. 3 (2012).

[14] Yu Xiaoqiu [俞晓秋], "Network Deterrence Power is a Dangerous Game" [网络威慑力"是个危险的游戏], *People's Daily* [人民日报], July 25, 2011. Dong Qinglin [董青岭] and Dai Changzheng [戴长征], "Deterrence in the Network Space: Is Retaliation Feasible?" [网络空间威慑: 报复是否可行?], World Economics and Politics [世界经济与政治], No. 7, 2012. See also Kang Yongsheng [康永升], "'Prism Gate' Sounds the Alarm on the Implementation of Cyber Weapons" ['棱镜门'敲响对赛博武器实施管控警钟], *China Youth Daily* [中国青年报], July 19, 2013.

[15] Liang Kui [梁逵], "Network Deterrence: Difficult to Employ" [网络威慑: 威而难慑], *China National Defense Daily* [中国国防报], August 08, 2011, and Yang Yanbo [杨延波], "Focusing on the U.S. Military's 'Network Deterrence' Strategy" [聚焦美军"网络威慑"战略], *China National Defense Daily* [中国国防报], January 9, 2012. Dong Qinglin [董青岭] and Dai Changzheng [戴长征], "Deterrence in the Network Space: Is Retaliation Feasible?" [网络空间威慑: 报复是否可行?], World Economics and Politics [世界经济与政治], No. 7, 2012.

[16] Peng Guangqian [彭光谦] and Yao Youzhi [姚有志], eds., *Science of Military Strategy* [战略学], Academy of Military Sciences Press, 2001 Chinese version / 2005 English version, pp. 220–221.

[17] Peng Guangqian [彭光谦] and Yao Youzhi [姚有志], eds., *Science of Military Strategy* [战略学], Academy of Military Sciences Press, 2001 Chinese version / 2005 English version, pp. 220–221. Similar views are also conveyed in Science of Military Strategy [战略学] ed. Shou Xiaosong [寿晓松] (Academy of Military Sciences Press, 2013), pp. 191–195.

[18] Zhang Mingzhi [张明智] (National Defense University) and Hu Xiaofeng [胡晓峰] (National Defense University), "Building a model for cyberspace operations and wartime simulation" [赛博空间作战及其对战争 仿真建模的影响], *Military Operations Research and Systems Engineering* [军事运筹与系统工程] 26.4 (2013).

[19] Yuan Ke [袁轲] (PLA Unit 93501 Command Automation Station), Zhang Hai [张海娟] (Unit 95972 Control Station), and Liu Zhe [刘哲] (Unit 93501 Informatization Office), "Research on the New Trend of Information and Network Warfare" [信息网络战新趋势研究], Digital Technology and Applications [数字技术与应用] No. 12 (2012). Zhao Ming [赵明] (Electronic Engineering Institute), Dai Lichao [代立超] (Electronic Engineering Institute), and Wang Jinsong [王劲松] (Electronic Engineering Institute), "A Research on ECM in Cyberspace" [应对网络空间电子战对策研究], National Defense Science and Technology [国防科技] 34.2 (2013).

[20] Science of Military Strategy [战略学] ed. Shou Xiaosong [寿晓松] (Beijing: Academy of Military Sciences Press, 2013), pp. 188–198.

[21] Remarks by Xi Jinping at first meeting of Network Security and Informatization Leading Small Group, 2014.

[22] Science of Military Strategy [战略学] ed. Shou Xiaosong [寿晓松] (Beijing: Academy of Military Sciences Press, 2013), pp. 188–198.

[23] "The Location of Information Operations" [信息作战定位] in Lectures on the Science of Information Operations [信息作战学教程] ed. Ye Zheng [叶征] (Beijing: Academy of Military Sciences Press, 2013), pp. 21–41.

[24] Peng Guangqian [彭光谦] and Yao Youzhi [姚有志], eds., *The Science of Military Strategy* [战略学], (Beijing: Military Sciences Press), 2001 Chinese version / 2005 English version, pp. 220–221.

Joe McReynolds

25 "The Location of Information Operations" [信息作战定位] in *Lectures on the Science of Information Operations* [信息作战学教程] ed. Ye Zheng [叶征] (Beijing: Military Sciences Press, 2013), pp. 21–41.

26 Science of Military Strategy [战略学] ed. Shou Xiaosong [寿晓松] (Beijing: Academy of Military Sciences Press, 2013), p. 192.

27 "Information Operations Guidance" [信息作战指导] in *Lectures on the Science of Information Operations* [信息作战学教程] ed. Ye Zheng [叶征] (Beijing: Military Sciences Press, 2013), pp. 84–106.

28 Deng Zhifa [邓志法] (National University of Defense Technology) and Lao Songyang [老松杨] (National University of Defense Technology), "Research on Cyberspace Conceptual Framework and Cyberspace Mechanisms" [赛博空间概念框架及赛博空间作战机理研究], Military Operations Research and Systems Engineering [军事运筹与系统工程] 27.3 (2013).

29 Zhang Mingzhi [张明智] (National Defense University) and Hu Xiaofeng [胡晓峰] (National Defense University), "Building a model for cyberspace operations and wartime simulation" [赛博空间作战及其对战争仿真建模的影响], *Military Operations Research and Systems Engineering* [军事运筹与系统工程] 26.4 (2013).

30 Liu Haifeng [刘海峰] (National Defense University) and Cheng Qiyue [程启月] (National Defense University), "Analyzing Joint Operation in Cyberspace's View" [从赛博空间视角探析联合作战], Fire Control and Command Control [火力与指挥控制] 38.5 (2013).

31 "Information Operations Guidance" [信息作战指导] in *Lectures on the Science of Information Operations* [信息作战学教程] ed. Ye Zheng [叶征] (Beijing: Military Sciences Press, 2013), pp. 84–106.

32 "Information Operations Guidance" [信息作战指导] in *Lectures on the Science of Information Operations* [信息作战学教程] ed. Ye Zheng [叶征] (Beijing: Military Sciences Press, 2013), pp. 84–106, "Information Operations Offense" [信息作战进攻] in *Lectures on the Science of Information Operations* [信息作战学教程] ed. Ye Zheng [叶征] (Beijing: Academy of Military Sciences Press, 2013), pp. 170–199.

33 Zhang Mingzhi [张明智] (National Defense University) and Hu Xiaofeng [胡晓峰] (National Defense University), "Building a model for cyberspace

258

operations and wartime simulation" [赛博空间作战及其对战争 仿真建模的影响], *Military Operations Research and Systems Engineering* [军事运筹与系统工程] 26.4 (2013). Lu Jianxun [陆建勋] (China Ship Research and Development Academy), "The Impacts of Cyber Operation on Future Development of Military Communication" [赛博作战对军事通信未来发展的影响], Ship Science and Technology [舰船科学技术] 34.1 (2012).

34 Yu Zhonghai [于中海] (Equipment Department of Nanjing Military District), "Study and Grasp the Winning Mechanisms in Modern Warfare Based on the Latest Developments of Technology and Equipment" [基于技术 和装备最新发展研究把握现代战争制胜机理], *National Defense Science and Technology* [国防科技] 35.1 (2014).

35 Science of Military Strategy [战略学] ed. Shou Xiaosong [寿晓松] (Academy of Military Science) (Beijing: Academy of Military Sciences Press, 2013), pp. 190–191.

36 See, for example, Yang Xiaobo [杨晓波], "Realization and Application of Deterrence in the Network Domain" [网络空间威慑的实现与应用], *Small Arms* [轻兵器], No. 10, 2013.

37 "The Location of Information Operations" [信息作战定位] in *Lectures on the Science of Information Operations* [信息作战学教程] ed. Ye Zheng [叶征] (Academy of Military Sciences) (Beijing: Academy of Military Sciences Press, 2013), pp. 21–41.

38 Peng Guangqian [彭光谦] and Yao Youzhi [姚有志], eds., Science of Military Strategy [战略学], Academy of Military Sciences Press, 2001 Chinese version / 2005 English version, pp. 220–221.

39 Huang Dafu [黄大富], ed., "Joint Defensive Warfare under Informatized Conditions" [信息化条件下联合防 御作战], (Beijing: National Defense University Press, PLA Internal Distribution [军内 发行], 2005), 183.

40 *Science of Military Strategy* [战略学] ed. Shou Xiaosong [寿晓松] (Beijing: Academy of Military Sciences Press, 2013), pp. 188–198.

41 "Information Operations Guidance" [信息作战指导] in *Lectures on the Science of Information Operations* [信息作战学教程] ed. Ye Zheng [叶征] (Beijing: Academy of Military Sciences Press, 2013), 84-106.

42 See, for example, Meng Hongwei [孟宏伟] (China Academy of Electronics and Information Technology) and Song Wenlue [宋文略], (China Academy

of Electronics and Information Technology), "A War without Gun Smoke" [没有硝烟的 战争], Military---Civil Dual---Use Technologies and Products [军民两用技术与产品] No. 9 (2012).

43 Peng Guangqian [彭光谦] and Yao Youzhi [姚有志], eds., Science of Military Strategy [战 略学], Academy of Military Sciences Press, 2001 Chinese version / 2005 English version, pp. 220–226.

44 Liu Jinxing [刘金星] (Air Force First Aviation Academy and Photoelectric Control Key Laboratory), Chen Shaodong [陈哨东] (Photoelectric Control Key Laboratory), and Wang Fang [王芳] (Photoelectric Control Key Laboratory), "The Tactical Maneuver in Cyber Space" [赛博空间的战术机 动], Electronics, Optics, and Control [电光与控制] 21.9 (2014).

45 Yang Xiaobo [杨晓波], "Realization and Application of Deterrence in the Network Domain" [网络空间威慑 的实现与应用], Small Arms [轻兵器], No. 10, 2013.

46 "The Location of Information Operations" [信息作战定位] in Lectures on the Science of Information Operations [信息作战学教程] ed. Ye Zheng [叶 征] (Beijing: Academy of Military Sciences Press, 2013), pp. 21–41.

47 Huang Hanwen [黄汉文] (Shanghai Research Institute of Satellite Engineering), "Concept of Aerospace Electronic Warfare and Its Development" [航天电子对抗的概念与发展], Aerospace Electronic Warfare [航天 电子对抗] 23.2 (2007). Zeng Wei [曾炜] (PLA Wuhan National Defense Information Academy), and Zou Jianjin [邹剑金] (PLA Wuhan National Defense Information Academy), "Research on Developments in Military Information Warfare Technology and Equipment" [军事信息对抗技术与装备的发展研究], Science and Technology Information [科技信息] No. 15 (2014). Wang Haoyu [王滴宇] (School of Astronautics, Beihang University), Fan Hongshen [范宏深] (Second Department, Equipment Research Institute, PLA Second Artillery Force), and Zhao Guowei [赵国伟] (School of Astronautics, Beihang University), "The Function Demand of Spacecraft by the Integration of the Net Electric for Space Warfare" [空间作战融合网电力量对航天器的功能 需求], Aerospace Electronic Warfare [航天电子对抗] 30.5 (2014).

48 Li Yunlong [李云龙] (PLA Equipment Academy) and Yu Xiaohong [于小 红] (PLA Equipment Academy), "美 军'空海一体战'空间作战行动探析"

[Journal of Academy of Equipment], Journal of Academy of Equipment [装备学院学报] 24.4 (2013).

⁴⁹ "The Location of Information Operations" [信息作战定位] in *Lectures on the Science of Information Operations* [信息作战学教程] ed. Ye Zheng [叶征] (Beijing: Academy of Military Sciences Press, 2013), pp. 21–41.

⁵⁰ "Information Operations Guidance" [信息作战指导] in *Lectures on the Science of Information Operations* [信息作战学教程] ed. Ye Zheng [叶征] (Beijing: Academy of Military Sciences Press, 2013), pp. 84–106.

⁵¹ "The Location of Information Operations" [信息作战定位] in *Lectures on the Science of Information Operations* [信息作战学教程] ed. Ye Zheng [叶征] (Beijing: Academy of Military Sciences Press, 2013), pp. 21–41.

⁵² Science of Military Strategy [战略学] ed. Shou Xiaosong [寿晓松] (Academy of Military Science) (Beijing: Academy of Military Sciences Press, 2013), pp. 188–198.

⁵³ Ye Zheng [叶征], *Lectures on the Science of Information Operations* [信息作战学教程], Academy of Military Sciences Press, 2012, p. 252

⁵⁴ Science of Military Strategy [战略学] ed. Shou Xiaosong [寿晓松] (Academy of Military Science) (Beijing: Academy of Military Sciences Press, 2013), pp. 188–198.

⁵⁵ "Information Operations Forces" [信息作战力量] in *Lectures on the Science of Information Operations* [信息 作战学教程] ed. Ye Zheng [叶征] (Beijing: Academy of Military Sciences Press, 2013), pp. 107–126.

⁵⁶ "Information Operations Guidance" [信息作战指导] in *Lectures on the Science of Information Operations* [信息作战学教程] ed. Ye Zheng [叶征] (Beijing: Academy of Military Sciences Press, 2013), pp. 84–106. Lu Jianxun [陆建勋] (China Ship Research and Development Academy), "The Impacts of Cyber Operation on Future Development of Military Communication" [赛博作战对军事通信未来发展的影响], Ship Science and Technology [舰船科学技术] 34.1 (2012). Zhang Mingzhi [张明智] (National Defense University) and Hu Xiaofeng [胡晓峰] (National Defense University), "Building a model for cyberspace operations and wartime simulation" [赛博空间作战及其对战争仿真建模的影响], *Military Operations Research and Systems Engineering* [军事运筹与系统工程] 26.4 (2013).

⁵⁷ See, for example, Nie Songlai [聂送来], "From Network Attacks to Network Warfare?" [从网络攻击到网络 战争?], *Network Communications*

Joe McReynolds

[网 络 传 播], July 25, 2010. Qiu Hongyun [邱 洪 云] (Chongqing Communication Institute), Zhang Yanwei [张彦卫] (China Satellite Guo Mai Communications Co.), Guan Hui [关慧] (PLA Unit 95899), Tian Li [田莉] (Chongqing Communication Institute), Wang Lizhi [王 立 志] (Chongqing Communication Institute), and Zhu Jibing [祝 继 兵] (Chongqing Communication Institute), "The Basic Characteristics of the Cyberspace" [论赛博空间的基本特征], Space Electronic Technology [空间 电子技 术] No. 2 (2013).

58 Tang Lan [唐岚], "The Contest in the Network Domain Between the U.S. and China" [网络空间较量中的美 国和中国], August 08, 2011. Qiu Hongyun [邱洪云] (Chongqing Communication Institute), Zhang Yanwei [张彦卫] (China Satellite Guo Mai Communications Co.), Guan Hui [关慧] (PLA Unit 95899), Tian Li [田莉] (Chongqing Communication Institute), Wang Lizhi [王立志] (Chongqing Communication Institute), and Zhu Jibing [祝继兵] (Chongqing Communication Institute), "The Basic Characteristics of the Cyberspace" [论赛博 空间的基本特征], Space Electronic Technology [空间电子技术] No. 2 (2013). "A Summary of Information Operations" [信息作战学综述] and "The Location of Information Operations" [信息作战定位] in Lectures on the Science of Information Operations [信息作战学教程] ed. Ye Zheng [叶征] (Beijing: Academy of Military Sciences Press, 2013), pp. 1–41.

59 See, for example, Science of Military Strategy [战略学] ed. Shou Xiaosong [寿晓松] (Academy of Military Science) (Beijing: Academy of Military Sciences Press, 2013), pp. 188–198.

60 "Information Operations Guidance" [信息作战指导] in Lectures on the Science of Information Operations [信息作战学教程] ed. Ye Zheng [叶征] (Beijing: Academy of Military Sciences Press, 2013), pp. 84–106.

61 Science of Military Strategy [战略学] ed. Shou Xiaosong [寿晓松] (Academy of Military Science) (Beijing: Academy of Military Sciences Press, 2013), pp. 188–198.

62 "The Location of Information Operations" [信息作战定位] in Lectures on the Science of Information Operations [信息作战学教程] ed. Ye Zheng [叶征] (Academy of Military Sciences) (Beijing: Academy of Military Sciences Press, 2013), pp. 21–32.

[63] Huang Hanwen [黄汉文] (Shanghai Institute of Satellite Engineering), Lu Tongshan [路同山] (Shanghai Institute of Satellite Engineering), Zhao Yanbin [赵艳彬] (Shanghai Institute of Satellite Engineering), and Liu Zhengquan [刘正全] (Shanghai Institute of Satellite Engineering), "Study on Space Cyber Warfare" [空间赛博 战研究], Aerospace Electronic Warfare [航天电子对抗] No. 6 (2012).

[64] Liu Jinxing [刘金星] (Air Force First Aviation Academy and Photoelectric Control Key Laboratory), Chen Shaodong [陈哨东] (Photoelectric Control Key Laboratory), and Wang Fang [王芳] (Photoelectric Control Key Laboratory), "The Tactical Maneuver in Cyber Space" [赛博空间的战术机动], Electronics, Optics, and Control [电光与控制] 21.9 (2014).

[65] Qiu Hongyun [邱洪云] (Chongqing Communication Institute), Zhang Yanwei [张彦卫] (China Satellite Guo Mai Communications Co.), Guan Hui [关慧] (PLA Unit 95899), Tian Li [田莉] (Chongqing Communication Institute), Wang Lizhi [王立志] (Chongqing Communication Institute), and Zhu Jibing [祝继兵] (Chongqing Communication Institute), "The Basic Characteristics of the Cyberspace" [论赛博空间的基本特征], Space Electronic Technology [空间电子技术] No. 2 (2013).

[66] Wang Liping [汪立萍] (No. 8511 Research Institute, China Aerospace Science and Industry Corporation) and Zhang Ya [张亚] (PLA Unit 73677), "Development of Space War based on Space Operations Exercises" [从 太空作战演习看天战的最新发展], Aerospace Electronic Warfare [航天电子对抗] 27.3 (2011).

[67] "The Location of Information Operations" [信息作战定位] in *Lectures on the Science of Information Operations* [信息作战学教程] ed. Ye Zheng [叶征] (Beijing: Academy of Military Sciences Press, 2013), pp. 29–30.

[68] Liu Jinxing [刘金星] (Air Force First Aviation Academy and Photoelectric Control Key Laboratory), Chen Shaodong [陈哨东] (Photoelectric Control Key Laboratory), and Wang Fang [王芳] (Photoelectric Control Key Laboratory), "The Tactical Maneuver in Cyber Space" [赛博空间的战术机动], Electronics, Optics, and Control [电光与控制] 21.9 (2014).

[69] "The Location of Information Operations" [信息作战定位] in *Lectures on the Science of Information Operations* [信息作战学教程] ed. Ye Zheng [叶征] (Beijing: Academy of Military Sciences Press, 2013), pp. 21–41.

[70] Science of Military Strategy [战略学] ed. Shou Xiaosong [寿晓松] (Academy of Military Science) (Beijing: Academy of Military Sciences Press, 2013), pp. 188–198. Chen Baoquan [陈保权] (PLA Unit 65301), Yang Guang [扬光] (PLA Unit 65301), and Li Xuefeng [李学锋] (PLA Unit 65301), "Research on System Combat Effects and Develop Policy of Space Electronic Attack" [空间电子攻击的体系作战效用及发展对策], Aerospace Electronic Warfare [航天电子对抗] 28.1 (2012).

[71] "The Location of Information Operations" [信息作战定位] in *Lectures on the Science of Information Operations* [信息作战学教程] ed. Ye Zheng [叶征] (Beijing: Academy of Military Sciences Press, 2013), pp. 21–41.

[72] Science of Military Strategy [战略学] ed. Shou Xiaosong [寿晓松] (Academy of Military Science) (Beijing: Academy of Military Sciences Press, 2013), pp. 188–198.

[73] Wang Hongbiao [王洪表] (GSD Third Department, Special Operations Academy), "Requirements and Countermeasures of Soldiers' Physical and Psychological Qualities in Networks Warfare" [信息网络战对军人 身心素质的需求及对策研究], *Journal of Military Physical Education and Sports* [军事体育学报] 32.3 (2013).

Chapter 8: The Conceptual Evolution of China's Military Space Operations and Strategy

Kevin Pollpeter and Jonathan Ray

Over the past decade and a half, China's space program has been one of the most dynamic of the world's major powers. China is just one of three countries to have independently launched humans into space and to have landed a probe on the moon. It has made important progress in establishing a global satellite navigation system, and has launched a large number of remote sensing satellites suited for a variety of missions. China has also conducted a series of counterspace and counterspace-related tests and operations.

This time period has also witnessed an evolution in the PLA's thinking on the military use of space, as seen through authoritative documents such as the multiple editions of the *Science of Military Strategy* (SMS) that have been released during this time frame. This evolution is apparent in the increasing amount of attention devoted to outer space in PLA writings as well as in characterizations of the role that space will play in China's future military operations. Successive editions of the book have increased the amount of coverage of outer space from short descriptions in the 1999 edition to an entire section in the 2013 edition, and have moved from treating space as a mere extension of the air domain to viewing space as an indispensable and independent domain with unique characteristics that carry clear strategic implications.

This evolution appears to be driven by three factors. The first is a widespread belief among Chinese military strategists that the United States plays an activist and destabilizing role in world affairs that is intended to restrict China's rise as a world power. As a result, many PLA officers believe China must develop space and counterspace capabilities as a part of an overall strategic deterrent that can prevent the United States from interfering with this rise. A second and related factor is the PLA's need to develop a warfighting force capable of defending China's expanding interests globally and in outer space. This includes the development of space-based C4ISR capabilities to enable long-range precision strikes to defend China's interests far from its coastal waters, as well as counterspace capabilities that can threaten and degrade an adversary's space assets. A third factor is the increasing utility of China's own space capabilities. Military space capabilities are no longer the exclusive purview of other countries, and now play a more instrumental role in China's military operations and economic development. As authoritative PLA writings put it, outer space is now a "commanding height" in modern warfare, and along with nuclear and cyber capabilities it plays a crucial strategic role in the outcome of warfare.

The Military Application of Outer Space Depicted in the 1999 and 2001 Editions of the Science of Military Strategy

The 1999 and 2001 editions of SMS present initial examinations of the military uses of outer space, and provide an evolving but sometimes equivocal treatment of the role and importance of the domain to modern warfare. In the 1999 SMS, authors at the PLA's National Defense University (NDU) treated space primarily as an extension of the air domain that provides support capabilities to the traditional domains of air, land and sea. With the publication of the Academy of Military Sciences' (AMS) more authoritative 2001 edition, however, the SMS authors had begun to characterize space warfare as inevitable, and spent considerably more time assessing its role in future wars.

The 1999 SMS edition was the culmination of almost of a decade of teaching by NDU strategists who observed transitions in the international strategic environment after the Cold War.[1] Looking abroad, the authors saw a global shift toward a multipolar international power structure with increasing competition by multiple actors for influence with the greatest threat to world peace being hegemonism and power politics.[2] The authors did not foresee a new world war occurring from this competition, but instead believed such competition would more likely result in local wars, particularly wars of intervention by multinational coalitions. Key drivers fueling these conflicts were (1) major Western powers trying to secure regions with strategic resources or trade routes, (2) Western intervention in the internal conflicts of developing countries, and (3) the rapid development and application of new technologies for conventional arms that facilitate armed intervention.[3]

The primary example of these trends was the 1991 Gulf War, which demonstrated the effectiveness of high-tech weaponry against less-advanced opponents.[4] That war caused the PLA to reevaluate the types of wars it would need to prepare to fight and in 1993 resulted in the PLA's Military Strategic Guidelines being changed from the PLA fighting "local, limited wars" to "local wars under modern, especially high tech conditions." This rubric envisioned the Chinese military fighting a technologically sophisticated opponent in a conflict that would be intense, mobile, and highly lethal with a greater reliance on C4ISR capabilities.[5]

This transition to the new strategic guidelines and debates among Chinese military strategists strongly influenced the 1999 edition of SMS, which draws from teaching materials used at NDU throughout the 1990s.[6] At that time, NDU strategists understood the importance of space assets to military operations, but recognized that at the time China had only limited interests and capabilities in space. As a result the 1999 SMS contains chapters for air, sea, and nuclear strategies, but does not dedicate a chapter to the space domain. Instead, the authors treated space as an extension of the air domain, with space capabilities understood as being imperative for intelligence, communications, and precision strike capabilities.

The authors of the 1999 SMS clearly understood the importance of space capabilities to information warfare capabilities. They note that from the 1980s to 1990s, information superiority (制 信息权) became increasingly important to operations in all domains, as demonstrated in the first Gulf War.[7] Additionally, they observed that "militaries operate in an integrated multidimensional battlefield on land, sea, air, space, and the electromagnetic spectrum."[8] In keeping with this integration the authors argue that "the significance of air (and space) operations is rapidly rising; outer space is becoming a very important strategic high ground (战略制高点)."[9] In their view, this trend as well as the growing importance of electromagnetic warfare are creating a transition from mechanized to informatized forces. Consequently, they argue that in the initial phase of any war, China must contest "information, air (and space), and sea superiority."[10]

Despite the increasing importance of space to China's military capabilities, in 1999 space was still a secondary domain for analysis purposes due to China's limited interests and capabilities. The 1999 SMS authors do not designate space as an independent domain, opting instead to treat air and space as an integrated and continuous spectrum. As a result, space threats were treated as an extension of air warfare.[11] The most illustrative example is the 1999 SMS's concept of "integrated air and space" (空天一体化), which emphasizes the benefits that superiority in air and space can provide to other forces, and likely reflects strong influence by the PLA Air Force in the drafting of the text.[12] Other discussions indicate a subordination of space to the air domain, such as a description of air defense operations including threats that originate from the air and space.[13] For Chinese air power, increases in both air and space technologies were helping facilitate major changes in the PLA Air Force's role and capabilities through the use of "surgical strikes," making air power a key part of joint operations and aiding in the execution of independent air campaigns.[14] Discussions of counterspace operations were limited in the 1999 edition, however, with just brief mentions of "space superiority" (制天权).[15]

Continuing the 1999 SMS theme, the 2001 SMS presents the post-Cold War transition toward a multipolar world order as fraught with uncertainty, and considers other countries' attempts to prevent China's rise, most likely by the United States, as one of the gravest national threats.[16] The authors, however, depict China's threat environment in primarily regional rather than global terms, describing China's geographic position between Eurasia and the Pacific as constituting a geopolitical center that will naturally face many potential threats.[17] These concerns include sharing a common border with numerous countries, the possibility of Taiwan independence, and other national sovereignty issues.[18] In this view of the threat environment, China's primary goal must be to prevent or deter external aggression in order to ensure continued development and stability.[19] No specific mention is made of protecting China's interests in space; instead, the focus is on ecological and maritime resources and maintaining access to petroleum.[20]

Departing from the 1999 NDU edition, the 2001 AMS-authored SMS portrays the military use of space as a possible threat that China may need to address in the future. Although its discussion of space remains limited and sometimes contradictory, the 2001 edition marks the rise of a theme in Chinese military strategic thought that would become increasingly prominent over the coming decade: the expansion of the battlefield into outer space through the use of satellites, space planes, laser weapons, and other high-tech technology systems.[21] Citing the 1991 Gulf War as an example, the authors write of the importance of space to strategic information operations, including intelligence, command and control, computer networks, and information warfare.[22] With these capabilities the authors conclude that "military satellites may provide future operations with strong operational command and control capabilities, and military satellites may become a target for direct attack using electronic operations; space electronic warfare may become a new domain for electronic warfare."[23]

With this conclusion, the 2001 SMS appears to refer to outer space as a separate domain of warfare. Outer space, also referred to as near space (近地太空 and 近地宇宙空间), is one of three "major strategic spaces" (战略大空间) along with the ocean and air.[24] By the text's definition, air extends to 100 km in altitude to include lower atmosphere, stratosphere, and ionosphere.[25]

The 2001 SMS text is also the first edition to include a section on "space assaults" (太空进攻) and multiple references to space superiority (制天权) and space force deterrence (空间力量威慑).[26] The text is ambiguous about the meaning of space assault, but claims that no country at that time had a capability to strike strategic targets using space assaults, though such capabilities were being developed by "certain countries."[27] Consequently, the authors believed, "in future wars, space battles will be difficult to avoid, and space assaults very possibly will become a future and new means of strategic attack."[28] The authors stated that space assaults must follow three guidelines: meeting the fundamental objectives of the strategic assault; matching the reality of one's own strategic forces; and matching the reality of the ground situation and conditions.[29] The authors did not provide specific elaboration on these guidelines, however, perhaps reflecting China's nascent understanding of space warfare and limited space capabilities.

Despite apparently designating space as a separate domain, the 2001 SMS continues the theme of air and space as an integrated medium seen in the earlier 1999 edition.[30] Recognizing the importance of aviation and space technologies, the authors of the 2001 SMS conclude that:

> The high degree of development of aviation and space technologies and weapons provides a technological and material basis for the establishment of a dominant air-space battlefield. The air-space military struggle dominates the military struggles for air, sea, and electromagnetic supremacy of local war under high technology conditions. The development of theory for air-space military struggle is an importance aspect of developing theory for local wars under high-tech conditions.[31]

It is noteworthy that the authors appear to allocate a secondary role to the space mission, with parenthetical references to "air (space) defense systems" and "air (space) forces" ("防空 [防天] 系统" and "防空 [防天] 力量," respectively). They also call for the PLA to deploy integrated defenses against aircraft, missiles, and spacecraft capable of defending against near, medium, and long-range targets.[32]

Despite this seemingly contradictory treatment of space, the 2001 SMS authors recognized that strategic theory needed to be expanded to include the space domain, describing Chinese space strategy as being in a "gradually developing and maturing phase."[33] They stated that the most prominent example of this transition would be the subsequent expansion of the PLA's air superiority concept to include space superiority. As a model they cite the U.S. Air Force's goal at the time of transitioning from being an air-centric "air and space force" to becoming a space-centric "space and air force," as well as the U.S. Air Force's goal of achieving space control and space superiority. The authors of the 2001 SMS concluded that "[t]hese [examples] presage space strategic theory becoming an important direction for the development of strategic theory."[34] Ultimately, however, the authors refrained from offering an in-depth explanation of China's approach to space strategic theory; only in the 2013 SMS was such a discussion offered for the first time.

The Depiction of the Military Application of Space in the 2013 SMS

The 2013 edition of SMS represents a great leap forward in our understanding of how China sees outer space as fitting into modern warfare. It jettisons the equivocal nature of the discussion of space operations presented in the 1999 and 2001 editions in favor of a much more certain assessment of its fundamental role in modern warfare. No longer do the authors write that space "may provide" critical information support to the PLA and for this reason "may" become targets in a future conflict. Instead, the 2013 SMS concludes that outer space is an independent domain, that space-based C4ISR systems are an essential element of modern military operations, and that countries are developing counterspace technologies to deny this capability to adversaries. In fact, the authors of the 2013 SMS appear to conclude that space is so important to military operations that space forces will form, along with nuclear and cyber force, a strategic counterbalance to potential adversaries. In this assessment, one sees much the same conceptual taxonomy that was written into the PLA's organizational structure several years later through the creation of the Strategic Support Force (战略支援部队, or SSF).

The authors' conclusion is driven by the growing role and importance of outer space as a national interest. Here the book draws upon the PLA's "New Historic Missions" concept first elucidated under Hu Jintao, an attempt to broaden the PLA's understanding of its necessary core competencies which among other things tasks China's military with expanding the defense of China's interests from its land borders, airspace, and territorial waters to the distant oceans, outer space, and cyber space.[35] Outer space is described by the 2013 SMS as a strategic high point for a country's economic and military development, a "'high frontier' for maintaining national security," an important region for China's expanding national interest, "a new source of growth for comprehensive national power," and an indispensable economic and military domain.[36] According to the 2013 SMS, the growing role of space as a military and economic interest requires the PLA to protect its interests there by creating capabilities that can serve both deterrent and warfighting missions.[37]

According to the 2013 SMS, the Chinese military must develop its military space program based on both an assessment of its strategic situation and the expansion of China's national interests.[38] Indeed, the strategic concepts for the employment of military space capabilities discussed in the 2013 SMS have direct corollaries in China's overall military strategy, rooted in PLA strategists' overall assessments of the current security situation and the state of China's military capabilities. While threat assessments describe what types of conflicts a country may face, military capabilities determine how it will actually fight those conflicts.[39]

The threat assessment provided by the authors of the 2013 SMS paints a complicated picture of the world situation. On one hand, economic cooperation has lessened the possibility of great power conflict by enmeshing the interests of countries to such an extent that containing one country can have negative consequences for all countries. On the other hand, the authors of the 2013 SMS assess that the international situation is changing from a unipolar world led by the United States to a multipolar world where other countries, such as China, will play a more consequential role in world politics. Citing history, the authors of the 2013 SMS note that "the fiercest competition" between major powers occurs during periods of geopolitical transition involving a rising power attempting to overtake an existing hegemon."[40] Despite this pessimistic conclusion, the 2013 SMS concludes that this dynamic will not result in a new Cold War between the United States and China, but that "conflicts of interests and structural contradictions between China and the United States will not be resolved easily."[41]

This cautionary threat assessment is placed against a background of China's increasing and expanding search for resources to fuel its rise. According to the 2013 SMS, "[t]he full establishment of a well-off society and the realization of the Chinese nation's great rejuvenation is the national strategic objective for the first half of the 21ˢᵗ Century. A secure, stable, and persistent expansion of the nation's interests is the basic condition and important channel for realizing this objective."[42] As a result, "the competition between great powers is ultimately a competition that revolves around the realization of maximizing national interests."[43]

According to the 2013 SMS, this kind of competition will increasingly focus on control of various global commons: the open ocean, the arctic and Antarctic, outer space, and cyber space.[44] To adapt to this new situation, the PLA must expand its strategic view and "provide a strong and powerful strategic support within a greater spatial scope to maintain national interests."[45] As a result, "the possibility of requiring the flexible employment of the armed forces due to the difficulty of reconciling conflicts of interests or major threats facing [China's] interests outside of [its] national boundaries cannot be eliminated."[46]

This period of great power transition also coincides with a period when advances in weapons technology, led by the United States, are occurring at an ever more rapid pace. According to the 2013 SMS, the use of long-range strike platforms and "new type weapons" such as electromagnetic and laser weapons is expected to be increasingly common, compelling the integration of ground, air, naval, and space forces and expanding warfare to the distant oceans, outer space, and cyber space.[47] The 2013 SMS asserts that this emphasis on long-range and new types of weapons has resulted in the United States establishing a new "new triad" based on nuclear, space, and cyber forces.[48]

The 2013 SMS assessment of the world situation and the threats China faces is reflected in its assessment of the threats surrounding the use of outer space. It argues that countries which both "seek world hegemony" and have a high degree of reliance on outer space will attempt to control outer space through expansionary, militaristic, and non-inclusive activities.[49] The 2013 SMS, by contrast, describes China as taking a defensive national military strategy focused on defending its legitimate rights and interests in space by ensuring that space can support its economic and military interests while "not harming the security and interests of other countries."[50] According to the 2013 SMS:

China's military activities in the space domain have the distinctive features of being defensive and inclusive: it takes as the basis maintaining its rights and interests in space and maintaining space security. It does not take the initiative to infringe upon the space rights and interests of other states, and does not seek space hegemony. It emphasizes development and not offensive action. China adopts the mode of benefitting itself and not harming others while exercising its legitimate space rights and ensuring space security. Only when another state conscientiously infringes upon China's space rights and interests and causes harm to national space security, may China implement space deterrence against the enemy and launch a space counterattack. In the space domain, what China still follows is the principle of we will not attack unless we are attacked.[51]

The authors argue that outer space is becoming more competitive and contested, with established players becoming more active and new countries entering the field. In their view, Russia has made the development of its space program a major priority. Europe, Japan, India, and Brazil continue to develop their space programs while other countries such as South and North Korea, Pakistan, and Iran are viewed as being at the beginning phases of their space programs.[52] The United States, however, is characterized as the main impediment to China's pursuit of its interests in outer space by "attempting to seize control of outer space in order to achieve absolute security." The

United States is said to stress a doctrine emphasizing space control, including the creation of counterspace units, the development of plans for space operations, carrying out space exercises, and developing counterspace weapons such as the X-37B and missile defenses.[53]

According to the 2013 SMS, "the United States, as the nation with the most advanced space technology and strongest space capabilities, on one hand ensures that other nations may not carry out the weaponization of space, while on the other hand it ceaselessly advances its own progress on space weapons."[54] Meanwhile, China's space capabilities are portrayed as inadequate relative to those of the United States. If accurate, this places China's military in a difficult position. Although the PLA must prepare for conflict across the full-spectrum of modern war, its lack of advanced space technologies on par with those of the United States could impede Chinese attempts to defend itself against hypothetical U.S. aggression.

Based on these assessments, the authors of both the 2013 SMS and other authoritative Chinese writings assign a more prominent role for outer space in military operations than in past authoritative works, including previous editions of SMS. For example, the authors of the book argue that the PLA must be able to deter the United States from attacking China, prevent Taiwan from declaring independence, and deter peripheral countries from infringing upon its interests. Deterrent capabilities also need to be developed to not only protect China's interests on the land, but also in the distant oceans, outer space, and cyberspace.[55] As a result, the PLA must transform itself from being a strictly continental army to a military force that can operate in all domains, including outer space.[56] According to the 2013 SMS, "looking toward future space defense operations, [we must] establish a space operational force that is integrated, has high fidelity, has great depth, and multi-layered and combines space launches, tracking telemetry and control, support, defense, and strategic deterrence."[57] The 2013 SMS also states:

> In focusing on seizing the strategic high point of future military conflict, we must defend our country's space security and ensure access to space, bring into play the role of military space systems as a central point of our military's joint operations and accelerate the construction of space and near space systems. In the short term, we should accelerate the development of space-based information support systems so that space strengthens ground operations, space strengthens naval operations, space strengthens air operations, and space strengthens nuclear operations. In the long-term, we must focus on the prevention and containment of possible space military confrontations, and develop reliable and usable operationally defensive space force systems that have a certain level of space strategic early-warning capability and a limited comprehensive space dominance capability.[58]

Fitting Space into China's Broader Military Strategy

The 2013 SMS assessment that the PLA must both protect its interests in outer space and develop space and counterspace capabilities appears to necessitate the development of a strategy for the employment of these capabilities. In fact, the close correlation between the 2013 SMS assessment of the security situation in space and its overall assessment of the international security situation is matched by the close correlation of its discussion of space strategy with China's national military strategy (centered on the "active defense" concept) and its assessment of the nature of the wars that China is likely to fight ("informatized" conflicts).

China's national military strategy of active defense was first developed by Mao Zedong during China's civil war period. According to Mao, active defense is "offensive defense or defense through decisive engagements ...for the purpose of counter-attacking and taking the offensive." [59] Mao more colloquially explained the strategy as "if people do not attack us, we will not attack them; if people attack us, we inevitably will attack them."

During the decades after the founding of the People's Republic of China, the active defense strategy was geared toward defeating ground invasions from the United States and the Soviet Union by stressing "fighting early, fighting hard, and fighting a nuclear war." In more recent times, the active defense strategy has been adapted to meet the challenges of modern war. With the end of the Cold War and the strengthening of China's military, the settlement of most of China's land border disputes, and the expansion of China's interests discussed above has now focused the PLA on protecting national interests farther away from its land borders, especially in the maritime domain, and providing a stable environment for China's economic development. As a result, although China's nuclear deterrent continues to serve as the ultimate backstop to the country's security, the probability that China will be involved in a nuclear war is now judged as remote.[60] Similarly, the possibility of a ground invasion of China is nearly completed ruled out.[61] As a result, the practical focus of China's military strategy has begun to shift toward the maritime, outer space, and cyber domains.[62]

Under this new situation, China's active defense strategy is now geared toward "prioritizing the land borders, stabilizing the periphery, controlling the near seas, advancing outer space, and focusing on information." Defense of the land borders and the near seas will remain the top priority, but outer space and cyberspace will be "critical."[63] According to the 2013 SMS, this restructuring of the substance of active defense should not be unexpected: "active defense is a dynamically developing strategic concept...regardless of the past, present, or future, one cannot equate it to a pure territorial home defense. Looking at it in terms of development trends, in order to support the expansion of the national interest in all domains and to win future wars we may face, it is necessary for us to establish a forward defense guiding thought."[64]

The adjustment of the types of conflicts the PLA is called upon to fight has also coincided with its conception of the changing nature of warfare. The PLA is no longer focused on conducting campaigns similar to its past efforts in Korea, India, and Vietnam, where mass force was used to overwhelm its opponents. Instead, the types of wars the PLA has been tasked to fight have undergone a steady adjustment since the early 1990s from local wars under modern conditions, to the version of local wars under high-tech conditions discussed in the 2001 SMS, to local wars under informatized conditions as discussed in the 2013 SMS. These changes have progressively stressed the growing role of advanced technologies in modern warfare, in particular information technologies. The current formulation of fighting "informatized wars," announced in the 2015 Defense White Paper (DWP), appears to be a culmination of this evolution where the ability to use information and deny it to an enemy is now regarded as the most critical factor for achieving victory in war.[65]

Recognizing the importance of information systems, the 2013 SMS concludes that the PLA must further integrate information technologies with its weapon systems and become capable of denying an adversary the use of their own information technology if it is to adequately carry out its missions. This new way of war with information as the core moves away from the PLA's previous platform-centric approach to military operations and toward what the PLA has termed a 'system-of-systems' approach. Under this concept, warfighting is a contest between networks of systems, and the operation of every system and subsystem affects the performance of the entire system. Together the synergistic qualities of this system-of-systems configuration can yield a result greater than the sum of its parts, enabling joint operations through the use of networked information systems that provide each operational element with a real-time Common Operating Picture (COP) of the battlefield and allowing units to be more flexible and adaptive.[66]

Although system-of-systems operations can greatly increase the effectiveness of a fighting force, there is also a potential for dependencies to develop wherein the entire system is overly reliant on any one sub-system, creating choke points and thus vulnerabilities. The PLA believes these vulnerabilities can be exploited using synchronized strikes against key nodes, such as critical command and control centers and C4ISR systems, paralyzing the enemy and creating a "shock and awe" effect.[67] As a result, "system vs. system" warfare is characterized by both belligerents trying to disrupt each other's systems in order to degrade the decision-making ability of the opponent. As the 2013 SMS states, the purpose of system vs. system warfare is to "transform information superiority into decision-making superiority and transform decision-making superiority into operational superiority" and "to disrupt the enemy's operational pace and upset the enemy's operational disposition and firmly grasp taking the initiative in regards to time."[68]

A system-of-systems operations approach also takes long-range precision strikes as a key and potentially deciding factor in modern war.[69] The PLA, however, is cognizant that its ability to carry out long-range precisions strikes remains limited relative to the U.S. military. Consequently, the 2013 SMS argues that the PLA must rely on its land borders and coastal waters to conduct long-range precision strikes as the main form of attack supplemented by smaller scale strikes by forward-deployed units. These long-range strike forces will be composed of Second Artillery (now Rocket Force), Air Force, and Navy units supported by space-based C4ISR assets conducting kinetic and non-kinetic attacks from multiple domains supplemented by counterspace, computer network attack, and electronic warfare operations against select C4ISR and logistics nodes.[70]

In carrying out these operations, the PLA will take an asymmetric approach characterized by strikes against an adversary's weak points and avoiding direct attacks against its strengths. Asymmetric operations are regarded as especially important when a weaker military is facing a stronger military.

In this case, the authors of the 2013 SMS counsel the PLA to stress joint operations against the single service operations of an adversary as well as to remain flexible in regards to the conduct of operations. As the 2013 SMS states, "In order to fully create the conditions [for victory], [we] must absolutely not adopt the timing or place and methods and operations dictated by the enemy; and [we] must avoid battles where the enemy has the superiority in high-tech areas."[71]

Although the conventional wisdom of Western observers is that the PLA must use an asymmetric strategy against a superior U.S. military, the 2013 SMS asserts that the nature of system vs. system warfare is fundamentally asymmetric and not entirely dependent on the balance of forces. The key to victory lies not just in the overall superiority of a fighting force, but also in the nature of its adversary's vulnerabilities and the ability of an opposing side to strike these vulnerabilities to produce decisive effects.[72] It states that "local war under informatized conditions is system vs. system warfare," and thus "in the future, no matter whether we will face an enemy with superior equipment or an enemy with inferior equipment, we will always need to focus on paralyzing enemy warfighting systems and emphasize 'striking at systems,' 'striking at vital sites,' and 'striking at [key] nodes'," with the "most universal and practical" method of doing so being "asymmetrical operations."[73]

The Role of Space Missions in Asymmetric System-of-systems Warfare

The role of space in modern warfare described by the authors of the 2013 SMS is based upon their assessment that outer space is an essential element of modern war whose "position and role within the overall national strategic situation have constantly risen."[74] The development of military space forces is described as being "of important significance for building informatized armed forces, winning informatized wars, and for propelling the PLA's strategic transformation."[75] This assessment follows in part from the PLA's understanding of the increasing role that information in all its forms plays in modern warfare.[76] Space-based information support is now assessed to be an indispensable capability for a military. According to the 2013 SMS, the U.S. military uses satellites for "100 percent of its navigation and 90 percent of its communication needs."[77] Moreover, because of the proliferation of a wide-range of rapid strike methods, "especially space and network attack and defense methods," China must prepare for an enemy to attack from all domains, including space.[78] Because of the strategic importance of outer space, the 2013 SMS assesses that future wars may begin in outer space and cyberspace and that "achieving space superiority and [cyber] superiority are critical for achieving overall superiority and being victorious over an enemy."[79]

Recognizing the new threats from space and cyberspace, the authors of SMS 2013 recommend that the PLA "expand the strategic depth of active defense" to encompass these non-traditional domains.[80] They elevate space operations to one of nine "main operational activities" along with information operations, joint strike operations, air and missile defense, air and sea blockades, island seizure operations, area denial operations, border defense operations, and cyber operations. In this thinking, space-based threats are one of five major military deterrent threats the PLA faces, along with nuclear, conventional, cyber, and nuclear-conventional threats. The

2013 SMS then goes on to recommend that the PLA must adapt to the "new forms of warfare and to the characteristics of new operational domains" and "closely track the world's strong powers in the development of military technologies, weapons and equipment, operational forces, and strike methods" by developing unmanned aerial vehicles, counter-stealth and cruise missile technologies, aircraft carrier strike units, counterspace platforms as well as tactics for countering ISR, precision strike, network attacks, space weapons, and other new attack methods.[81]

These technologies will be used to conduct three types of missions for space forces: space information support, space attack and defense operations, and space deterrence.

Space Information Support (空间信息支援)

Space information support is achieved through the use of space-based ISR, early warning, communication, and navigation capabilities. Space information support is described as the basis of a space program. Consequently, conflict in space revolves around the ability of a military to derive support from space-based assets.[82]

Space Deterrence (空间威慑)

Space deterrence is the use of space forces to carry out deterrent activities and is one of five delineated military deterrent activities, alongside nuclear deterrence, conventional deterrence, cyber deterrence, and nuclear-conventional deterrence. [83] According to the 2013 SMS, space deterrence capabilities are increasingly important due to the increasing use of space for both military and civilian applications. As the 2013 SMS states, "even in a relatively peaceful period, under circumstances where a hostile relationship is unclear, the presence and development of one side's space systems and the boosting of its space capability can still potentially influence and constrain the military activity of other nations and generate a certain deterrent effect."[84]

The purpose of space deterrence is to prevent the outbreak of war in general and attacks against China's space systems specifically. It is conducted to ensure the normal operation of China's space systems, as well as to keep enemy actions within a limited, acceptable scope in order to control the enemy's intentions and actions.[85] The 2013 SMS cautions, however, that the PLA should not take the initiative to escalate a space conflict and should not initiate an attack against the space assets of a powerful adversary. Only when deterrent actions are seen as having failed and the enemy is conducting strikes against China's space assets, they believe, should China consider striking an enemy in space. If counterspace actions are required, the PLA should not conduct an all-out attack against a powerful enemy and instead should choose critical nodes that can paralyze the system as a whole.[86] This includes the possible use of kinetic methods that can serve to warn an adversary and "prevent losing control of the situation and conflict escalation."[87]

The 2013 SMS describes two ways in which space can be used to deter an adversary. The first way is through the use of space-based ISR to monitor the activities of potential adversaries to provide advanced warning of conflicts and thus give time for China to take preemptive military and diplomatic measures.

This advance notice can be so crucial to the outcome of a conflict that even the mere presence of space-based ISR systems can potentially deter adversaries from even contemplating taking provocative actions. A second deterrent measure is the application of counterspace measures. According to the 2013 SMS, China can "conduct limited space operations with warning and punishment as goals in order to stop the adversary from willfully escalating the intensity of a space confrontation."[88]

To carry out these actions, the 2013 SMS calls for "constantly strengthening space deterrence capabilities, grasping different deterrence mechanisms, innovating deterrent methods" and "upholding various principles to restrict adversaries' space interests, counter activities that threaten China's own space security, and form a strategic deterrent force" and also calls for actions to reveal China's counterspace capabilities and intent to take counterspace actions.[89] At the same time, the 2013 SMS argues that China should continue to oppose the weaponization of space, but should also selectively develop counterspace technologies so as to impose costs on countries that are developing space weapons.[90] In this manner of thinking, China should not seek to acquire a military space capability that is the equal of the United States in order to demonstrate to the world to that it is a different, more peaceful, space power. At the same time, however, China should have sufficient capability to carry out required military missions.[91] According to the 2013 SMS, the most efficient method to develop operational space capabilities is for the PLA to "[do] some things while leaving some things undone" and "play to its strengths while avoiding weaknesses."[92]

Space Attack and Defense (空间攻防)

Space attack and defense operations are described as a type of "direct military confrontation activity carried out mainly in outer space by opposing sides." The main goal of space attack and defense operations is to achieve space supremacy within a certain period of time and certain location.[93] It includes both offensive and defensive counterspace capabilities involving ground and air capabilities as well as offensive and defensive operations between space-based platforms. It also includes attacks from space against surface or air targets.[94]

Although the majority of applications for space are now associated with intelligence collection, the 2013 SMS sees a trend toward a greater role for offensive strike operations to degrade or destroy space-based assets.[95] In taking this approach, the 2013 SMS states that space support capabilities should receive priority over the development of counterspace capabilities[96] with China developing a small but capable space force that can serve its C4ISR requirements and a limited counterspace force.[97]

Based on the weapons employed and the type of operation, space attack and defense operations can be divided into the following:

- *Satellite attack and defense operations:* the use of ground-based, air-based, and space-based weapons to attack enemy satellites and defend friendly satellites;
- *Space anti-missile operations:* Operations using space-based laser and kinetic energy weapons to intercept and destroy enemy missiles passing through outer space;

- *Space operational platform attack and defense*: Offensive and defensive operations conducted against space-based platforms through the use of weapons systems based on space-based platforms, such as space planes and space stations;
- *Space-based attack operations against ground (air) targets*: Operations employing laser, particle-beam, or kinetic energy weapons from space-based platforms to attack and destroy enemy targets on the ground, sea surface, or in the air.[98]

Command of Space Forces

The development of nascent strategic principles and the call for the building of a strong space program would also appear to necessitate the designation of certain services or units to command the space mission. On December 31, 2015, the PLA announced the creation of a Strategic Support Force (战略支援部队, or SSF) to command "new type operational forces,"[99] a term that has in the past been used to encompass space, cyber, and electronic warfare forces.[100] According to semi-official news reporting, the SSF consists of space, cyber, and electronic warfare units that will provide information support capabilities to other operational units. In regards to the space mission, this appears to include the management of satellites, including launch, space-based ISR, satellite communications, and satellite navigation functions. Unstated in these news reports is which PLA unit(s) now command counterspace forces.[101]

The establishment of the SSF would appear to somewhat settle the question of how China's space enterprise will be commanded. The establishment of some sort of "space force" has been talked about for years with a focus on the potential involvement of the Air Force and the Second Artillery (now the Rocket Force) in providing launch and counterspace capabilities as well as their use of space-based C4ISR capabilities. [102] However, despite these two services having positioned themselves for some time to take on an increasing role in the PLA's space mission, it now appears that no one service will control all of the PLA's space forces.

The PLA Air Force and Space Operations

The Air Force strategy section in the 2013 SMS continues the theme found in other editions that the Air Force will develop into an air and space force as China's "national security environment changes and its national interests" expand into the air and space domain. In 2004, the PLAAF established as its strategic requirements "integrated air and space, simultaneous offense and defense," which appeared to inherently tie the Air Force with space. According to the 2013 SMS, this will necessitate the PLAAF transitioning from an aviation force into an integrated air and space force.[103] Analysts writing after 2004 have offered several reasons for why the Air Force should take over the space mission. The first is that since the PLA Air Force is the 'most technical' branch of the Chinese military, it is best suited to lead the military's space effort. A second argument is that as space warfare evolves it will one day involve the use of manned space planes, a capability uniquely suited to the Air Force mission with its experience piloting aircraft. A final argument draws on the experiences of foreign militaries, holding that the space programs of most militaries are operated by their nations' respective air forces and the Chinese military should be no different.[104]

The discussion of the PLAAF's role in space in the 2013 SMS, however, is much more limited in its scope than that found in these less authoritative writings and is to some extent contradictory. For example, it states that the PLAAF should develop into a service able to shape the air and space situation, control air and space crises, and win air and space wars. In doing so, it should carry out air and space defense as well as air and space deterrence. At the same time, however, the authors of the book discuss the PLAAF's current core mission of seizing air superiority without any mention of a current corresponding mission to seize space superiority.[105]

Instead, the authors of the 2013 SMS describe a PLAAF that is currently more geared toward being a consumer of space-based C4ISR capabilities than a service directly responsible for the development and operation of space-based platforms. They state that in carrying out its transition to an integrated air and space force, the PLAAF should develop into a force with "one system possessing five forces and seven operational capabilities." The "one system" refers to an informatized system that combines air, space, and ground-based C4ISR capabilities into an integrated strategic, campaign, and tactical-level system-of-systems in which space-based information platforms are essential. The authors of the 2013 SMS also mention that the PLAAF *utilizes* (as opposed to controls or is developing) "all-Army space-based information sources." In contrast, the PLAAF is developing air-breathing platforms such as fourth generation aircraft, airborne refueling aircraft, long-distance reconnaissance aircraft, early warning aircraft, and unmanned air aircraft, among other capabilities.[106]

However, this does not necessarily preclude the PLAAF from taking a more active role in space operations in the future. The 2013 SMS notes that the PLAAF's strategic missions are expanding from its traditional air defense mission to encompass integrated air defense, missile defense, and space defense missions that will eventually include the use of ground-based and airborne space defense, counterspace, and space superiority operations.[107] The 2013 SMS calls for the PLAAF to focus on future operational requirements and develop air-spacecraft, near-space strike weapons, and airborne laser weapons as well as capabilities to deliver assets to orbit via space planes.[108] The 2013 SMS states: "With the mature development of space planes, the transportation of space-based forces will become an important method of Air Force strategic transportation."[109]

The PLA Rocket Force and Space Operations

The 2013 SMS takes a much more forward-leaning approach to the role of the Second Artillery (now the Rocket Force) in carrying out space operations. The 2013 SMS describes the Second Artillery as "an important reliance for the expansion of our military's operational capabilities"[110] and states that as national interests expand military competition in the space domain is only increasing and has placed new requirements on military capabilities. It notes that because of the nature of its ballistic missile mission, the Second Artillery is inherently a space organization. Ballistic missile warheads, for example, pass through space to reach their targets. Consequently, ballistic missile defense capabilities and the means to defeat them are also associated with space operations. The 2013 SMS also notes that ballistic missiles, with little modification, can also launch satellites into space and serve as anti-satellite weapons. As a result, the text concludes that "the Second Artillery...possesses the basic infrastructure and hardware, as well as the personnel, and knowledge to rapidly develop space capabilities" and "has a solid foundation and the favorable conditions to both develop space capabilities and implement space operations, and is an important cornerstone for the expansion of our military's operational capabilities into the space domain."[111]

In carrying out this role, the 2013 SMS states that initial strikes conducted by the Second Artillery will be aimed at paralyzing an adversary's operational systems, possibly including satellites.[112] This first strike would target reconnaissance and early warning, electronic warfare, and air and missile defense systems, and aviation targets. The text also states:

> Under special circumstances, it may also exploit the distinct advantage of missiles by attacking an adversary's military satellites and other space network and information system nodes; [this would] influence the adversary's operations systems, awe the opponent, and create conditions for us to gain the strategic initiative and quickly achieve strategic goals.[113]

Conclusion

The examination conducted here of the role of outer space in China's military strategy reveals an evolution of thinking among scholars at the PLA's top think tank, the Academy of Military Science and its top school, the National Defense University. The conceptualization of outer space as a military domain has transitioned from an integrated, but secondary element of the air domain that had the *potential* to provide salient effects on the battlefield to an independent and essential domain that has real and consequential implications for the outcomes of modern wars. These assessments of the importance of outer space is based on its importance to the national interest and the global political situation.

According to AMS, outer space is a domain of increasing economic and military utility whose importance has reached a critical mass. The United States, however, is seen as improving its advantage in space and actively seeking to contain China and suppress its rise as a political, economic, and military power in general and as a space power in particular. China, consequently, must develop technologies to both exploit the benefits of space and defend its interests there.

Indeed, the apparent conclusion that space will form one leg of a new triad involving nuclear, space, and cyber forces suggests that AMS analysts see the PLA being substantially committed to the use of space as an instrument of national power. This conclusion is based on their assessment that these three capabilities have an overall effect on a country's economy, society, and national security.[114]

Moreover, AMS's assessment appears to be substantiated by a real commitment to the PLA's space capabilities. China's military strategy not only set the requirements for the development of space and counterspace technologies, but is also product of their development. In this sense, although the authors of the three editions of the SMS do not discuss specific technology developments, it appears likely that Chinese developments in space technology have reached a level of utility that required the authors of the 2013 SMS to contemplate its ramifications at the strategic level of war.

Indeed, China has made tremendous advancements in space technologies since the 1999 SMS was published. China had conducted just four launches in 1999 and had just a handful of operating satellites in orbit that were of minimal utility. Since 2010, however, China has regularly launched at least 14 rockets and as of August 2015 had 142 operating satellites in orbit of relevant and increasing utility. As of August 2015, China had a 17-satellite navigation constellation that could provide regional capabilities, 43 remote sensing satellites with varying types of sensors, and 14 communication satellites.[115] Moreover, China appears to be developing a wide variety of counterspace capabilities, including direct ascent, co-orbital, and cyber, which are intended to threaten the satellites of potential adversaries.

The conclusions reached by the 2013 SMS on space operations, however, must be tempered by the fact that a body of Chinese literature already exists on the military uses of space and that many of the assessments provided by authors of the various editions of SMS, especially the 2013 edition, have already been proposed by numerous other researchers in studies published between 2000 and 2013. Although important differences exist, especially in regards to the description of space as part of an air-space domains, the 2013 SMS appears to draw from these previous works and in this respect demonstrates that PLA thinking on space remains largely consistent even though it has transitioned from less authoritative works written by individual authors to the more authoritative SMS.

The assessments by the authors of the 2013 SMS are also reflected in statements by top Chinese leaders as well as the 2015 Defense White Paper, *China's Military Strategy*, suggesting that the analysis of AMS researchers influence official policy making. The 2013 SMS assessment of the importance of space, for example, is buttressed by CMC Vice Chairman Xu Qiliang, who wrote in a 2015 article that "China is on its way to building itself into a maritime, space and cyber power" and that "the ocean, outer space, and cyberspace are strategic areas for military competition." [116] Similarly, both the 2013 SMS and *China's Military Strategy* view the world with trepidation. Like the 2013 SMS, *China's Military Strategy* sees factors for peace as increasing, but also maintains that "new threats from hegemonism, power politics and neo-interventionism" have emerged and that "international competition for the redistribution of power, rights and interests is tending to intensify." The 2015 DWP concludes that "the world still faces both immediate and potential threats of local wars." One important threat facing China is the increasing speed of the revolution in military affairs that presents "new and severe challenges to China's military security."

This unsettled view of the world situation is brought about by an expansion of threats to China's interests. According to the white paper, "In the new circumstances, the national security issues facing China encompass far more subjects, extend over a greater range, and cover a longer time span than at any time in the country's history." To deal with these expanding security issues, the military must be able to "safeguard China's security and interests in new domains," be able to deal with "a wide variety of emergencies and military threats" and "prepare for military struggle in all directions and domains." One of these new domains is outer space, which the white paper calls "a commanding height in international strategic competition" and states that "threats from such new security domains as outer space and cyber space will be dealt with to maintain the common security of the world community."

The 2013 SMS, however, takes a much more cautionary approach to space than sources focusing on space at the operational level of war. References to counterspace actions in the 2013 SMS are often prefaced by the caveats "when necessary" or "under special circumstances" that are not only not used by earlier, but admittedly less authoritative sources, but also by the more recent but more authoritative *Study of Space Operations Textbook*, also published by AMS. The 2013 SMS states, for example, that the first shots in space *may* occur in outer space and cyber, whereas the authors of *Study of Space Operations Textbook* write that China will "do all it can at the *strategic* level to avoid firing the first shot" (emphasis added), [117] but then recommend that China should "strive to attack first at the campaign and tactical levels in order to maintain the space battlefield initiative." [118] They also argue that fighting a quick war with a quick resolution is one of the "special characteristics of space operations" and that a military should "conceal the concentration of its forces and make a decisive large-scale first strike." [119]

This discrepancy is especially apparent in the 2013 SMS discussion of space deterrence, where the authors state explicitly that China should not initiate an attack in space, especially against a strong opponent like the U.S. military. The discrepancy could be the result of individual PLA-authored books dealing with war at different levels—some taking a strategic focus, others more operational. The 2013 SMS, for example, recognizes that the pace of modern wars is much quicker than wars in the past[120] and that "the struggle to seize the battlefield initiative is unusually fierce"[121] which places a premium on seizing the initiative as quickly as possible at the outset of a war. Indeed, the 2013 SMS acknowledges the importance of seizing the initiative as early as possible in a campaign and that information superiority is the foundation for seizing the initiative.[122]

Further muddying the waters are other passages in the 2013 SMS that appear to contradict this more cautionary approach to deterrence. One way stated by the 2013 SMS for the PLA to overcome a superior enemy is to "create a favorable posture for the initiative prior to combat" not only through economic and diplomatic means, but also by degrading an enemy's command system through "military deterrent measures" against space and cyber forces.[123] These include an assessment by the authors that future wars may possibly begin in outer space and cyber space and that achieving space and cyber space superiority will be essential to winning future wars.

One way to square this circle is that Chinese strategists may consider the crossing of certain red lines, and not actual combat, as the start of a war. For a potential Taiwan contingency, this includes a declaration of independence by Taiwan, the development of nuclear weapons, or the stationing of foreign forces on the island, but for other contingencies these red lines are unknown. It may also be that Chinese strategists view the escalation of a crisis past some turning point as the start of war. According to the 2013 SMS, "containing war requires being sufficiently prepared and having reliable capabilities, both materially and spiritually, to win the war. But once war is unavoidable, there should be a decisive shot and war should be used to stop war."[124] This was seen in China's entry into the Korean War where the crossing of the 38th parallel by United Nations forces triggered an unannounced commitment of Chinese forces.

These questions aside, the main thrust of sources designating outer space as an independent domain suggests that the PLA will be required to develop a concept of operations for the use of space. This may also require designating space as a distinct operational campaign, something which has yet to be done.[125] Although it may be too early to determine the specifics of a space doctrine for the PLA, based on the three editions of the *Science of Military Strategy* examined here as well as the 2015 Defense White Paper, it may be possible to identify the broad contours of a doctrine. This doctrine could include as its basis a necessity to achieve space superiority, defined as the ability to use space and deny its use to an enemy. This would entail developing a robust space-based C4ISR system to enable the PLA to defend China's interest far from its land borders, including through the use of long-range precisions strikes. It would also entail taking an offensive approach to space that emphasizes degrading or destroying an adversary's space assets early in a conflict. This would differ from the U.S. military's approach, which emphasizes the use of counterspace measures to maintain access to space capabilities.[126]

Finally, the apparent conclusion that space will form one leg of a new triad involving nuclear, space, and cyber forces further suggests that AMS believes that China should be substantially committed to space as an instrument of national power. As a result, AMS appears to advocate the development of strategic-level capabilities that can serve to inoculate China's rise from U.S. military action. Its nuclear deterrent prevents the United States from conducting "nuclear blackmail" against China by threatening devastating retaliation against U.S. society in general. Its space and cyber forces, on the other hand, while not as destructive as nuclear weapons, are directed at the technological underpinnings of the U.S. military and economy by threatening the ability of the U.S. military to wage modern war and the U.S. economy to function effectively. As a result, space is a strategic-level capability that not only helps drive China's rise, but is also a strategic deterrent that prevents others from derailing China's plans to become a major power.

NOTES

[1] M. Taylor Fravel, "The Evolution of China's Military Strategy: Comparing the 1987 and 1999 Editions of Zhanluexue" in James Mulvenon and David Finkelstein (eds.), *China's Revolution in Doctrinal Affairs: Emerging Trends in the Operational Art of the Chinese People's Liberation Army*, RAND, Washington, DC, p. 81.

[2] Wang Wenrong, ed., Science of Strategy [战略学], (Beijing: National Defense University Press, 1999), pp. 99–100. Hereafter SMS 1999.

[3] SMS 1999, pp. 100–101.

[4] SMS 1999, pp. 68–69.

[5] David M. Finkelstein, "China's National Military Strategy," in James Mulvenon and Richard Yang, *The People's Liberation Army in the Information Age*, (Santa Monica: RAND, 1999), pp. 127–128.

[6] For a discussion of how the 1999 and 2001 editions of SMS compare and contrast, see M. Taylor Fravel, "The Evolution of China's Military Strategy: Comparing the 1987 and 1999 Editions of Zhanluexue" in James Mulvenon and David Finkelstein (eds.), *China's Revolution in Doctrinal Affairs: Emerging Trends in the Operational Art of the Chinese People's Liberation Army*, RAND, Washington, DC, pp. 79–99.

[7] SMS 1999, pp. 273–274.

[8] SMS 1999, pp. 273–274.

[9] SMS 1999, p. 274.

[10] SMS 1999, p. 228.

[11] SMS 1999, p. 322.

[12] SMS 1999, pp. 325–326; 340–341.

[13] SMS 1999, p. 333.

[14] SMS 1999, p. 341.

[15] SMS 1999, pp. 325–326.

[16] Peng Guangqian and Yao Youzhi, The Science of Military Strategy [战略学], (Beijing: Academy of Military Sciences Press, 2001), pp. 465–466. Hereafter SMS 2001.

[17] SMS 2001, p. 467.

[18] SMS 2001, pp. 468–470.

[19] SMS 2001, pp. 472–476.

[20] SMS 2001, p. 475.

[21] SMS 2001, p. 443.

[22] SMS 2001, pp. 361–362.

[23] SMS 2001, p. 363.

[24] SMS 2001, p. 71.

[25] SMS 2001, p. 71.

[26] SMS 2001, pp. 132–133, 237, 234–240, 243, 303.

[27] SMS 2001, p. 304.

[28] SMS 2001, p. 304.

[29] SMS 2001, pp. 304–306.

[30] SMS 2001, p. 303.

[31] SMS 2001, p. 443.

[32] SMS 2001, p. 323.

[33] SMS 2001, p. 19.

[34] SMS 2001, p. 133.

[35] For more on the New Historic Missions, see Daniel M. Hartnett, "The 'New Historic Missions:' Reflections on Hu Jintao's Military Legacy," in Roy Kamphausen, David Lai, and Travis Tanner, *Assessing the People's Liberation Army in the Hu Jintao Era,"* (Carlisle: U.S. Army War College Press, 2014), pp. 31–79.

[36] China Academy of Military Science (AMS) Military Strategy Studies Department, [战略学], (Beijing: Academy of Military Sciences Press December 2013), pp. 242 and 247.

[37] SMS 2013 , 182.

[38] SMS 2013 , 247.

[39] SMS 2013 , p. 21.

[40] SMS 2013 , p. 72.

[41] SMS 2013 , p. 78.

[42] SMS 2013 , p. 105.

[43] SMS 2013 , pp. 105–106.

[44] SMS 2013 , pp. 105–106.

[45] SMS 2013 , p. 105.

[46] SMS 2013 , p. 105.

[47] SMS 2013 , p. 73.

[48] SMS 2013 , p. 73.

[49] SMS 2013 , 185.

[50] Ibid.

[51] Ibid.

[52] SMS 2013 , p. 180.

[53] SMS 2013 , pp. 180 and 183.

[54] SMS 2013 , p. 184.

[55] SMS 2013 , p. 254.

[56] SMS 2013 , p. 255.

[57] SMS 2013 , p. 255.

[58] SMS 2013 , p. 258.

[59] Mao Zedong, *Selected Military Writings of Mao Zedong*, Beijing: Foreign Languages Press, 1967, p. 105.

[60] SMS 2013 , p. 170.

[61] SMS 2013 , p. 149.

[62] SMS 2013 , p. 246.

[63] SMS 2013 , p. 246.

[64] SMS 2013 , p. 105.

[65] State Information Council, *China's Military Strategy*, May 26, 2015, http://eng.mod.gov.cn/Database/WhitePapers/.

[66] SMS 2013 , p. 125.

[67] SMS 2013 , p. 93.

[68] SMS 2013 , p. 97.

[69] SMS 2013 , p. 94.

[70] SMS 2013 , p. 108.

[71] SMS 2013 , p129.

[72] SMS 2013 , pp. 127–129.

[73] SMS 2013 , p. 129.

[74] SMS 2013 , p. 179.

[75] SMS 2013 , p. 179.

[76] SMS 2013 , p. 179.

[77] SMS 2013 , p. 96.

[78] SMS 2013 , p. 102.

[79] SMS 2013 , p. 96.

[80] SMS 2013 , p. 102.

[81] SMS 2013 , pp. 100, 118, 130.

[82] SMS 2013 , p. 181.

[83] SMS 2013 , p. 100.

[84] SMS 2013 , p. 182.

[85] SMS 2013 , p. 186.

[86] SMS 2013 , p. 187.

[87] SMS 2013, p. 186.

[88] SMS 2013, p. 182.

[89] SMS 2013, p. 185–187.

[90] SMS 2013, p. 187.

[91] SMS 2013, p. 187.

[92] SMS 2013, p. 188.

[93] SMS 2013, p. 182.

[94] SMS 2013, p. 182.

[95] SMS 2013, p. 183.

[96] SMS 2013, p. 187.

[97] SMS 2013, p. 188.

[98] SMS 2013, p. 183.

[99] Wang Shibin and An Puzhong, "习近平向中国人民解放军陆军火箭军战略支援部队授予军旗并致训词"[Xi Jinping Confers Military Flags to

Chinese People's Liberation Army Ground Force, Rocket Force, and Strategic Rocket Force," 中国军网 (China Military Net), January 1, 2016, http://www.81.cn/sydbt/2016-01/01/content_6839896.htm.

[100] See, for example, "战略支援部队其实就是天网军：将改变战争"[The Strategic Support Force is actually a Space and Cyber Service: It Will Change Warfare], accessed at http://war.163.com/16/0104/08/BCFMF4HF00014J0G.html and "Expert: Strategic Support Force Will Be Involved in the Entire Operation and will be Critical to Achieving Victory," [专家:战略支援部队将贯穿作战全过程 是致胜关键]人民网 (People's Net), January 5, 2016, http://military.people.com.cn/n1/2016/0105/c1011-28011251.html.

[101] David Finkelstein, "2015 Should be an Exciting Year for PLA-Watching," *Pathfinder Magazine*, Vol. 13, No. 1 (Winter 2015), pp. 10–11.

[102] For a discussion of the role PLA analysts see for the PLA Air Force in China's space program, see, Kevin Pollpeter, "The PLAAF and the Integration of Air and Space Power," in Richard P. Hallion, Roger Cliff, Phillip C. Saunders, *The Chinese Air Force Evolving Concepts, Roles, and Capabilities*, (Washington, DC: National Defense University Press), 2012, pp. 165–190.

[103] SMS 2013, p. 218.

[104] Kevin Pollpeter, "The PLAAF and the Integration of Air and Space Power," in Richard P. Hallion, Roger Cliff, and Phillip C. Saunders, *The Chinese Air Force: Evolving Concepts, Roles, and Capabilities*, (Washington, DC: NDU Press, 2012), pp. 176–178.

[105] SMS 2013, p. 221.

[106] SMS 2013, pp. 223–224.

[107] SMS 2013, pp. 226, 227.

[108] SMS 2013, p. 224.

[109] SMS 2013, p. 227.

[110] SMS 2013, p. 229.

[111] SMS 2013, pp. 229–230.

[112] SMS 2013, p. 236.

[113] SMS 2013, p. 236.

[114] SMS 2013, p. 169.

[115] See the Union of Concerned Scientists satellite database at http://www.ucsusa.org/nuclear-weapons/space-weapons/satellite-database#.Vp-yemf2YqQ.

[116] Xu Qiliang, "许其亮: 推进国防军队改革 重塑军队组织形态," [Xu Qiliang: Promote National Defense and Military Reform Adjust the Military Organization], 人民网 [People's Net], November 12, 2015 accessed http://military.people.com.cn/n/2015/1112/c1011-27805432.html.

[117] Jiang Lianju and Wang Liwen (Eds.), *Textbook for the Study of Space Operations* (空间作战学教程), Beijing: Academy of Military Sciences Press, 2013, p. 42.

[118] Jiang Lianju and Wang Liwen (Eds.), *Textbook for the Study of Space Operations* (空间作战学教程), Beijing: Academy of Military Sciences Press, 2013, p. 52.

[119] Jiang Lianju and Wang Liwen (Eds.), *Textbook for the Study of Space Operations* (空间作战学教程), Beijing: Academy of Military Sciences Press, 2013, pp. 142–143.

[120] SMS 2013, p. 97.

[121] SMS 2013, p. 127.

[122] SMS 2013, p. 130.

[123] SMS 2013, p. 129.

[124] SMS 2013, p. 50.

[125] Office of the Secretary of Defense, *Military and Security Developments Involving The People's Republic of China*, 2015, p. 35.

[126] *Joint Publication 3-14: Space Operations*, May 29, 2013, II-8.

Chapter 9: Modernizing Military Intelligence: The PLA Plays Catchup

Peter Mattis

Since the Central Military Commission revised the military strategic guidelines in 1993, directing the People's Liberation Army (PLA) to prepare for "local wars under high-tech conditions," intelligence from the strategic to the tactical level has played an increasingly important role in Chinese thinking about military operations. The critical role of information in modern warfare has been further emphasized in the subsequent conceptual shift from operating under "high-tech conditions" to "informatized conditions (信息化条件下).[1] As noted in previous chapters, the PLA understands intelligence work to be one component of a broader concept of information warfare that encompasses network warfare, political warfare, and electronic warfare. Most of the intellectual groundwork for this theory was laid by the early 2000s, with the publication in 2001 of the *Science Military Strategy* (hereafter *SMS 2001*) and *Science of Military Intelligence*, but the organizational structure and responsibilities of the PLA's intelligence apparatus under the General Staff Department (GSD) initially lagged behind. However, signs of an operational shift in this direction can be seen in both authoritative writings such as the 2013 edition of *Science of Military Strategy* (hereafter SMS 2013) and recent structural changes within the PLA.

By the mid-2000s, the tension between the PLA's conceptual emphasis on intelligence and its actual ability to provide intelligence support across the spectrum of military operations had reached a breaking point. From the Cultural Revolution onward, military intelligence came to occupy a central role in China's national intelligence system, because of long-standing personal relationships to senior party leaders, unique capabilities, and the dissolution of the Chinese Communist Party's (CCP) Central Investigation Department, a bureaucratic rival, in 1968. When the first generation of PLA intelligence leadership finally passed from the scene in the late 1980s and early 1990s, however, a generation of defense attachés without combat or other traditional military experiences took the leadership mantle of military intelligence. A mismatch developed between the PLA's intelligence capabilities and military commanders' information support needs for both situational awareness and targeting precision-guided munitions and missiles. Starting in 2005, the PLA slowly began to reassert itself over its principal intelligence departments, bringing military operators into leadership positions. If military intelligence needed new leadership who understood military operations and the role of intelligence within system of systems operations and winning informatized local wars, then military units at all levels also required officers who understood intelligence. Signs from the top of the military intelligence leadership indicated that intelligence no longer was a terminal career and that options existed for PLA intelligence officers to move into deputy commander positions up to the service level.

Personnel moves, however, would not be enough, and larger organizational changes would be required to reorient the PLA's intelligence apparatus toward military operations. On November 26, 2015, CCP General Secretary and CMC Chairman Xi Jinping announced the most significant organizational overhaul of the PLA since the post-1949 transition from an army geared to fight for control of China to one focused on protecting China's territory. As of July 2016, the full scope and implications of the reforms for intelligence have yet to be established. Xi's reforms included the creation of the Strategic Support Force (SSF) to bring a number of intelligence-related assets, reportedly including satellites and computer network operations, under one roof. Alongside the new SSF, the restructuring of the military regions and the creation of a new ground forces headquarters will have additional effects on the organization of PLA intelligence.

This chapter addresses the evolution of PLA thinking on intelligence in three parts. The first addresses the conclusions that the PLA has developed about intelligence as it prepares to engage in modern warfare under informatized conditions. The second addresses why military intelligence became disconnected over time from the PLA's operational decision-making processes. Finally, the chapter concludes with observations on how the PLA's broader structural reform is affecting its intelligence functions.

Intelligence: Supporting Decision-makers at All Levels

In most Western analysis and media commentary, discussion of China's approach to intelligence has largely focused on human intelligence operations by civilian intelligence agencies and cyber-enabled theft of technological information, almost entirely overlooking the PLA's growing need to use intelligence to drive operations. Most analyses, on the basis of these human and cyber-enabled intelligence operations, have described China as taking an exotic approach wherein intelligence collectors have free reign to gather any information that might potentially be valuable in the present or future, sometimes referred to as a 'grains of sand' strategy.[2] The PLA's approach to intelligence-gathering, however, is more in line with the practice of its counterparts in the United States and other Western militaries.

Intelligence, for the PLA, is knowledge that allows a decision-maker to resolve the specific dilemmas holding them back from reaching a decision. The most influential Chinese concept of intelligence originated with Dr. Qian Xuesen, the U.S.-trained scientist who led China's rocket program from the 1950s onward, and it has been widely used in PLA writings. Qian observed: "Intelligence is the knowledge necessary to solve a specific problem. This view embodies two concepts. One is that [intelligence] is knowledge, not false, nor random. And the other? It is for a specific requirement and also for a specific question, so timeliness and relevance are very important..."[3] Variations of this definition appear in both PLA publications and professional information science journals to which PLA officers contribute. For example, without specific attribution to Qian, the book *Military Informatics* stated that "intelligence is knowledge, the knowledge necessary to solve a specific problem and knowledge that can be transmitted and satisfies [information] needs... the goal of the collection, transmission, and use of intelligence is to understand the situation and resolve problems." From this perspective, the decision-maker and his/her needs are central to the successful production of intelligence. This point was stated explicitly in *Military Informatics*: "the value of intelligence is determined by its degree of usefulness to consumers."[4]

Since decision-makers' needs define its value, intelligence has several characteristic qualities that inform its functioning. Among these qualities are its purposefulness or target-oriented focus (目的性), timeliness (时效性), and confidentiality (保密性). The first two qualities are obvious in the context of supporting decision-makers. Intelligence cannot be random, but must be directed, and intelligence must arrive in advance of a decision for it to be useful. The need for confidentiality in intelligence stems from the role of intelligence in the broader conduct of information warfare; intelligence operations, whether offensive or defensive, occur in an explicitly competitive domain where success is zero-sum and relative to the success of one's adversary.[5]

Perhaps the most important quality of intelligence, however, is the need for selectivity (选择性) at every step of the process from collection to its final delivery to decision-makers. At each step, intelligence officers must make decisions about what to collect, what to validate, and how much effort to expend doing so. After collection, analysts must determine which information requires analysis, and then which information should be forwarded to decision-makers. The consequence of not being selective in the intelligence business is to overload both the intelligence system and decision-makers with unnecessary or irrelevant information, potentially paralyzing the system. Technical sensors in the various battlespaces of future warfare are likely to become more numerous, making this an important trend in intelligence. Unlike the technical solutions to this problem proposed in some U.S. writings, *SMS 2001* suggests improving strategic judgment "to effectively curtail the phenomenon of information overload." Accurate strategic judgment provides guidance for collectors pursuing strategic intelligence and bears no direct relationship to the volume of information available.[6] As China continues to launch satellites, deploy a variety of fixed and mobile radars, airborne-early warning and command and control systems, and several different models of unmanned aerial vehicles for reconnaissance, the amount of information arriving in PLA headquarters is rising steadily.

A final feature of conducting intelligence work, according to both the *Science of Military Intelligence* and *SMS 2001*, is the need to account for one's own side. This offers a distinct counterpoint to the U.S. approach to intelligence that assumes objective, reality-based intelligence support requires distinct operational and intelligence staffs with latter focused on the adversary. The *Science of Military Intelligence* notes "military intelligence should take the enemy's situation as the primary task, but also should not be limited to the adversary's situation (it also should include [one's own] side and related objective circumstances)."[7] *SMS 2001* explains that intelligence plays a role in matching one's specific strengths to an adversary's weakness, and also in helping calibrate coercive measures to control escalation. This cannot be done without being informed as to one's own capabilities.[8]

It is worth noting the ways in which the terms intelligence (情报) and reconnaissance (侦察) are employed in China's intelligence apparatus. These terms sometimes appear to be used interchangeably when referring to intelligence-related units in the PLA. Intelligence bureaus from the Joint Staff Department's Intelligence Bureau (formerly the GSD Second Department, or 2PLA) on down are places where information is compiled, analyzed, and disseminated in some form. These units also may have some collection responsibilities, but this is not definite. In some cases, however, a distinction is made between the two. Military reconnaissance units, such as the technical reconnaissance bureaus previously associated with the services and military regions, perform the "action taken to obtain the required intelligence for national security and military conflicts." Technical reconnaissance (技术侦察) refers specifically to "the use of technical equipment or technical means to carry out reconnaissance."[9] Although this distinction has little to do with how the PLA views intelligence in the Information Age, it is a critical component for understanding how the Chinese military is reorganizing intelligence work within the Joint Staff Department and the Strategic Support Force.

The Roles of Intelligence in an Informatizing World

Intelligence serves three basic roles for the PLA. The first, as noted above, is supporting decision-making at all levels from the Central Military Commission (CMC) down to the tactical level. It is a recognized and valued military staff function. The second is enabling deterrence and compellence, so that controlled pressure can be applied to a foreign country without triggering a war. The third is enabling information warfare in which intelligence plays a role at every level, including how to understand an adversary's society and social structures, and across each information warfare discipline.

First, intelligence supports strategic decision-making at the level of the Central Military Commission (CMC) and other military command and management responsibilities, such as army building. It is a recognized and valued general staff function.

Without elements of a general staff to handle intelligence, the PLA could not function on the basis of "calculations, scientific evaluations, and verifications" and could not coordinate their activities to execute a chosen strategy. This has remained a consistent point through the release of the 2013 edition of the *Science of Military Strategy*, which emphasizes strategic intelligence as a necessary component of both the art and science of strategy.[10]

Going forward, the PLA has held since at least 2001 that the proliferation of technical sensors and digital forms of intelligence data will continue to reshape the discipline, both in terms of what intelligence can do and how to organize intelligence support. Data stored and communicated in electronic form allows the pluralization of intelligence users, because of the ease with which it can be collected and disseminated.[11] In a later set of observations, PLA scholars also noted that local informatized war places a burden on intelligence collection to be flexible enough to deal with rapidly-changing circumstances.[12]

In the early 2000s, the PLA expected that several other related qualities of intelligence would also change under modern, informatized conditions. The first was the thoroughness in reconnaissance, which is moving the battlefield toward greater transparency. Intelligence needs greater comprehensiveness and precision to exploit the opportunities and vulnerabilities of informatized warfare. The second was the need for the capability to disseminate intelligence to commanders in real time for their decision-making and support precision strikes as those responsible for firing weapons needed targeting information and bomb damage assessment. The traditional model of intelligence involves a lengthy process of collection, assessment, and dissemination that cannot keep up with the modern battlefield. The third was the automation of information management. The explosion of information that modern intelligence could gather threatens to overwhelm existing intelligence procedures and could not be managed by human hands, alone and unaided. The fourth was the integration of information systems across different military services. At the time, each service operated on different networks with different hardware and software protocols. Integrating these different systems allows for a shared intelligence picture and joint operations as well as the ability to exploit the potential of automation.[13]

Nothing in the more recent PLA publications, like SMS 2013, suggests PLA thinkers misunderstood where the world of intelligence was going. These publications focus on applying intelligence in this world rather than developing any new ideas.

Second, the PLA considers intelligence to be a critical component of deterring would-be adversaries and conducting coercive diplomacy, both of which are encompassed by the same Chinese term weishe (威慑). SMS 2001 highlights several tasks that intelligence must perform to guide decision-makers in these endeavors. The first is to provide a systematic understanding of the other side's decision-making, including both organizational and psychological factors. This enables the formulation of actions that will result in psychological shock. The second is to help China's leaders calibrate and match Chinese objectives to the right strength of coercive or deterrent measures. Keeping these two objectives in balance is necessary in order to avoid missteps that might mistakenly escalate a situation. The third is to target deterrent measures against "a target that the enemy must save," forcing the adversary to cede the initiative, take defensive action, and/or withdraw. Such targeting hides the vulnerabilities of one's own side. Finally, intelligence provides a feedback mechanism that alerts Chinese decision-makers to how the adversary is responding to the PLA's coercive or deterrent measures. A properly working intelligence feedback mechanism helps Beijing maintain the initiative, because intelligence allows decision-makers to respond promptly and with confidence to the inevitable crises and contingencies that arise when force is used against an adversary.[14]

Third, supporting deterrence operations highlights the expansive nature of intelligence support to information warfare in the broadest sense. Placing intelligence within this framework links it directly to the creation and use of covert power apart from its uses to support decision makers. Chinese military thinkers label intelligence as one of the four components of information warfare, which also includes network warfare, political/psychological warfare, and electromagnetic warfare. Each of these areas, including intelligence warfare, is where the PLA seeks an advantage over an adversary's decision-making processes, ranging from how information is collected to how it is understood, communicated, and used. Because an adversary is not transparent about any of these areas, intelligence is required to map the adversary's networks, society, sensors, and intelligence apparatus. Surveying the adversary's information landscape is prerequisite for all other elements of information warfare. Thus, as the *Science of Military Intelligence* described it, modern information warfare has shifted intelligence from a "subordinate and protective" role to a leading role in identifying what operational goals to pursue and targets to strike.[15]

This connection to information warfare also highlights that in the Chinese view intelligence encompasses not only specific information about an adversary's capabilities and intentions, but also the broader aspects of how an adversary's government, military, and other systems process information and function at a social level. While this latter element may not appear in Chinese descriptions of the work of the general staff, it has appeared in the *Political Work Regulations for the People's Liberation Army* consistently since at least 1963. [16] The regulations include an imperative "to investigate and study the condition of the enemy forces, and to lead in the work designed to dis-integrate enemy forces." [17] In Ye Zheng's *Lectures on Information Operations Studies*, this kind of intelligence work includes "the enemy's national state of affairs, the circumstances of the enemy's military, the psychological warfare situation of the enemy's military, the circumstances that the enemy currently faces, and the real psychological state of our own military and the state of our own equipment and materials, etc." [18] The targets of information warfare go beyond purely military targets and methods, encompassing a broad array of targets in the political, economic, diplomatic, and technological arenas from the strategic down to the tactical level.[19]

Embedding intelligence within information warfare emphasizes the competitive aspects of intelligence that are not always evident in the context of decision support functions. Beyond collection capabilities, it extends to protective measures designed to ensure the integrity of one's own information processing system. Apart from preventing the adversary from collecting intelligence effectively on one's own side, the defensive side of intelligence includes concealing sources, methods, and results.[20] This is one of the reasons PLA writers emphasize the importance of space-based intelligence assets for signals and electronic intelligence collection in addition to imagery. Satellites may be easy to identify, but their specific capabilities and operations are not readily discernible by an outside observer. This helps preserve the viability of the collection effort, even if identified by the adversary.[21]

Most importantly, key PLA writings imply that this integration means that intelligence should work closely with the units responsible for the other aspects of information warfare in the network, psychological, and electromagnetic fields. At the time these ideas were expressed in the early 2000s, the PLA intelligence and information warfare apparatus included the following:

- GSD Second Department (Intelligence);
- GSD Third Department (Technical Reconnaissance);
- GSD Fourth Department (Electro-magnetic Warfare);
- GSD Communications Department (renamed the Informatization Department in 2011);[22]
- General Political Department Liaison Department;
- Intelligence bureaus and technical reconnaissance bureaus within the Military Regions and services.

This organizational landscape created multiple lines of effort reporting to several different senior officers. Relatedly, the command and control of Chinese military satellites also presents a complex picture, because various reports suggest several different departments may have had competing authorities over how they were employed.[23] The GSD chief, assisted by the deputy chief responsible for foreign affairs and intelligence, was the closest the PLA had to an officer capable of coordinating a large body of activities across the spectrum of information warfare. These officers, however, also had a broad set of responsibilities, like representing the PLA on central leading small groups, meeting with foreign militaries, and operational oversight for routine military operations. There was no top-level information warfare staff or other organizational apparatus to bring these lines of effort together—at least from the peacetime organizational chart.

How the PLA Lost Its Intelligence Apparatus

The PLA's intelligence apparatus slowly drifted from military control beginning in the late 1960s as it became the principal intelligence provider to the central leadership. A series of reinforcing developments limited the PLA's control over its intelligence apparatus and prevented military intelligence from evolving alongside the rest of the PLA as the military moved toward 'system-of-systems' operations beginning in the 1990s.

Intelligence services operate within a larger national context that places additional demands on their members beyond their own chain of command. Regardless of whether intelligence services are national or departmental, their capabilities to collect and analyze intelligence are national resources that can be called upon by national leadership as desired. From 1966 through at least 1976, the PLA's intelligence organizations were among the only functioning services that could support the party leadership. The turmoil caused by the Cultural Revolution led to the dissolution of the Central Investigation Department and the Ministry of Public Security's foreign intelligence units. Those in any kind of routine contact with foreigners often faced espionage accusations, and the tight compartmentalization with which sources were handled ensured that few if any other officers could vouch for or defend those accused. As the state ministries and the party bureaucracy shut down, the civilian intelligence organizations appear to have turned their sources and operations over to military intelligence.[24]

The intelligence leadership within the General Staff Department (GSD) also underwent a generational turnover that privileged the general foreign affairs expertise of defense attachés over expertise gained through operations or providing direct intelligence support to PLA commanders. These officers were exemplified by Xiong Guangkai (熊光楷), who served tours in East and West Germany as a defense attaché. Xiong served as deputy director and then director of 2PLA (1984–1988 and 1988–1992, respectively) before becoming the deputy chief of the general staff responsible for overseeing intelligence and foreign affairs from 1998 to 2005.[25] Prior to Xiong's rise to the top of 2PLA, the department's chiefs had operational intelligence experience in combat during the Chinese Revolution, War of Resistance against Japan, or the Korean War. From Xiong's directorship onward, however, only one of the seven 2PLA directors, Chen Xiaogong (陈小工), had any combat or operational experience.[26]

The centrality of military intelligence remained even after the Cultural Revolution and the reestablishment of party-state intelligence functions in a briefly reconstituted Central Investigation Department and, in 1983, the Ministry of State Security (MSS). Several reasons account for the PLA's overall importance to Chinese policymakers. First, the PLA possesses the only all-source intelligence capability within the Chinese system, and there is no reason to believe intelligence is shared across the divide between the civilian ministries and the PLA on a routine basis. Shared operational platforms suggest the civilian and military intelligence services share intelligence in at least one area, but the need to keep building new intra-governmental centers for security operations suggests intelligence is not routinely integrated.[27] Second, the senior-most PLA intelligence officer, who up until the recent reorganization was a GSD deputy, sits on the leading small groups (LSG) that guide foreign and security policy, such as the Foreign Affairs and the Taiwan Affairs LSGs. The MSS would not join the Foreign Affairs LSG until the mid-1990s, more than twelve years after the MSS was formed. Third, in 1985, Deng Xiaoping placed draconian restrictions on the MSS that reduced its presence in China's embassies and ability to recruit sources abroad. These constraints were not lifted until at least the 2000s.[28] Despite having its own presence in the embassies and other official platforms like Xinhua, the PLA was not subject these restrictions.

Personal relationships also helped isolate the PLA intelligence apparatus from military's direct control. From Deng Xiaoping's rehabilitation as GSD chief in 1975 to Xiong's ascension to GSD deputy in 1998, the intelligence leadership were all veterans of the 8th Route Army with a direct personal connection to Deng. These close personal ties and relaxed operational restrictions suggest Deng was comfortable relying on the PLA for his intelligence needs.[29] The close relationship between General Secretary Jiang Zemin and Xiong also boosted the centrality of military intelligence and probably cemented the drift between the PLA as a whole and its intelligence apparatus. Reportedly, this relationship was close enough that Jiang attempted to install Xiong at the MSS to assert control and boost the ministry's intelligence collection against Taiwan.[30] Other rumors suggest Xiong turned PLA signals intelligence and other intelligence capabilities on the PLA leadership to help Jiang outmaneuver the military bureaucracy in implementing de-commercialization and oversee day-to-day management of the PLA.

These factors held back the PLA's intelligence apparatus from adapting to the changing requirements for intelligence work within an informatizing military. After the retirement of Xiong in December 2005, however, the PLA slowly began reasserting control over military intelligence. The changes began at the leadership level, where senior intelligence leaders now had the opportunity for promotion or lateral moves into operational roles as deputy commanders. Intelligence stars like Chen, Yang Hui (杨辉), and Wu Guohua (吴国华), who might have retired early in view of their terminal career prospects, moved to the PLA Air Force, Nanjing Military Region, and Second Artillery, respectively. The GSD deputy chiefs after Xiong all came from operational backgrounds, such as former GSD Operations Department chief Zhang Qingsheng (章沁生) and former pilot and now PLA Air Force Commander Ma Xiaotian (马晓天).[31] Anecdotal evidence also has started to emerge that such interchanges between operations and intelligence personnel are occurring at lower levels, giving some officers time abroad in military attaché billets and moving mid-career intelligence officers into deputy unit commander billets.

Reforming the Military, Reforming Intelligence

On November 26, 2015, CMC Chairman Xi Jinping announced far-reaching military reforms to reshape and reorganize the PLA. Old structures, like the military region system, were wiped away, and the ground forces, long dominant in every major but ostensibly "joint" PLA department, appear to have lost their pride of place. Amid the propaganda fanfare over new organizational structures, the PLA made almost no announcements that explicitly noted how the military organized and reorganized intelligence work. However, a tentative analysis is still possible, because of how systematically the PLA has organized itself and intelligence work. The definitive changes as of this writing are relatively few, but this section addresses what is known from the portions of the PLA restructuring already announced, what can be deduced from information that is definitively known, and speculation regarding additional changes that may emerge in the future.

Chinese sources suggest three main changes have taken place since the announcement of the PLA reforms in last November. First, many of the now-defunct General Staff Department's (GSD) intelligence functions have been transferred to the new Joint Staff Department (JSD). The GSD deputy chief responsible for intelligence and foreign affairs, Admiral Sun Jianguo (孙建国), is now a JSD deputy chief and continues to represent the PLA to foreign audiences in Beijing and at forums like the Shangri-La Dialogue in Singapore.[32] Sun also continues to serve as the president of the China Institute for International and Strategic Studies (CIISS), a position with some authority in the military intelligence community.

Second, the JSD includes an intelligence bureau (情报局), a unit that is most likely a renamed 2PLA.[33] Historically, Chinese organizational charts have included 2PLA as the intelligence department and listed the GSD Third Department (3PLA) as the technical reconnaissance department. None of the sources identifying the JSD organizational structure identifies any bureau still within the department that could be 3PLA. While some reports suggest that 3PLA has moved elsewhere, possibly into the Strategic Support Force (SSF), no definitive Chinese sources have yet clarified how 3PLA's intelligence capabilities have been disposed.

Third, based on personnel movements, the 2PLA's Aerospace Reconnaissance Bureau appears to have moved over to the SSF as part of a broader move to bring space assets under one command.[34] The most visible movement occurred from the now-defunct General Armaments Department, where the department's space organizations have moved over to the new force.

Inferences about the future of PLA intelligence also can be made on the basis of the broader structural changes. The most important of these is the creation of a new headquarters department for the ground forces. Previously, the GSD served as both the joint staff for the PLA as a whole as well as the headquarters for the ground forces. The ground forces' dominance of GSD leadership positions probably skewed most of the staff work toward supporting their operational needs and political desires. Splitting the JSD and the ground forces headquarters allows each to focus on their respective responsibilities without muddling the two. The split almost certainly breaks up elements of the GSD's intelligence departments in order to send them over to either the ground forces or the newly-created theater commands. The most likely GSD elements to move are the units that provide tactical level support, such as an unmanned aerial vehicle (UAV) regiment and other technical reconnaissance units.[35] The ground forces headquarters also is likely to host at least an intelligence department/bureau to provide strategic intelligence support to ground forces leadership.

More speculatively, the PLA will likely divide the former military regions' intelligence and technical reconnaissance bureaus between the five new theater commands and the SSF. Intelligence is a common headquarters component and a recognized staff function. One of the lessons the PLA drew from its experiences during the Chinese Revolution and Civil War was the need to keep intelligence close to decision-makers, and modern PLA writings, as noted above, emphasize the need for a close connection. Even if the military region's collection capabilities were given wholly to the SSF, their intelligence bureaus probably would be reconstituted among the theater commands' headquarters to process incoming information for the command's specific needs.

The PLA appears unlikely to resolve the contradiction between the need to centralize information warfare capabilities and the different bureaucratic rice bowls in intelligence work. Intelligence always will be a military staff function, and the JSD should rightfully have a stake in both intelligence capabilities and supporting decision-makers at senior levels. The real question of bureaucratic conflict lies between the SSF and the Political Work Department (previously the General Political Department).

The SSF appears likely to aggregate a number of information warfare capabilities under a single command structure, especially those relating to network warfare and electromagnetic warfare. The SSF also appears to be taking control over several space-related units that once belonged to the General Armament Department and the General Staff Department, suggesting the SSF now controls the PLA's intelligence satellites. This gives the SSF important resources in three of the four information warfare disciplines. The principal department responsible for political/psychological warfare as well as the intelligence-related functions outlined in the Political Work Guidelines is the Liaison Department (probably now the Liaison Bureau within the Political Work Department). The changes to the guidelines in 2003 and 2010 emphasized the importance of political officers becoming part of the PLA's warfighting capability, and other publications about modular force groupings within evolving system of systems operations included political/psychological warfare units.[36] So long as the Liaison Department (or its successor) remains within the Political Work Department, information warfare will operate under divided commands that only unify at the CMC level.

The unknowns remain quite substantial. For example, as of June 2016, many of the technical reconnaissance bureaus (TRB) for the services and military regions appear to be in existence, but no information published online after the reorganization links them to the services, the new theater commands, or the SSF. The guiding phrase for the reform, "the CMC leads, the theater commands fight, and the services equip" (军委管总、战区主战、军种主建), suggests the TRBs will be moved over to or carved up for the SSF or the theater commands. If the services should be focused on equipping their forces, then it makes little sense for them to possess tactical intelligence collection capabilities.

The building of an alternative center for intelligence work also raises the question of how the PLA will train the intelligence personnel for the SSF to better support military operations at the tactical level. The traditional intake into the military intelligence services comes from the Nanjing International Relations Institute and the Luoyang Foreign Language Institute as well as the PLA Information Engineering University. Technical and area studies education may work well for training the staff of the old 2PLA, 3PLA, and 4PLA; however, these programs do not translate well into the kind of tactical intelligence support needed for targeting and bomb damage assessment. If intelligence is being integrated more broadly to support operations, then new training programs will need to be created.[37]

Conclusion

PLA thinking on intelligence has evolved remarkably little over the last fifteen years, because, in many respects, it has not been necessary. The PLA's steady modernization effort to conduct joint operations on shared knowledge of the battlefield with precision-guided munitions demanded more from the PLA's intelligence apparatus than it could give without a serious overhaul. The intelligence organizations at the General Staff Department level were ill-suited to provide tactical support, so little in the way of experimentation could be done to develop tactical intelligence doctrine using GSD resources. In a sense, the PLA has not yet seen or tested its thinking about intelligence in any serious way. Though the possibility that intelligence has been tested through exercises cannot be ruled out, there are enough other potential drivers of the current reform drive and the creation of the SSF to view intelligence as an ancillary issue—or only as one part of the broader changes to information operations.[38]

The ambitious set of intelligence missions—supporting decision-making at all levels of command, calibrating deterrence operations, and guiding information warfare—suggests the challenges for PLA intelligence is not in the concepts but the organizational infrastructure to execute. The broad range of intelligence work that goes into these missions requires an equally broad set of training programs that will teach skills that cannot readily transfer from one kind of decision support to another. If the intelligence organizations are centralized, then the new organizations need to be able to reach across the PLA and also tailor its support for the different challenges facing different military units. Moreover, unless the PLA moves away entirely from supporting the Party leadership on foreign affairs, military intelligence also needs to keep officers capable of doing collecting, analyzing, and presenting intelligence to the leadership on foreign countries.

For analysts, the challenge will be identifying the PLA's evolving intelligence posture and how it resolves the challenges it faces. Chinese security authorities are allowing fewer and fewer slipups as they become accustomed to the ways in which researchers and foreign intelligence services exploit the Internet. If the PLA reorganization proceeds down some of the aforementioned lines, then many of the unit identifiers will change over. Many of the PLA's lower-level intelligence bureaus in the services and military regions barely had a public or online footprint, and the lag time in identifying the new units could be months if not years. Moreover, the tools for identifying what is included in military training and education are blunt, especially on a sensitive topic like intelligence. Top-level changes at the level of the JSD and the theater commands probably will be visible; however, the nuts and bolts of making intelligence successful are unlikely to be available.

NOTES

[1] For a summary of these changes to the Military Strategic Guidelines from 1993 onward, see, M. Taylor Fravel, "China's New Military Strategy: 'Winning Informationized Local Wars'," *China Brief*, July 2, 2015.

[2] Peter Mattis, "Assessing Western Perspectives on Chinese Intelligence," *International Journal of Intelligence and Counterintelligence* 25, No. 4 (Fall 2012), pp. 678–699.

[3] Chen Jiugeng, "Regarding Intelligence and Information [关于情报与信息]," *Journal of Information* (情报杂志) 19, No. 1 (January 2000), pp. 4–6.

[4] Yan Jinzhong, ed., *Military Informatics Revised Edition* [军事情报学修订版] (Beijing: Shishi chubanshe, 2003), p. 13.

[5] Ibid., pp. 4–5.

[6] Peng Guangqian and Yao Youzhi, eds., *Science of Military Strategy* [战略学] (Beijing: Military Sciences Press, 2001), p. 218. Hereafter, SMS 2001.

[7] Zhang Shaojun, chief editor, Zhang Shaojun, Li Naiguo, Shen Hua, and Liu Xinming, eds., *The Science of Military Intelligence* [军事情报学] (Beijing: Junshi kexue chubanshe, 2001), p. vi.

[8] SMS 2001, p. 191.

[9] Liu Zonghe and Lu Kewang, eds., *Military Intelligence: China Military Encyclopedia* (2nd Edition) [军事情报: 中国军事百科全书 (第二版)] (Beijing: Zhongguoda baike quanshu chubanshe, 2007), pp. 22, 95.

[10] SMS 2001, p. 214; SMS 2013, p. 264.

[11] Ye Zheng, *Lectures on Information Operations Studies* [信息作战学教程] (Beijing: Academy of Military Sciences Press, 2013), p. 51; Zhang et al, *Science of Military Intelligence*, p. 195.

[12] Xiao Tianliang, ed., *The Science of Military Strategy* [战略学], (Beijing: National Defense University Press, 2015), p. 260.

[13] Zhang et al, Science of Military Intelligence, pp. 195–197.

[14] SMS 2001, pp. 191–193.

[15] Zhang et al, Science of Military Intelligence, pp. 188–189.

[16] David Finklestein, "The General Staff Department of the Chinese People's Liberation Army: Organization, Roles, and Missions," in James Mulvenon and Andrew N.D. Yang, eds., *The People's Liberation Army as Organization Version 1.0* (Santa Monica, CA: RAND, 2002). pp. 126–128.

[17] "Political Work Regulations for the Chinese People's Liberation Army," in Ying-mao Kau, Paul M. Chancellor, Philip E. Ginsburg, and Pierre M. Perrolle, *The Political Work System of the Chinese Communist Military: Analysis and Documents* (Providence, RI: Brown University East Asia Language and Area Center, 1971).

[18] Ye, Lectures on Information Operations Studies, p. 185.

[19] Zhang et al, Science of Military Intelligence, p. 190.

[20] SMS 2001, pp. 297–298.

[21] Ye, Lectures on Information Operations Studies, p. 50.

[22] "PLA General Staff Department's Communications Department Reformed into Informatization Department [解放军总参谋部通信部改编为总参谋部信息化部]," Xinhua, June 30, 2011.

[23] Ian Easton and Mark Stokes, "China's Electronic Intelligence (ELINT) Satellite Developments: Implications for U.S. Air and Naval Operations," Project 2049 Institute, Occasional Paper, February 23, 2011.

[24] David Ian Chambers, "Edging in from the Cold: The Past and Present State of Chinese Intelligence Historiography," *Studies in Intelligence* 56, No. 3 (September 2012), pp. 31–46.

[25] Defense Intelligence Agency, "China: Lieutenant General Xiong Guangkai," Biographic Sketch (Washington, DC, October 1996) Digital National Security Archive.

[26] Chen Xiaogong served as a unit commander again Vietnam, either in 1979 or in the border skirmishes that flared up most noticeably in 1984. His unit reportedly lost more than 20 percent of its strength, suggesting Chen witnessed serious fighting. See, James Mulvenon, "Chen Xiaogong: A Political Biography," *China Leadership Monitor*, No. 22 (Fall 2007).

[27] On the former, see, Peter Mattis, "China's Espionage against Taiwan (Part II): Chinese Intelligence Collectors," *China Brief*, December 5, 2014. On the latter, see, Peter Mattis, "New Law Reshapes Counterterrorism Policy and Operations," *China Brief*, January 25, 2016; Sarah Cook and Leeshai Lemish, "The 610 Office: Policing the Chinese Spirit," *China Brief*, September 16, 2011.

[28] Peter Mattis, "The New Normal: China's Risky Intelligence Operations," *The National Interest*, July 6, 2015; Lu Ning, "The Central Leadership, Supraministry Coordinating Bodies, State Council Ministries, and Party Departments," in *The Making of Chinese Foreign and Security Policy in the Era of Reform 1978–2000*, ed. David Lampton (Stanford, CA: Stanford University Press, 2001), p. 414.

[29] Peter Mattis, "PLA Military Intelligence at 90: Continuous Evolution," Paper presented at Annual CAPS-RAND-NDU Conference, Taipei, Taiwan, November 2015.

[30] Willy Wo-Lap Lam, "Surprise Elevation for Conservative Patriarch's Protégé Given Security Post," *South China Morning Post*, March 17, 1998.

[31] Peter Mattis, "PLA Personnel Shifts Highlight Intelligence's Growing Military Role," *China Brief*, November 5, 2012.

[32] "Senior Military Official Elaborates on China's Regional Security Policy at Shangri-La Dialogue," *Xinhua*, June 5, 2016.

[33] "Central Military Commission Joint Staff Department Internal Structure Gradually Appears [军委联合参谋部内设机构渐次露面]," Duowei News, April 10, 2016.

[34] Yue Huairang [岳怀让], "Chinese Academy of Sciences Academician Zhou Zhixin Moves Over to Strategic Support Force as Bureau Director [中科院院士周志鑫出任战略支援部队某局局长]," The Paper, April 9, 2016.

[35] Elsa Kania and Kenneth Allen, "The Human and Organizational Dimensions of the PLA's Unmanned Aerial Vehicle Systems," China Brief, May 11, 2016.

[36] Kevin McCauley, "System of Systems Operational Capability: Operational Units and Elements," China Brief, March 15, 2013.

[37] The author would like to thank Kenneth Allen for raising this point in November 2015.

[38] John Costello, "The Strategic Support Force: China's Information Warfare Service," China Brief, February 8, 2016; Phillip C. Saunders and Joel Wuthnow, "China's Goldwater-Nichols? Assessing PLA Organizational Reforms," U.S. National Defense University, Institute for National Strategic Studies, Strategic Forum, No. 294 (April 2016).

SECTION IV: CHINA'S STRATEGY BEYOND WARFIGHTING

Chapter 10: China's Evolving Approach to Strategic Deterrence

Dennis J. Blasko[1]

Deterrence is one of the most important elements of Chinese military strategy and doctrine. As part of its larger, self-proclaimed 'strategically-defensive' defense posture, through deterrence China seeks to defend its sovereignty, territorial integrity, and national interests by preventing foreign invasions, averting a variety of threats from "terrorists, separatists and extremists," and limiting conflict escalation in all domains of modern combat.

People's Liberation Army (PLA) strategists see deterrence as a military concept with political and psychological dimensions that requires the comprehensive use of all aspects of national power, leveraging not only military but also political, diplomatic, economic, and scientific/technological means to achieve its goals. They acknowledge that deterrence is based on the credible threat of violence and thus on warfighting capabilities. However, China characterizes its deterrence posture as qualitatively different from that of the United States and other nations.

Compared to the amount of attention paid to advances in PLA warfighting capabilities and military technologies over the past two decades, except for its nuclear deterrence policy, China's multifaceted concept of deterrence has received minimal attention from foreign analysts. Yet, despite having different objectives and indicating different intentions, deterrence and warfighting are intimately connected to one another.

Chinese military literature has frequent references to the tasks of the armed forces to *both* deter and win wars.[2] The series of command and control and force structure reforms announced in 2015 and beginning to be implemented in 2016 are intended to improve the PLA's warfighting capabilities, but they will take several years to execute and fine tune. In the meantime, many PLA personnel are likely to experience institutional instability and many of its organizations will undergo disruptions, which could result in temporary lapses in combat readiness. If successful, however, these reforms will improve the PLA's deterrence posture in the long term.

Most foreign interest naturally focuses on developments in PLA warfighting and technological capabilities and does not explore with equal enthusiasm the deterrence effects of the same developments. Moreover, the Chinese government has not done a particularly good job in explaining to the outside world the components, requirements, and intentions of its multidimensional deterrence posture.

Even the official Defense White Papers have not sufficiently described the theory and nuances of China's overall concept of deterrence. The white papers' first specific reference to deterrence is found in the 2000 edition under the heading of "implementing the military strategy of active defense":

> Strategically, China pursues a principle featuring
> defensive operations, self-defense and gaining
> mastery by striking only after the enemy has

struck. Such defense combines efforts to deter war with preparations to win self-defense wars in time of peace, and strategic defense with operational and tactical offensive operations in time of war.[3]

Subsequent white papers have spoken of deterrence to various degrees, but none of them have provided the theoretical underpinnings of the concept. The latest white paper on strategy again mentions the term in relation to active defense:

A holistic approach will be taken to balance war preparation and war prevention, rights protection and stability maintenance, deterrence and warfighting, and operations in wartime and employment of military forces in peacetime. They will lay stress on farsighted planning and management to create a favorable posture, comprehensively manage crises, and resolutely deter and win wars.[4]

The white paper does not go into further detail about how deterrence and warfighting are balanced holistically or exactly what that means. Though the white papers tell us that deterrence is part of the PLA strategy of "active defense" and China's "self-defensive defense" posture, and that it is linked closely to warfighting, they do not explain the objectives of deterrence, the factors necessary for deterrence, and the various types of deterrence employed by the Chinese armed forces. This information, however, can be found in a number of Chinese military textbooks available to the public, such as the 2001 and 2013 editions of *The Science of Military Strategy*, and articles in the Chinese military media. Moreover, once the theory of deterrence is understood, examples of deterrence in practice can be seen in actions taken by both the Chinese government and the PLA.

Deterrence: One of Three Basic Ways to Use Force

Like its 2001 predecessor, the 2013 edition of *The Science of Military Strategy* (SMS 2013) has an entire chapter dedicated to the topic of deterrence.[5] Deterrence is identified as one of the three basic ways (基本方式) to use force (力量运用): war (战争) or warfighting (作战), military deterrence (军事威慑), and military operations other than war (非战争军事行动, or MOOTW).[6] Accordingly, deterrence should be as much of a consideration as are warfighting or MOOTW in any analysis of PLA doctrine, strategy, objectives, or actions.

This triad of functions is found multiple times in a variety of forms throughout SMS 2013, and represents a fundamental expansion of SMS 2001's assertion that warfighting (实战) and deterrence (威慑) are the *two* major basic functions (基本功能) of the armed forces. The elevation of MOOTW to be part of this triad of functions is a major change in SMS 2013, as significant as the book's acknowledgement of the heightened threat from the maritime direction and the doctrinal adjustments that take into account the new advanced technologies now available to the PLA, such as those found in the aerospace and information warfare domains.

Figure 1 below illustrates this triad of functions and provides examples of the use of force on a spectrum moving, left to right, from peace to war. The vertical line labeled "intentional use of deadly force" is superimposed (by the author) to indicate that actions to the left of that line are not intended to result in casualties. For example, some limited deterrent actions and low-intensity operations could be planned to achieve their objectives through threat and intimidation without the use of deadly force. Nonetheless, somewhere along the spectrum of actions, even while attempting to control the use of force, mistakes or miscalculations can be made which result in death and destruction. Likewise, peacekeeping, anti-terrorism, and domestic stability operations may begin with the intention of not using force, but then escalate to the point where violent action is necessary or perceived to be necessary.

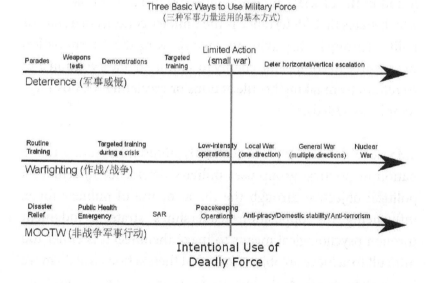

Three Basic Ways to Use Military Force
(三种军事力量运用的基本方式)

Regardless of whether the PLA is conducting warfighting, deterrence, or MOOTW, SMS 2013 stresses that military planners must "carefully estimate each type of difficulty that can be encountered" and prepare to overcome these difficulties.[7] In order to do so, the fundamental requirement of strategic judgment is to "know the enemy and know ourselves."[8] This guidance traces its roots back to Sun Tzu, and along with the objective of "winning without fighting" continues to be the basis for Chinese military strategy.[9]

The PLA's Definition of Deterrence

Perhaps the most succinct Chinese definition of deterrence is found in the official English-language translation of SMS 2001, which states that "deterrence is the military conduct of a state or political group in displaying force or showing the determination to use force *to compel* the enemy to submit to one's volition and *to refrain* from taking hostile actions or escalating the hostility" (emphasis added).[10]

SMS 2013 defines deterrence slightly differently, stating that a nation or political group uses military deterrence to achieve a political objective through the threat or use of military force, influencing the opposition leadership's strategic judgment through psychological means to make them feel it is either too difficult to achieve an objective or that their actions will do more harm than good, and thus to encourage them to give up hostilities.[11] From this perspective, the "nature of deterrence is a threat of violence."

By connecting the threat or use of force (i.e., coercion) to the objectives of either preventing/deterring an event from taking place or coercing/compelling an opponent to change its behavior, Chinese deterrence doctrine enters the semantic debate over the meaning of compellence, coercion, and coercive diplomacy. The late Alexander L. George summarized these distinctions as follows:

> Coercive diplomacy (or compellence, as some prefer to call it) employs threats of force to persuade an opponent to call off or undo its encroachment—for example, to halt an invasion or give up territory that has been occupied. Coercive diplomacy differs, therefore, from the strategy of deterrence, which involves attempts to dissuade an adversary from undertaking an action that has not yet been initiated.[12]

Professor David Lampton adds:

> There is a distinction between deterrence and coercive diplomacy, with the former using threat to <u>prevent an unwanted future action</u> and the latter using threat to persuade an adversary to <u>undo</u> an action already taken. The former is easier than the latter. [13] (Underline in the original)

Despite the distinction between deterrence and coercive diplomacy in the United States, the Chinese definition and theory of deterrence accounts for *both outcomes*, either preventing *or* undoing action through the threat or use of force. Notwithstanding the details of PLA doctrine, some observers prefer to call Chinese actions short of war "coercive diplomacy" instead of deterrence. The Chinese do not use this term to describe any of their activities in any of their official documents or statements.

Moreover, China considers its military deterrence to be fundamentally different from that practiced by the U.S. and other western countries. SMS 2001 compares "offensive strategic deterrence," which is "principally adopted by states or military groups that pursue an invasive expansion strategy," with China's strategic deterrence, which is "self-defense in essence." [14] SMS 2013 states that China's multi-dimensional deterrence posture is intended to deter foreign invasion, prevent conflicts from escalating to war, and counter hegemonic-type deterrence; it is not, they argue, a tool to dominate others. China does not see itself as seeking to use force to threaten or coerce other countries and does not seek regional or global hegemony. Because it obeys the strategic guidelines of active defense, China's deterrence posture is thus "not strategically offensive or pre-emptive" (而不是战略上的进攻和先发制人).[15]

The Fundamentals of Chinese Deterrence

Like the rest of PLA modernization, military deterrence is subordinate to and supports China's overall national security and development strategy. It must be adjusted or adapted according to changes in national security conditions. Though the Chinese government judges the previously-felt threat of large-scale invasion of China to have fundamentally been eliminated, other threats to China's national security are increasing, with some even more challenging and complex than actual war.[16] China faces the danger that crises and conflicts could escalate to become local wars, which could then interfere with or even destroy China's 'period of strategic opportunity' for national development. Thus, controlling crises and deterring (also translated as stopping, preventing, or containing) war are the basic tasks of military deterrence. Great effort must be made to foresee, defuse, and respond to crises. When crises and conflicts occur, all methods must be employed to control them and to deter and delay the outbreak of war.[17]

Deterrence consists of more than just the military component; it entails the use of all aspects of comprehensive national power, such as political, diplomatic, economic, and science and technological means, to achieve national objectives.[18] Actions should be unpredictable, causing the opponent difficulty in decision-making by making him guess constantly. Suitable deterrence objectives must be selected based on available means, and large objective should be avoided when capabilities are insufficient.[19]

SMS 2013 and other authoritative Chinese sources are very clear that deterrence capabilities are based on combat capabilities and that there is no qualitative difference between the form of deterrence forces and combat forces.[20] In short, deterrence capabilities reside in combat capabilities. The integration of deterrence and warfighting (慑战一体), which is called "the soul of war" (其魂在战), is a theme found throughout SMS 2013.[21] This relationship is sometimes described in Marxist terminology, through the assertion that "deterrence of war and winning the war are a dialectical unity."[22] This is what the 2015 Defense White Paper means when it speaks of China's "holistic approach" to deterrence and warfighting.

In addition to possessing effective military capabilities, deterrence also requires the determination to use that force and an information exchange between both the deterring side and the side to be deterred.[23] In other words, for deterrence to be credible, those China seeks to deter must be aware of actual Chinese capabilities and in some way express to China that they have an accurate understanding of Chinese willingness to use its capabilities. Seeking to intimidate through bluffing is ineffective.[24]

Even within the context of the active defense precept of "striking only after being struck," PLA strategists believe it may be necessary to "dare to use war to stop war" (敢于以战止战) or fight a small battle to deter a large war.[25] Throughout the course of deterrent actions, controlling the situation through the timing, intensity, and type of deterrence operations is imperative in order to avoid a crisis escalating into war. Preventive deterrence actions (预防性威慑行动) may be taken to influence the opponent not to act rashly. At the appropriate time, limited but effective warning firepower and information attacks (有限而有效的警示性火力打击和信息攻击) may be employed to stop the enemy from taking further actions.[26] While acknowledging that deterrence may not be effective, i.e., that escalation leading to war may occur, SMS 2013 underscores the preference of resolving issues through deterrence without resorting to warfighting (既要争取慑而不打解决问题), in part by leaving the enemy a route of retreat.[27] Deterrence is to be employed both before and after fighting begins, preferably to avoid war, but also to avoid horizontal escalation (to other regions or strategic directions) or vertical escalation (up the spectrum of violence, especially to nuclear war).

China's Multi-dimensional Deterrence Posture

When many foreigners write about China's deterrence posture, often they consider only its nuclear deterrent. However, SMS 2013 speaks of many types of deterrence, including conventional and nuclear deterrence, space and information deterrence, direct and indirect deterrence, peacetime and 'contingency' deterrence, combat and non-combat deterrence, and local and overall deterrence.[28] In addition to deterring a nuclear strike on the mainland, China seeks to prevent many types of behavior that may damage its core and major interests (核心利益和重大利益).[29]

Threats to China's interests may take many forms, including the activities of separatist forces for "Taiwan independence," "Tibet independence," and "East Turkistan independence."[30] The most possible threat of war is defined as a "limited military conflict" from the direction of the sea, whereas the most serious conceivable threat is a large-scale strategic raid initiated by a powerful enemy seeking to destroy China's war potential. On the spectrum between these two possibilities, the threat that requires the greatest preparation is a relatively large-scale, relatively high-intensity local war in the sea direction against the backdrop of nuclear deterrence.[31] China seeks to prevent a small problem leading to a major concern, to prevent crises from escalating to war, and to deter major military crises.[32]

Based on their historical experience in employing deterrent capabilities, Chinese leaders have determined that they must focus on all types of real as well as potential security threats in order to accurately grasp the country's overall strategic situation. China first seeks to gain the initiative in the overall strategic situation and build strategic momentum through its peacetime actions, thus dissuading the opponent from acting recklessly. [33] SMS 2001 specifically identified "large-scale military reviews, joint military exercises, and military visits" as "deterrent forms" that demonstrate this sort of momentum.[34] In addition to parades, exercises, and international military exchanges, weapons tests could be added to the list, whether they are first made public by China or by the foreign media. Senior CCP and PLA leadership consider the periodic military parades held in Beijing to be part of their deterrence effort. For example, the first display and public acknowledgement of the nuclear and conventional DF-26 intermediate-range ballistic missile and the DF-16 medium-range ballistic missile, along with other ballistic and cruise missiles and advanced weaponry, in the September 2015 "Victory Day Parade" sought to create momentum by demonstrating credible military capabilities for both warfighting and deterrence purposes.

China's multi-dimensional deterrence posture emphasizes the integrated use of a variety of forces, including "the overall strength of the people's war," as well as political, diplomatic, economic, and other military and non-military means.[35] All of these elements of power form a deterrence system, which is tasked to maintain the global strategic balance, to deter local conflicts and wars under informatized conditions, and to safeguard China's maritime sovereignty, rights and interests, and sea lane safety.[36]

These tasks require the PLA's deterrence system to focus on five elements: 1) the peacetime enhancement of the defense of islands and reefs, maritime patrols, declarations of sovereignty, maritime rights, etc., and the needs of maritime military operational capabilities, 2) to improve the effectiveness of maritime and air force projection as the core, 3) to enhance the basic fundamentals of integrated offshore (near sea) operations and distant/far sea defensive operations capabilities, 4) to be able to execute international joint maritime patrols, maritime escort, anti-piracy and maritime strike against terrorist activities (such as the Gulf of Aden escort mission now performed continuously by a series of naval task forces since late 2008), and 5) to create forces and capabilities to project the dual effects of maritime and air power systems.[37]

It goes without saying that China has conducted all of the activities listed above in recent years, many of which have been characterized by foreigners as "assertive" or "aggressive" behavior. Moreover, much routine PLA training, such as amphibious operations, naval task force training beyond the first island chain, and long-distance air operations, are necessary to develop the skills necessary for modern warfare and are now conducted throughout the entire calendar year. Most such training is part of an annual training plan developed in the year before implementation. In order to demonstrate PLA capabilities and determination as an element of "public opinion/media warfare," (one of the PLA's "Three Warfares") China's media now covers many of these exercises more than they were reported in the past and in greater detail.

Quite frequently outside observers unfamiliar with the PLA training cycle and objectives misinterpret routine training as intimidation directed at a variety of foreign actors due to the timing and circumstances of the exercises. For example, in December 2013 and early 2014 some foreign media portrayed winter training in northeast China as an attempt to send a message to North Korea.[38] In fact, that training was routine and similar to other training being conducted by all services in all parts of China at exactly the same time. On the other hand, the PLA has long been willing to carry out more specifically targeted military demonstrations and exercises, such as in the series of exercises at Dongshan Island and in the Taiwan Strait in the 1990s and early 2000s, to send deterrence messages. In order to understand the signals Beijing may or may not be sending, a basic background in PLA doctrine, including deterrence and training practices, is necessary.

In the future, not every PLA exercise in the air or at sea will be intended to intimidate China's neighbors; many will be drills to establish basic operational proficiencies in a force that has not fought a proper war in decades. As new weapons and technologies are introduced into the force, more such exercises can be expected in places the PLA has not been seen before. With the 2015 Defense White Paper's announcement that the PLA's "traditional mentality that land outweighs sea must be abandoned," such exercises will likely be more frequent in the future than they have been in past decades, becoming the "new normal" for PLA training. The first purpose of PLA training, therefore, is to develop a credible military force with the intention of deterrence, which will also be a force capable of winning informatized wars if deterrence fails.

New Technologies and Fine Traditions

SMS 2013 notes that new military technologies and operational capabilities have resulted in innovation in its methods of deterrence.[39] For example, SMS 2001 stated that "the day of employing deterrence of space force is not far off."[40] In SMS

2013, space is now considered a combat domain (领域军事斗争) where space deterrence (空间威慑) is practiced.[41] China further seeks to expand its deterrence capabilities through the "integration of the nuclear and conventional, deterrence and warfighting, and deterrence and war control." [42] New technologies and capabilities now available to the PLA can be used in all these realms.

China's nuclear forces are its "fundamental means for deterring large-scale enemy invasion" and necessary to support China's position as a major power. Conventional strength constitutes the principal instrument for deterring crises, controlling war situations, winning wars, and achieving strategic military objectives. China seeks to integrate its information, space, ground, sea, and air conventional forces to deter threats of dissimilar intensities, origins, and forms.[43]

At the same time, SMS 2013 emphasizes the "fine tradition of people's war," the expansion of strategies and tactics of people's war under new historical conditions, and using various measures to increase the efficiency of new-type people's war deterrence.[44] It is no coincidence that the book concludes by discussing the consolidation and development of civil-military integration (军民融合) under China's new historical conditions to develop a strong foundation for people's war.[45]

Conclusions

Overall, the 2013 edition of *The Science of Military Strategy*'s treatment of the concept of deterrence is consistent with the 2001 edition of the book, but reflects the expanded traditional and nontraditional security missions, terminology, and technology that the PLA adopted over that time period. While SMS 2013 emphasizes the availability of new technologies to the PLA and the requirement for the military to expand its maritime and aerospace capabilities and operations, the fundamental principles of Chinese strategy retain their relevance, including active defense and people's war, even as they are being adapted to the country's new conditions. None of the PLA's command and control or organizational reforms currently underway appears to change the fundamental principles of Chinese strategy.

As one of the three basic ways to employ military force, deterrence should not be overlooked as the PLA continues to make advances in technology and warfighting and structures itself to be better able to conduct joint operations in all domains. Analysts who focus on improvements in the PLA's warfighting capabilities are not wrong to do so, but they should not dismiss the book's references to "a cautious attitude toward war" or that "war is a last resort."[46] The same developments that improve the PLA's warfighting capabilities are also the basis for it to perform deterrence and MOOTW missions, the other two of the three fundamental ways to use military force.

This version of *The Science of Military Strategy* may contain trial balloons that have not yet been formally adopted by the PLA leadership. For example, in the section concerning PLA Air Force missions a "three-line control" pattern/deployment ("三线控制"的布局) is mentioned. It suggests establishing a "limited deterrence area" (有限威慑区) from the first island chain to the second island chain to monitor military forces and bases in the western Pacific to maintain a necessary deterrent state.[47] That is the only reference to the term "limited deterrence area" in the book and the term is not readily apparent in other PLA literature. As such, this notion may be more aspirational than descriptive of current doctrine. It is also worth noting that the term Air Defense Identification Zone (ADIZ, 防空识别区) is not mentioned in SMS 2013.

Finally, SMS 2013's discussion about enhancing the maritime dimensions of the PLA's deterrence system is significant, as the stated objective is to "safeguard China's maritime sovereignty, rights and interests, and sea lane safety."[48] Each of the five elements of maritime deterrence discussed in SMS 2013 can be directly observed in the variety of actions undertaken by Chinese government, civilian (commercial), military, and paramilitary organizations in the East China and South China Seas over the past several years. China's land reclamation activities in the Spratly Islands, in particular, fall under the first element of "peacetime enhancement of the defense of islands and reefs, maritime patrols, declarations of sovereignty, and maritime rights."

Consistent with its military doctrine, China has executed a series of activities within the action-reaction dynamic of 'active defense' and military deterrence with the aim of gaining the initiative in the overall situation in the East China and South China Seas. However, China's deterrence actions have not been successful in achieving its goals and have instead resulted in the continuous escalation of tensions in the region. Many observers now categorize the situation as a classic security dilemma.[49]

Few of China's neighbors or observers in the United States would agree that Chinese actions have conformed to the intentions stated in SMS 2013, the 2015 Defense White Paper,

Dennis J. Blasko

and other official policy documents that China does not seek to use force to threaten or coerce other countries and that it does not seek regional hegemony. As a result, it is no surprise that the first priority of the United States Asia-Pacific maritime security strategy issued in 2015 is to strengthen U.S. "military capacity to ensure the United States can successfully deter conflict and coercion and respond decisively when needed."[50]

NOTES

[1] Author's note: Thanks to Joe McReynolds and Brian Waidelich for their assistance in navigating difficult portions of the Chinese text of SMS 2013. Any translation or analytical errors are my own.

[2] The Chinese armed forces consist of the active and reserve forces of the PLA, the People's Armed Police (PAP), and the militia. All three components of the armed forces have a role in deterrence, warfighting, and military operations other than war.

[3] Information Office of the State Council, "China's National Defense in 2000," October 2000, http://www.gov.cn/english/official/2005-07/27/content_17524.htm.

[4] Information Office of the State Council, "China's Military Strategy," May 26, 2015, http://www.china.org.cn/china/2015-05/26/content_35661433_3.htm.

[5] The 2001 edition of *The Science of Military Strategy* was translated into English and released to the public by the Academy of Military Sciences Press in 2005. All quotes from SMS 2001 are taken from the official Chinese translation. SMS 2013 is approximately half as long as SMS 2001. SMS 2013 updates much of the terminology found in SMS 2001 and makes adjustments for technological advances in the PLA and developments in China's international environment. Nonetheless, most of the basics found in SMS 2001 are repeated in SMS 2013, sometimes using slightly different wording (reflecting different authors). Analysts interested in SMS 2013 should also

read SMS 2001 for background and sometimes for more in-depth discussion on certain topics.

[6] The first citation of these three terms together is found on p. 6 and then occurs multiple times later in the book in various forms.

[7] SMS 2013, p. 22.

[8] SMS 2013. p. 23.

[9] See Dennis J. Blasko, "Sun Tzu Simplified: An Approach to Analyzing China's Regional Military Strategies," AsiaEye, April 10, 2015, http://blog.project2049.net/2015/04/special-sun-tzu-simplified-approach-to.html.

[10] SMS 2001, p. 213.

[11] SMS 2013, pp. 134–135.

[12] Alexander L. George, "Foreword," to *The United States and Coercive Diplomacy*, eds Robert J. Art and Patrick M. Cronin, United States Institute of Peace Press, Washington, D.C., 2003, p. vii.

[13] David M. Lampton, "PacNet #63 - The US and China: sliding from engagement to coercive diplomacy," Center for Strategic and International Studies, August 4, 2014, http://csis.org/publication/pacnet-63-us-and-china-sliding-engagement-coercive-diplomacy.

[14] SMS 2001, p. 217.
[15] SMS 2013, p. 145.
[16] SMS 2001, p. 116.
[17] SMS 2001, p. 149.
[18] SMS 2001, pp. 135–136.
[19] SMS 2001, p. 151.
[20] SMS 2013, p. 147.
[21] SMS 2013, pp. 109, 119, 147, 153, 195.
[22] SMS 2013, p. 49.
[23] SMS 2013, p. 135. SMS 2001 (pp. 213–215) has a parallel discussion of the three basic conditions for strategic deterrence.

[24] SMS 2001, p. 152.

[25] SMS 2001, pp. 113, 145.

[26] SMS 2001, p. 119.

---

[27] SMS 2013, p. 153

[28] SMS 2013, p. 134

[29] SMS 2013, p. 150

[30] SMS 2013, p. 79. China's 2005 Anti-Secession Law (http://www.china.org.cn/english/2005lh/122724.htm) begins with a list of five objectives in Article 1. The first objective is stated as "opposing and checking Taiwan's secession from China by secessionists in the name of 'Taiwan independence,'" in other words China's first objective is *to deter* further movement toward Taiwan independence. The second objective is "promoting peaceful national reunification." The use of force (or as stated in the Law "non-peaceful means and other necessary measures") is not mentioned until Articles 8 and 9. The underlying Chinese position was stated in the 2004 white paper, "Should the Taiwan authorities go so far as to make a reckless attempt that constitutes a major incident of 'Taiwan independence,' the Chinese people and armed forces will resolutely and thoroughly crush it at any cost." Here use of force to crush at any cost would come after a major incident of "Taiwan independence."

[31] SMS 2013, p. 100.

[32] SMS 2013, pp. 114, 119.

[33] SMS 2013, pp. 113, 150.

[34] SMS 2001, p. 223.

[35] SMS 2001, p. 145.

[36] SMS 2001, pp. 145–146

[37] SMS 2013, p. 146.

[38] Lee Kyung-min, "China emphasizes military readiness," *Korea Times*, January 15, 2014, http://www.koreatimes.co.kr/www/news/nation/2015/11/205_149838.html.

[39] SMS 2013, p. 150. Adapting PLA doctrine to advances in technology frequently is described as "technology determines tactics" (技术决定战术) in Chinese military literature.

[40] SMS 2001, p. 220.

[41] SMS 2013, p. 181.

[42] SMS 2013, pp. 147–148.

[43] SMS 2013, p. 152.

[44] SMS 2013, p. 151.

[45] SMS 2013, p. 272.

[46] SMS 2013, p. 32.

[47] SMS 2013, p. 224.

[48] SMS 2013, p. 146.

[49] For example, see Simone Orendain, "China Stages Huge Military Drills in South China Sea," Voice of America, July 30, 2015, http://www.voanews.com/content/china-stages-huge-military-drills-in-south-china-sea/2886590.html.

[50] U.S. Department of Defense, "The Asia-Pacific Maritime Security Strategy: Achieving U.S. National Security Objectives in a Changing Environment," p. 19, http://www.defense.gov/Portals/1/Documents/pubs/NDAA%20A-P_Maritime_SecuritY_Strategy-08142015-1300-FINALFORMAT.PDF.

Chapter 11: PLA Thinking on Military Operations Other Than War

Morgan Clemens[1]

The first two decades of the 21st century have seen the dramatic re-emergence of China as a great power. A key element of this rise, alongside economic reform and development, has been an intensive process of military modernization. In a relatively short period of time, China's political and military leaders have positioned their country as a regional military power second only to the United States, with ambitions to achieve a global reach. This comes at a time when China's economic and political interests have begun to reach all corners of the earth.

And yet, even as their country's interests have expanded and military capabilities have increased, Chinese political and military leaders face a fundamental contradiction. Due to the changing nature of national security threats in the post-Cold War world, their strenuous efforts to develop fully-modernized armed forces are finally bearing fruit in an era when direct, large-scale application of military force is increasingly ineffective as a means of achieving national goals and advancing national interests. Given the fact that a large and powerful military is perceived as absolutely essential to defend the Chinese Communist Party (CCP) against both internal and external threats to its power, the question remains: what role are those expensive and well-equipped armed forces to play in advancing China's national interests (and those of the Party) in the modern era?

In answering this question, China's political and military leaders have fixed upon the concept of "military operations other than war" (非战争军事行动, or MOOTW).[2] Although the PLA was only dimly aware of MOOTW some fifteen years ago (at least doctrinally), under Hu Jintao it was catapulted into becoming a critical element of China's national strategy, as evidenced by references to MOOTW in official documents such as the annual Defense White Papers on China's military strategy and the in-depth treatment given to the topic in the 2013 edition of the *Science of Military Strategy* (战略学, or SMS). This chapter examines the rise of the MOOTW concept in the thinking of the People's Liberation Army (PLA), first by charting its historical progression and then examining the roots of PLA perceptions of MOOTW's rising importance. The chapter then explains how the PLA conceives of such operations and what their fundamental strategic purpose is.[3]

A Brief History of MOOTW and the PLA

PLA writings typically trace the origins of the MOOTW concept back to American military thinking during the 1980s, identifying it as an outgrowth of the "low-intensity warfare" concept.[4] The MOOTW concept became more prominent globally during the 1990s, after the end of the Cold War, and was explicitly adopted by countries such as Russian and Japan.[5] Across the world, the PLA observed an increase in military operations focused on the peacetime utilization of armed forces to combat non-traditional security threats (such as civil wars, epidemics, natural disasters, and transnational crime), resulting in a sizable body of academic literature and military thought on the subject. Yet, by the PLA's own admission, this new wave bypassed China, where the armed forces' non-war missions remained confined largely to disaster relief, supporting domestic economic development, and maintaining "social stability" and the rule of the Communist Party.[6] PLA sources are often at pains to point out that since its foundation the PLA has always been engaged in MOOTW-type missions, but that (like most other militaries) it had not thought of them as being part of a discrete, self-contained operational or strategic concept.[7]

For China, this began to change in 2001, when an authoritative PLA document used the term "military operations other than war" for the first time. The document in question was the new edition of the *Outline of Military Training and Evaluation* (军事训练和考核大纲, or OMTE), the basic policy document guiding training activities across the whole of the PLA.[8] The next September, the newly-enacted *Military Training Regulations* (军事训练条例), which deal with PLA personnel training in more granular detail than the OMTE, also made preliminary provision (初步规定) for MOOTW-specific training.[9] In the PLA's view, these two events together marked the PLA's entry into a "period of profound change" (深刻变化期) in terms of MOOTW.[10]

Despite this apparently promising start, however, it was clear that the PLA's understanding and conception of MOOTW was still in its early stages. While the term appears in the 2001 edition of the *Science of Military Strategy*, it is mentioned only four times, and then only in largely unconnected and logically disjointed ways.[11] Indeed, even an aspect of military affairs as unrelated to active operations as arms control is presented as an important form of MOOTW, although the 2001 edition already identifies MOOTW (alongside small-scale, low-intensity operations more generally) as a means to avoid escalating or aggravating a crisis and a way to engage in military deterrence, thereby definitely pointing to the future.[12] All in all, MOOTW was a negligible aspect of the PLA's strategic thinking as expressed in the 2001 edition, indicating the low starting point for China's theoretical development of the concept. Unsurprisingly, early PLA writings on MOOTW were heavily reliant on previous foreign (especially American) work on the subject. One of the earliest published attempts to grapple with how the concept might be relevant to the PLA is a 2003 article produced by the Nanjing Institute of Politics (南京政治学院学) which makes constant reference to American thinking on the subject, while at the same time identifying those aspects of foreign MOOTW doctrine that might be useful for guiding the PLA's thinking going forward.[13]

In the years following, the PLA began to take its first tentative steps in conducting MOOTW overseas while at the same time building up its capacity for domestic operations. Although at first the PLA's progress with MOOTW proceeded relatively slowly, 2008 saw another series of important milestones. In that year, the MOOTW concept was included in the National Defense White Paper for the first time, indicating its elevation to a key military task. As of 2016, MOOTW has been consistently referenced in every successive white paper. At the same time, a 2008 issue of the authoritative PLA academic journal *China Military Science* (中国军事科学) carried a special research series analyzing the nature, significance, and purpose of MOOTW.[14] Together, these articles explore the strategic and legal rationale for engaging in such operations, as well as how they specifically relate to naval operations, counter-terrorism, and disaster relief, representing perhaps the first in-depth expression of the PLA's thinking on subject. Other indications of increasing emphasis from that time include the General Logistics Department organizing an "all-army training course on logistical support strategy for military operations other than war" (全军非战争军事行动后勤保障战略集训班) in Beijing, and the General Staff Department Military Training and Service Arms Department's (军训和兵种部) development in 2009 of a MOOTW "force system" (力量体系) encompassing a wide range of operation types.[15]

Just as importantly, 2008 saw the establishment of the first departments dedicated to MOOTW studies at various military academic institutions, providing an organizational basis for deepening the PLA's theoretical and doctrinal grasp pf the concept.[16] According to PLA sources, the immediate motivating factor for the establishment of these academic departments (and for the increased overall effort to refine the PLA's theoretical framework for MOOTW) was the armed forces' experiences with domestic MOOTW during that period, most especially the 2008 Wenchuan earthquake relief efforts and the security operations associated with the 2008 Olympic Games in Beijing.[17]

A further critical inflection point came in late 2011, with the establishment of a MOOTW Research Center (非战争军事行动研究中心) within the Department of Operational Theory and Doctrine (作战理论和条令研究部) of the Academy of Military Science.[18] The center's primary tasks include undertaking research in order to provide decision-making advice regarding "non-traditional security" (非传统安全威胁) and MOOTW, as well as conducting basic research on and establishing a theoretical system for MOOTW (非战争军事行动理论体系).[19] Under the leadership of its director, Senior Colonel Zheng Shouhua (郑守华), the Center helps draft and edit regulations, text books, and dictionaries related to MOOTW, producing monographs and instructional texts which serve to encapsulate and synthesize the PLA's official thinking on the topic. [20] The importance of the Center's formation is apparent in the fact that MOOTW appears as a major component of the 2013 SMS less than two years later, a decision very likely dependent upon their practical and theoretical contributions. Theoretical development continued apace when, in March 2012, the CMC issued the 'Instructions for PLA Participation in UN Peacekeeping Operations' (中国人民解放军参加联合国维持和平行动条例), while the General Logistics department issued the "Armed Forces MOOTW Financial Support Regulations" (军队非战争军事行动财务保障办法). In the following months, the General Staff Department established an Emergency Office (应急办公室) with primary responsibility for organizing the command of MOOTW (though it is not yet known how such specialized command institutions will be constituted in the aftermath of the PLA's 2016 reorganization). [21]

Finally, in 2013, the PLA's thinking on the nature and role of MOOTW came to its fullest fruition with the publication of two critical official texts. The first of these, in January of that year, was *A Textbook for Military Operations Other Than War* (非战争军事行动教程), an AMS instructional text produced by its MOOTW research center. [22] Shortly after came the publication of the 2013 edition of the SMS, also edited and compiled by the staff of the AMS, which dedicated some fifteen pages to the discussion of military operations other than war. Given the nature of the research center's duties, it is almost certain that the center's staff was directly involved in drafting the 2013 edition's chapter on MOOTW. Together, these two publications represent the highest development of the PLA's authoritative thinking on military operations other than war, constituting the basic principles upon which Chinese military operations other than war will be carried out going forward.

The Need for MOOTW

Having reviewed the progress of the MOOTW concept within in the PLA, it would behoove us to consider why exactly the Chinese military believes such operations to be vital and necessary. As alluded to in the introduction, this belief stems from an assessment on the part of the Chinese that international conditions have radically changed since the end of the Cold War, a change brought about first and foremost by the end of the conflict itself. In the Chinse view, the dissolution of the Soviet Union and the cessation of U.S.-Soviet military confrontation made non-traditional security problems much more noticeable and salient to the international community. In this view, the end of that bipolar system also caused the collapse of the old mechanisms of global governance, increasing global disorder, while certain countries (meaning the United States) pursued unilateral policies to benefit themselves, creating conflicts and "stirring up trouble" (制造矛盾和挑起事端). This weakened many states, exposing underlying non-traditional security issues.[23] Likewise, in the absence of Cold War bipolarity, ethnic and religious conflicts became increasingly prominent.[24] Thus the international system faced increasing instability with a whole host of complex causes, including regional unrest arising from local conflicts, hegemonism, power politics and increasing neo-interventionism, terrorism, transnational organized crime, and problems of information network security. In Chinese writings, it is also frequently alleged that the American pivot to Asia and the American tendency to "frequently manufacture regional tension" (频繁制造地区紧张局势) are further exacerbating factors, contributing to global instability by their willingness to intervene in territorial disputes.[25]

These changes in the international system were amplified by the processes of economic globalization and broader worldwide informatization.[26] Economic globalization in particular has increased interdependence between even countries and regions distant from one another, thereby increasing the vulnerability of all countries to disruptions in the global economic system.[27] Globalization and informatization mean that the myriad problems of each region are contagious, quickly and strongly affecting other regions. Moreover, the modes of living of modern societies are often fragile, compounding the damage wrought by natural disasters, public health crises, and unexpected security challenges.[28] This became readily apparent in the 1990s, as disasters and crises of a non-military nature increasingly presented the international community with serious obstacles to sustainable development.[29] As a result, PLA strategists have come to take non-traditional security problems as seriously as conventional military threats, since in some cases their impact can be equally powerful.[30]

At the same time, the Chinese perceive increased globalization and interdependence as placing more and more restrictions on the use of war as a means of pursuing national interests, particularly as global economic integration has increased and broadened the negative economic impact of war.[31] Moreover, modern technology has made war so devastating that it is often no longer a rational means of achieving political objectives, especially when seeking to maintain overall political and economic order.[32] In any event, peace and development are, together, the 'theme' of the current era; although military skirmishes and minor regional conflicts may still occur, in this view it is non-traditional security issues which present the primary threat to the security and sustainable development of the international community.[33] While the Chinese continue to view pure military strength as the primary guarantee of traditional security, they recognize that it is not well-suited to solving the problems of non-traditional security, as exemplified by the September 11th attacks and the SARS outbreak in 2003, thereby presenting states with new challenges. [34] Although technological development has increased the destructiveness of war almost to the point of uselessness, it has also increased the efficacy of military operations other than war themselves, especially in terms of advances in communications and mobility. Thus, in the Chinese view, with large-scale war between great powers unlikely unless the present international strategic environment changes radically, the utility of MOOTW will only persist and increase.[35]

Having seen how the Chinese view a changed international order, one must also take into consideration the basic calculus guiding their overall strategy. It must be remembered that China's political and military leaders continue to look upon their country as a developing nation, utilizing a relatively peaceful window of opportunity in the general international situation to effectively "catch up" with the world's more developed nations. Moreover, in the view of Xi Jinping and the central leadership, China's security problems are becoming increasingly "complex" (复杂性), "comprehensive" (综合性), and "multivariate" (多变性), while "the next decade or two is the key period for [China] to realize national rejuvenation, but [China] is also facing unprecedented challenges in the development process."³⁶ This is in line with Hu Jintao's earlier assertion that traditional and non-traditional security threats are increasingly intertwined, increasing instability and threatening China's peaceful rise.³⁷ Along China's periphery, where most of the country's core security interests are concentrated, it is thus necessary to undertake military deterrence and military presence operations as well as "military diplomatic action" in order to create a favorable atmosphere for strategic cooperation, reassure (or deter) neighboring countries, and reduce the risk of conflict while assuring China's territorial integrity.³⁸ According to the CMC's Strategic Guidelines for the New Period (新时期战略方针), the military should "provide a strong security guarantee for building a moderately prosperous society," because otherwise even in peacetime non-traditional security challenges will interfere with or even interrupt the development process.³⁹

Because they are inherently disciplined, organized, equipped, and trained for rapid response than civilians, in the Chinese view the armed forces are a natural tool for dealing with non-traditional security threats.⁴⁰ In this vein, the 2013 SMS argues that avoiding confrontation is essential to securing China's rise and presents MOOTW as a "tool for the times," an active means short of war which can shape the international environment to China's advantage.⁴¹ In the words of the 2013 SMS:

> The concept of "military operations other than war"... is closely connected to the formation of an informatized society and the development of globalization; it is the result of changes in the conception of national security and in military thinking; it is the product of the diversification

of choice in the means of protecting our national security and interests; and it is also inevitable in the historical process of the development of military operations. In an age of peace and development, control over warfare has been greatly strengthened, [while] costs have increased, difficulties have been amplified, and the scope in which [warfare] can be employed has been strictly limited. *Military operations other than war, which are characterized by non-violence, conform to the characteristics of the age...*[42]

According to SMS 2013, MOOTW can eliminate "hidden" internal security dangers and promote internal "social stability" and "harmony," while externally they can create a secure environment and protect China's national interests. It is important to note that SMS 2013 specifically describes the range of MOOTW operations as encompassing the "potential use," "embodiment," and "actual use" of force (通过力量的和平宣示、体现和运用), language that indicates a meaningful role for MOOTW in China's overall deterrence posture.[43]

Ultimately, China's political and military leaders see themselves as confronted with an increasingly complex strategic environment, one in which their armed forces will be compelled by the forces of globalization and national development to play an increasingly active role. This is an environment, however, in which the traditional application of military strength has declined in utility, thanks to a number of factors, including the proliferation of non-traditional security threats. It is for this reason that SMS 2013 emphasizes that military operations other than war will become more frequent, more important, and more complex, playing an "irreplaceable strategic role" (不可替代的战略作用).[44]

MOOTW with Chinese Characteristics

Having laid out the PLA's reasoning regarding the necessity of MOOTW, it is now incumbent to examine precisely what the concept means in the eyes of the PLA, and how that meaning has grown and evolved in the past decade and a half. In doing so, the logical starting point would be to examine the various formal definitions of the term which the Chinese have employed over those years. As noted in the previous section, the 2001 edition of the *Science of Military Strategy* makes only stray references to MOOTW, and does not explicitly define the term, merely describing such operations as a means to avoid escalating or aggravating a crisis and to engage in military deterrence,[45] and as "one part of the totality of warfare" (战争全局的部分).[46] Over time, however, the PLA has sought to explicitly define the term, and according to one count, the PLA has or has had as many as ten formal definitions of MOOTW.[47] Reviewing several of these is instructive as to how the definition has increased in scope and specificity over time. In 2002, the *China Military Encyclopedia* (中国军事百科全书) defined MOOTW as: "Military operations which, in peacetime and in wartime, employ means of implementation and organization different from [those of] war."[48] In 2008, an article on MOOTW in the authoritative PLA journal *China Military Science* gave a lengthier definition:

> Military operations other than war refer to a national, ethnic, class, or political group carrying

out military operations by directly or indirectly using armed force, employing non-violent methods, or under certain conditions using violent methods to a limited degree, in order to [achieve] a certain political, economic, or military objective, protect national interests, preserve social stability, withstand natural disasters, [and] defend the people's peaceful labor and the security of their lives and property.[49]

Finally, both the 2011 edition of the official *Military Terminology of the Chinese People's Liberation Army* (中国人民解放军军语, known as the 军语 / *junyu* for short) and the 2013 SMS give what may be considered the current, authoritative definition:

Military operations that the armed forces carry out to protect national security and developmental interests, but which do not directly constitute warfare. They include such actions as counter-terrorism, stability maintenance, disaster relief, safeguarding national interests, security alerts, international peacekeeping, and international rescue operations.[50]

Drawing Boundaries around MOOTW

The progression of these definitions from a bare description to more robust ones is indicative of the expansion of the PLA's official thinking on MOOTW, particularly between 2001 and

2008. The greater specificity from the 2008 definition to the 2011/2013 iteration indicates the deepening and refinement of the PLA's MOOTW concept. The newest authoritative definition, in particular, provides fairly clear and easy-to-define basic categories for different forms of MOOTW, a set of categories which is largely consistent with those provided other PLA sources. For instance, a military textbook from 2008 lists six types of MOOTW:[51]

1. Counter-terrorism operations (反恐怖行动)

2. Counter-disturbance operations (反骚乱行动)

3. Handling border, coastal, and air defense incident operations (处置边防、海防、空防事件行动)

4. Rescue and relief operations (抢险救灾行动)

5. Peacekeeping operations (维和行动)

6. Deterrence (武力威慑)[52]

A list published by AMS only a year later provides an essentially identical set of five categories, with 'deterrence' having been removed.[53] Another list from the Nanjing Institute of Politics, also from 2009, lists only four primary types:

1. Stopping political unrest and riots, maintaining social stability (维护社会稳定)

2. Responding to major natural disasters, providing emergency relief, and protecting people's lives and property

3. Rapidly handling major accidents (重大事故进行) and protecting the environment (保护生态环境)

4. Large-scale military exercises intended to increase combat effectiveness and enhance military deterrence (军事威慑)

While these lists do display some differences in detail and emphasis, taken together they nonetheless demonstrate the breadth of the PLA's conception of MOOTW in the period of 2008–2009, a conception that would only deepen and broaden in the following years. Indeed, the most detailed set of MOOTW missions is provided by another AMS publication, a 2013 textbook on MOOTW, which names seven major categories of military operations other than war, along with thirty subcategories, as shown in the table below.

Figure 1: 2013 AMS Textbook's Delineation of MOOTW Categories and Sub-categories

Categories	Sub-categories
Rescue and relief (抢险救灾行动)	Flood rescue (抗洪抢险行动)
	Earthquake relief (抗震救灾行动)
	Forest fire-fighting (森林灭火行动)
	Nuclear/biological/chemical contamination emergency (核生化泄漏抢险行动)
Counter-terrorism (反恐怖行动)	Attacking terrorist camps (进攻恐怖分子营地行动)
	Anti-gunfire attack (反火力袭击行动)
	Anti-conventional explosive attack (反常规爆炸袭击行动)
	Anti-nuclear and biochemical attack (反核生化袭击行动)
	Anti-information attack (反信息袭击行动)
	Anti-hijacking (反劫持行动)
	International joint counter-terrorism (国际联合反恐怖行动)
Stability maintenance (维护稳定行动)	Intimidation (震慑造势行动)
	Sealing off incident area (封控事发地区行动)
	Stopping large-scale mass incidents (制止大规模群体性事件)
	Combatting serious violent crime (打击严重暴力犯罪活动)
	Defending important targets (防卫重要目标行动)

	Medical rescue/evacuation (救护救援行动)
	Aftermath cleanup (善后工作)
Rights protection (维护权益行动)	Onshore rights protection (陆上维护权益行动)
	Maritime rights protection (海上维护权益行动)
	Aerial rights protection (空中维护权益行动)
	Overseas rights protection (海外维护权益行动)
	Space rights protection (太空维护权益行动)
	Network and electronic domain rights protection (网电领域维护权益行动)
Security and guarding (安保警戒行动)	Ground security (地面安保警戒行动)
	Aerial security (空中安保警戒行动)
	Maritime (water-borne) security (海(水)上安保警戒行动)
	Nuclear/biological/chemical attack rescue (核生化袭击救援行动)
International peacekeeping (国际维和行动)	none
International relief (国际救援行动)	Natural disaster relief (自然灾害救援行动)
	Accident disaster relief (事故灾难救援行动)

The 2013 edition of the SMS, by contrast, groups such operations into four broad categories based on their scale, location, objectives, and the nature of their targets (such as a friendly power, a hostile power, or a domestic problem):

- *Confrontational operations* (对抗性行动), which encompass counter-terrorism operations, armed drug enforcement, attacking transnational crime, anti-piracy operations, and preventing social unrest and riots. The targets are usually hostile individuals, groups, or countries, typically located in border regions or certain areas within China, but also sometimes abroad. Missions in this category generally take the form of low-intensity operations.[54]

- *Law-enforcement actions* (执法性行动), which entail border and coastal control (or blockades), air alerts (or blockades), defense of rights at sea, convoying, security alerts, international peacekeeping, and military patrols, the scope of which is mostly domestic, but also includes border regions and international hotspots.[55]

- *Relief operations* (救助性行动), which embrace emergency disaster relief (for natural disasters, epidemics, nuclear-chemical-biological incidents, etc.), the protection and evacuation of foreign and Chinese nationals overseas, and medical assistance. Targets go beyond specific groups and organizations to include physical facilities and the natural environment. Such missions are exceedingly complex due to multiplicity of factors and actors involved, as well as the intense time pressures of emergency situations, which do not allow for significant pre-planning. Typically they do not involve direct conflict, though they can take place against the backdrop of conflict.[56]

- *Cooperative operations* (合作性行动), primarily comprising international joint military exercises and mostly held in strategically important areas along the national periphery or on the high seas, by means of which "interactive exchanges are strengthened, military mutual confidence is strengthened, and the ability for joint operations is improved." Such operations moreover serve to "display resolve to jointly use troops and the power to do so, and they use shock and awe against their common opponent to control actual and potential crises and to stabilize regional situations."[57]

While these various formulations do differ to an extent in their specific wording and terminology, their general consistency over time is evident. But beyond these rather spare definitions and lists, we are left with the question of what the precise nature of MOOTW is. What, in the eyes of the PLA, distinguishes MOOTW from other forms of operations, and indeed from war itself?

Of course, the simplest and most basic answer provided by authoritative Chinese writings, aside from the fact that they are primarily undertaken peacetime, is that military operations other than war entail a lower level of violence. This lower level of violence in turn offers decision-makers a greater degree of precise control, at least in comparison to warfare.[58] Indeed, the idea of control and limitation permeated much of the PLA's early thinking on the topic. In 2003, the Nanjing Institute of Politics emphasized that MOOTW entailed strict control over offensive military means (对进攻性武力手段的使用有着严格的控制).[59] Restraint was seen as being necessary in order to avoid alienating international opinion, which was understood to be an essential precondition for continued success. A further advantage of this restraint and limitation is that of cost-effectiveness, with the fiscal cost of MOOTW being perceived as universally lower than the cost of full-scale war operations, making MOOTW a cost-effective alternative in situations where the political goals of MOOTW and warfighting operations would overlap.[60]

MOOTW and war operations also differ in other aspects as well, with the 2013 AMS textbook identifying several. Chief among them are differing "operational natures" (行动性质不同), mainly defined by their different foci (traditional security vs. non-traditional security). Moreover, their targets or objects are different (作用对象不同). The targets of MOOTW are hostile forces (very broadly defined, to include terrorists, criminals, etc.), as well as the effects of natural disasters, epidemics, accidents, etc., while the targets of wartime operations are enemy military forces and critical military targets (bases, ports, factories, and so on). Finally, the 2013 textbook points out that their basic means are different (运用手段不同). Military operations other than war primarily entail non-lethal means. Even in counter-terrorism and stability maintenance operations the emphasis is on deterrence and avoiding the use of force whenever possible, in large part because the excessive use of force (and resultant heavy casualties) will erode public support and negatively impact international perceptions.[61] Despite the differences between the two, the PLA recognizes that MOOTW and war operations are fundamentally connected, and in particular that each can transition into the other based on changing circumstances and requirements.[62] Likewise, non-traditional security problems in one place can trigger a war somewhere else, while active wars in one country, region, or area can cause non-traditional threats to affect other countries, regions, and areas.[63]

A further key aspect which PLA sources consistently identify as fundamental to the nature of MOOTW is the exercise of centralized, high-level command. They state emphatically that the highest-level national authorities should exercise direct control over such operations, and that the principle of "small actions, big command" (小行动, 大指挥) or "tactical actions, strategic command" (战术行动, 战略指挥) is (and should be regarded as) a universal practice in the command of military operations other than war. [64] This principle is just as strongly put in the 2013 SMS, which emphasizes the primary role of the Central Committee and the Central Military Commission in making decisions regarding MOOTW, with authority being delegated when necessary to relevant theater commands, service headquarters, or the People's Armed Police (PAP). [65] This centralization is due in large part to informatization and the nature of modern media, meaning that even relatively small and localized operations can have a global impact. Thus, given the fact that many MOOTW have a strongly political and highly sensitive nature, it is necessary to tightly control and vigorously manage the media wherever possible, while avoiding any operational mistake that could compromise public or international perceptions. Authoritative sources also note that in the course of MOOTW, it is necessary to understand and take into account international law, the political, economic, and military conditions of relevant countries, and local customs, with the contextual implication being that lower-level commanders cannot be trusted to do so reliably. In this view, since successful MOOTW can improve the image (and potentially the geopolitical position) of not only the armed forces but also China as a whole (and by extension, MOOTW failures can harm one's image), decisions about MOOTW must be made at the highest levels of the state and armed forces.[66]

Centralized command is also necessary in order to ensure that such operations are in line with the policies of the Party and the state, especially when operating inside China.[67] The 2013 AMS textbook identifies further distinctive features of MOOTW command and control, namely the degree to which it is made more difficult by the wide range of operational elements typically involved, including the military, the armed police, the militia, public security forces, and local professional rescue forces.[68] Thus it is that the 2013 SMS prescribes that military command organs engaged in MOOTW (especially within China) must establish close coordination mechanisms with relevant civilian ministries and agencies, as well as local governments, in order to coordinate operations and achieve objectives together.[69] To this end, the 2013 AMS textbook outlines four main MOOTW command methods (非战争军事行动指挥模式):

- *Joint command on the basis of local government* (以地方政府为主的联合指挥模式), since, according to Chinese law, disaster relief should be undertaken with the local People's Governments in the lead. Even in the case of anti-terrorism and stability maintenance, civilian authorities can be given a joint leadership role.[70]

- *Joint command with the armed forces in the lead* (以武装力量为主的联合指挥模式), which is necessary in situations such as air or ground hijacking, hijacking at sea, ocean escort, and combating large-scale terrorist attacks.

- *Joint command organized between Chinese and foreign forces* (中外军队共同组织的联合指挥模式), which can take three forms: (1) with a joint headquarters, (2) without a joint headquarters, but with coordination of plans, intentions, etc., and (3) a joint regional command structure (e.g. ISAF).

- *Joint command led by the United Nations* (由联合国主导的联合指挥模式), which is self-explanatory.

Ultimately, the centralization of leadership associated with military operations other than war is considered attractive because of the perceived controllability of such operations, indicating that senior national and military leaders should directly and effectively control military operations other than in pursuit of their policy aims. This is predicated on the belief that such a thing is possible; or in the words of one article from 2011, that "the implementation of military operations other than war is easy to plan, easy to control, easy to adjust."[71] This does not mean that the PLA views such operations as quite so simple, but rather that they believe they are capable of being very finely tuned and shaped to suit the needs of policy (certainly more finely tuned and shaped than is the case with full-scale war operations). This must be understood within the context of the ongoing tensions within the PLA as a whole between advocates of using modern, informatized C4ISR technologies to centralize command and control at the highest levels, and advocates of using those same technologies to enable lower level commanders and units to take greater initiative and flexibly adapt to evolving scenarios. In the specific case of MOOTW, it remains to be seen how this tension within the system will resolve itself.

MOOTW for What Purpose?

There remains before us the important question of what strategic purpose the Chinese concept of MOOTW is intended to play, beyond the basic function of enabling the armed forces to remain an effective instrument of policy in the post-Cold War era of globalization. In doing so, it must first be recognized that the PLA views war operations as restricting MOOTW (战争行动制约着非战争军事行动), meaning that war operations and their necessary capabilities take precedence in the event of any conflict between the requirements of the two.[72] In other words, fighting and winning local wars under informatized conditions is the core military capability from which all other capabilities must flow.[73] As characterized in some of the PLA's early writings on the subject, in a modern society military operations other than war serve to increase the social value (社会价值) of the armed forces, making them useful for achieving a broader range of policy objectives. The basic strategic benefits of MOOTW include imposing strict control over the use of force, helping to avoid conflicts and the escalation of crises, and generally reducing the chance of the outbreak of war.[74]

In the Chinese view, military operations other than war are a useful means by which the armed forces can contribute to safeguarding international peace. When utilized correctly, they can serve to improve the country's image abroad, break the military containment imposed by "certain countries" (对于打破某些国家对我国军事围堵, a thinly veiled reference to the United States and allies), consolidate regional peace and security, curb and combat terrorism, and help solve border/territorial disputes.[75] Likewise, such operations are an important means for the armed forces to maintain internal social stability and safeguard national interests and security in peacetime (非战争军事行动是和平时期军队维护社会稳定、保障国家利益安全的重要手段).[76] It must be remembered that the primary role of the PLA is still to maintain the Party's authority in the face of unrest, opposition, and subversion, though more recently it has also fallen to the armed forces to safeguard broader national interests across all domains, including the lives, interests, and property of Chinese citizens overseas.[77]

This line of thinking is maintained by the 2013 SMS, which contends that the purpose of the MOOTW concept is to enable the armed forces to respond to crisis situations, to uphold the international security environment, and to uphold the political, economic, and social order.[78] In line with the emphasis on cost effectiveness noted earlier, the 2013 SMS also points out that military operations other than war typically require only limited resource commitments, while the resulting strategic benefits are comparatively great, and indicates that maximization of strategic return-on-investment is part of the purpose of MOOTW.[79] Of course, if operations of this kind are to be used for such a purpose, then there must be proper governing principles for their initiation. The 2013 SMS lays out a basic self-interest test for any MOOTW activity; the objectives and tasks involved must be "rational and proportionate" in relation to the problem being solved or the interest being pursued.[80] As other PLA publications have pointed out, national armed forces are instruments of violence intended to protect their nations' interests, and all their actions are carried out to safeguard those national interests. Thus, for MOOTW just as much as for war operations, the decision to engage should be based solely on the rational calculation of national interest and on broader national strategy.[81] According to the Academy of Military Science, the decision to participate in military operations other than war must, for China, be an extension of the national strategy of peaceful development. Participation must be based on a rational understanding of overall national and military strength (国家和军队综合实力); in this view, since China is still a relatively weak developing nation, it is vital that resources only be spent on those operations directly related to national interests.[82]

Of course, part of MOOTW's efficiency is derived from its utility as a tool for heading off problems that can lead to greater conflict. In the words of the 2013 SMS: "One of the important goals of military operations other than war is to keep situations from escalating and avoiding the start of war."[83] The 2013 AMS textbook concurs, stating in the "new international environment," MOOTW serves to ease situations, defuse crises, curb war, and provide effective means of safeguarding world peace. [84] At the same time, however, the PLA also views MOOTW as being a potential tool for strategic confrontation. This line of thinking in regard to MOOTW was present in the earliest days of the PLA's thinking: "Although military operations other than war are often used by certain hegemonic countries as a means to interfere in the affairs of other countries, they are nonetheless a means for many countries to resist hegemony."[85] It has been sustained down to the present, with the Academy of Military Science warning that Western powers are inclined toward engaging in a containment strategy against China. Familiar Chinese complaints about Western policies are grouped under this umbrella, including "technology blockades" (export restrictions), cultural aggression, ideological infiltration, and support for separatist forces, all while China is supposed to be internally vulnerable because of ongoing economic and social transitions. Thus, in this view, the task of the armed forces is in part to keep hostile or unfriendly powers from pushing China too far during a crisis or non-military conflict, and the use of the armed forces in peacetime should be focused on combating the ill-effects to regional stability caused by "hegemonism, power politics, and neo-interventionism" (霸权主义、强权政治和新干涉主义, a typical Chinese reference to the alleged bad behavior of Western powers).[86]

A final major form of utility for MOOTW, in the eyes of the PLA, is its potential for improving operational and combat capabilities by providing a facsimile of actual combat experience. This is made possible by what Chinese sources describe as the "mutually beneficial and transformative relationship" (二者存在着相互利用、相互转化的关系) that exists between MOOTW and war operations, since not only are many types of MOOTW (counter-terrorism, stability maintenance, etc.) intended to prevent escalation to war, they are also likely to be needed in the wake of a conflict, once a war's aims have been successfully achieved. There also exists between them a "mutually inclusive relationship" (二者存在着相互包含的关系), with more intense MOOTW missions necessitating the limited use of full-scale war methods, and some tertiary wartime threats (such as terrorist or guerrilla attacks on the flanks and rear areas) being best handled by low-intensity methods more typical of MOOTW. [87] According to the PLA, military operations other than war are consistent with the fundamental purposes of core wartime military operations due to their connected essential capabilities and similar requirements, and since MOOTW capabilities are based on core military capabilities, improving MOOTW capabilities can thereby help improve core military capabilities.[88]

The PLA emphasizes that many MOOTW tasks, skills, operational processes, and command requirements are essentially the same as those of war,[89] and therefore performing military operations other than war can test the capabilities of troops and equipment, making it possible to find gaps in doctrine, learn lessons, and promote combat effectiveness generally.[90] The Academy of Military Science contends that, since MOOTW involves completing difficult and perilous tasks which are roughly equivalent to war and provides useful operational experience, active participation in MOOTW will strengthen China's defense S&T development strategy (国防科技发展战略), military strategic guidance (军事战略指导), and army building (军队建设).[91]

MOOTW is both a way for the Party and state to use the armed forces in service of national development, and also a means to build, develop, and strengthen the armed forces themselves,[92] and in this way carrying out MOOTW can itself serve as a deterrent. As a "low-intensity, high-efficiency" (低强度, 高效益) form of operations, MOOTW can warn, pressure, or deter an enemy.[93] Furthermore, because strength in MOOTW essentially represents strength in war operations, demonstrating proficiency in it can serve to strengthen deterrence.[94] Ultimately, the PLA views a strong MOOTW capability as vital to maintaining a secure environment for strategic deterrence, providing both the ability to control crisis development/escalation and the ability to rapidly deal with emergencies. Thus, improving the armed forces' capacity for MOOTW is an integral part of achieving great power status, and the requirements of MOOTW must be given serious consideration when making decisions regarding equipment, technology, procurement, and infrastructure.[95]

The Rubber Meets the Road: Real-world Chinese MOOTW

How, then, does the preceding discussion relate to Chinese MOOTW activities in the real world? It becomes clear upon examination that many of the principles, priorities, and concerns described above are well evidenced in China's actual military operations other than war. China's counter-piracy operations in the Gulf of Aden, for instance, have provided the PLA Navy with valuable learning opportunities. For nearly eight years, the continual maintenance of a multi-ship task force in a complex operational environment several thousand miles from China's coast has enabled the PLA Navy to gain solid experience in meeting the logistics requirements of distant force projection, long-distance communications, and operating in unfamiliar environments, all skills that are applicable to both war and non-war operations. At the same time, the counter-piracy mission has allowed the Chinese to portray themselves as a responsible international actor, develop collaborative relationships with countries both located in the region and operating there, and to protect Chinese economic interests by providing convoy escorts to thousands of commercial vessels, many of them Chinese.

Similar benefits are derived from the various mass evacuation operations which the PLA has undertaken overseas to protect Chinese nationals in conflict zones, including from East Timor in 2006, Libya in 2011, and Yemen in 2015. Generally undertaken in response to political violence or civil war, and entailing the evacuation of thousands of Chinese citizens (as well as non-Chinese foreigners), these operations provide the PLA with real-world experience in the rapid mobilization and movement of numerous transportation assets. They require the PLA to simultaneously organize and coordinate activities with limited warning or advance planning, experience which can easily translate to war operations. As with the counter-piracy missions, overseas evacuation operations also serve to help shape the diplomatic environment in China's favor (especially by burnishing China's image among those countries whose citizens her forces help evacuate) while also protecting the lives and safety of Chinese citizens living and working abroad, thereby serving the larger purpose of protecting China's growing national interests.

Involvement in humanitarian and disaster relief operations present many of the same benefits in terms of experience of rapid mobilization and power projection, as typified most recently by China's response to the April 2015 earthquake in Nepal. Engaging in domestic relief operations for affected areas of Tibet, the PLA, PAP, and militia mobilized nearly 7,000 personnel and hundreds of vehicles in response to the earthquake. This included deploying several hundred medical and rescue personnel to Nepal, transported and supplied by the PLA Air Force's main long-range logistics assets, namely its fleet of Il-76 heavy transports. [96] The operation, as with similar operations over the years in Pakistan, Indonesia, and elsewhere, is significant in that it took place along China's periphery, the set of countries whose stability and security conditions are identified as having the most direct (and potentially dire) impact on Chinese interests and national security. Indeed, the response to the 2015 earthquake in Nepal and many other natural disasters should be seen first and foremost as part of broader efforts to head off potential long-term instability in China's own backyard.

By contrast, the utilization of the so-called *Peace Ark*, a converted hospital ship operated by the PLA Navy that visits ports across East Asia, dispensing supplies and providing direct medical treatment, does not confer significant operational benefits, even indirectly. Rather, it serves as a form of military diplomacy and a pure exercise of soft power, winning hearts and minds among neighboring populations while providing useful grist for China's propaganda mill. Finally, the various presence operations undertaken in the East China Sea and South China Sea (including construction on occupied islands, asserting control over fishing grounds and sea-lanes, and observing/harassing foreign vessels and aircraft operating in claimed waters and airspace) represent MOOTW utilized as a tool of plain power politics. In particular, such operations are a manifestation of China's desire to break the perceived encirclement and containment orchestrated the United States and their close allies. By preventing the easy implementation of American policy priorities, China's MOOTW activities in disputed waters serve to combat the perceived policy of hegemonism pursued by the United States. These operations demonstrate the wide organizational reach of the MOOTW mission, entailing the participation of a wide range of naval militia forces from localities in China's southern provinces as well as various elements of the Chinese coast guard.[97]

Conclusion

In the end, and as the preceding sections have shown, China's military operations other than war do not have any one specific purpose or role in Chinese military and security strategy, but rather are intended to support multiple aspects of that strategy, from the maintenance of internal stability (i.e. Party rule) and the exercise of soft power to engaging in military diplomacy and deterrence. Such operations are further looked upon as the best available means to provide the armed forces with realistic operational experience, even experience approximating combat. They are thus critical to developing capabilities and honing the operational efficiency of the PLA and the rest of the armed forces. Should the Chinese manage to avoid major interstate war in the years ahead (as seems to be their objective), then it will be the case that the armed forces' primary operational activities (as opposed to training, maintenance, etc.) will be those which fall within the Chinese conception of military operations other than war.

We can thus expect the frequency of Chinese military operations other than war, and the importance of the MOOTW concept which guides them, to increase in the years ahead. The PLA's MOOTW capability will likely be increased by the major organizational and other reforms initiated by the PLA in early 2016. Though the primary purpose of these reforms is to increase the PLA's conventional warfighting capacity, it cannot be lost on China's political and military leaders that they will also serve to improve the PLA's MOOTW capabilities, especially in terms of undertaking and supporting joint operations at long distances. Ultimately, as with the militaries of other countries, the MOOTW concept is intended to enable the Chinese armed forces to play as active a role as possible in the shaping of China's security environment, even in the midst of an age in which the occurrence and salience of major interstate war has sharply declined. In this way, China's leaders are seeking to derive the maximum possible return on their considerable (and ongoing) financial and political investment in military modernization and reform.

NOTES

[1] The author is deeply indebted to his colleague Ken Allen, who helped to identify some of the sources used in this paper and provided critical comments on an early draft.

[2] Also translated by the Chinese as "non-war military operations".

[3] Drawing as it does almost entirely on publications of the PLA, the present chapter represents an analysis of *that* organization's thinking on the subject. In terms of which organizations will actually *engage* in MOOTW, the sources become notably inconsistent, variously referring to the PLA, the armed forces, and the military (军队 or 我军). For the sake of clarity, in such instances the present chapter will utilize the term "armed forces," thereby encompassing the PLA, the People's Armed Police, and the reserves/militia.

[4] Zhu Zhihong [朱之江], "On military operations other than war" [论非战争军事行动], *Journal of the PLA Nanjing Institute of Politics* [南京政治学院学报], 2003/05, pp.83–84; Song Guocai [宋国才], Shi Limin [石利民], and Yang Shu [杨树], chief eds., *Military Operations Other Than War Case Studies* [非战争军事行动实例研究], (Beijing: Academy of Military Sciences Press, 2009), pp.3–4.

[5] A contention made in many PLA writings on MOOTW (including the 2013 SMS) is that the U.S. military embraced MOOTW almost in desperation, as a means to obtain missions (presumably in order to justify budgets). SMS 2013, p.157.

[6] Zhu Zhihong [朱之江] and Wang Liming [王笠铭], "A review of military operations other than war by the people's military" [人民军队非战争军事行动述论], *Military Historical Research* [军事历史研究], 2010/01, p.38.

7 SMS 2013, pp.155–56; Zhou Meng [周萌], "Discussion of guiding the vigorous improvement of MOOTW capabilities on the basis of Hu Jintao's military innovative theory" [以胡锦涛军事创新理论为指导大力提高非战争军事行动能力], *Military Historical Research* [军事历史研究], 2009 special issue, p.25; Indeed, one source contends that Chinese troops have been engaged in military operations other than war since at least the Han dynasty, presumably to demonstrate that the Chinese were doing them before anyone else. Ma Yuezhou [马越舟] and Tian Yiwei [田义伟], "A discussion with AMS MOOTW Research Center director and researcher Zheng Shouhua" [与军事科学院非战争军事行动研究中心主任郑守华研究员一席谈], *PLA Daily* [解放军报], September 5, 2012.

8 Some PLA sources also emphasize that prior the PLA's MOOTW activities (such as they were), were primarily focused on maintaining internal stability. The leading example of this sort of MOOTW, according to an article published in 2010 by officers from the Nanjing Institute of Politics, was the suppression of the Tiananmen Square protests. They go so far as to state that "In 1989, quelling the political disturbance in Beijing was a landmark event in the structural development stage of the PLA's military operations other than war" (1989 年, 平息北京政治风波是我军非战争军事行动进入结构性拓展阶段的标志性事件), and that "In calming this disturbance, our military was put to the test, with military operations other than war playing a major role" (在平息这场风波中, 我军经受住了考验, 非战争军事行动发挥了重要的作用). Other examples from the 1990s include imposing martial law in Tibet, engaging in flood relief, establishing the Hong Kong and Macau garrisons, and the military exercises carried out during the 1995–96 Taiwan Strait crisis. Zhu and Wang, "A review of military operations other than war by the people's military," pp.38–39.

9 Another source indicates that the regulations provided for 30 days of training time dedicated to MOOTW. Cheng Guofeng [程果丰] and Zhang Xiaona [张孝娜], 'Focus on strengthening MOOTW training' [注重加强非战争军事行动训练], *National Defense* [国防], 2008/04, p.48.

10 Zhu and Wang, "A review of military operations other than war by the people's military," p.39.

11 The terms "*feizhanzheng junshi xingdong*" (非战争军事行动) and "*feizhanzheng xingdong*" (非战争行动) each appear twice, on p.214 and 500, and p.15–16 and 484 respectively.

12 SMS 2001, p. 500. SMS 2001, p. 214 also contends that that some states utilize arms control as a peacetime weapon which obfuscates their political and strategic intentions while "interfering with other states' ability to implement correct strategic decisions" (干扰别国作出正确的战略决策), likely indicating the suspicion with which the MOOTW concept was first met.

13 Zhu, "On military operations other than war"

14 *China Military Science* (CMS) is published by the Academy of Military Science in Beijing. Its articles are generally written by AMS staff and are used in the instruction of the PLA's officer corps. Therefore its contents are tantamount to official statements of policy.

15 Zhu and Wang, "A review of military operations other than war by the people's military," p.40

16 Ibid.

17 Ibid.

18 "Academy of Military Science establishes MOOTW Research Center" [解放军军事科学院成立非战争军事行动研究中心], December 13, 2011, http://www.china.com.cn/; By July of 2014, the center employed four permanent researchers (研究员) and four post-doctoral researchers (博士后), and had also at various times engaged more than sixty experts in related fields as well as visiting researchers (客座研究员). "Overview of the MOOTW Research Center" [非战争军事行动研究中心概况], July 29, 2014, AMS website, http://www.ams.ac.cn/.

19 "Academy of Military Science establishes MOOTW Research Center" [解放军军事科学院成立非战争军事行动研究中心], December 13, 2011, http://www.china.com.cn/.

20 According to internet reports, Zheng has over twenty years' experience in MOOTW work, and personally participated in the relief efforts in response to the 2013 Lushan earthquake (possibly as an observer). No author, "Academy of Military Science MOOTW Research Center director Zheng Shouhua—In order to win, what should be done?" [军事科学院非战争军事行动研究中心主任郑守华—— 为打赢，怎么"拼"都应该], August 26, 2014, http://news.china.com.cn/; Zheng also attended the 5th Xiangshan Forum in 2014. No author, "The Fifth Xiangshan Forum's Chinese experts,"

October 13, 2015, http://www.xiangshanforum.cn/artfive/fiveforum/fiveguests/fiveces/201510/499.html. Since its establishment, the center has produced various monographs and instructional texts, including *A Textbook for MOOTW* [非战争军事行动教程], *Research on Counter-terrorism Operations* [反恐怖作战研究], *Regulations for Counter-terrorism Exercises* [反恐怖演习规范], *Rescue and Relief Operations* [抢险救灾行动], and *The Yearbook of World MOOTW* [世界非战争军事行动年鉴]. English titles are author translations. No author, "Overview of the MOOTW Research Center" [非战争军事行动研究中心概况], July 29, 2014, AMS website, http://www.ams.ac.cn/

[21] Zheng Shouhua [郑守华], chief ed., *A Textbook of Military Operations Other Than War* [非战争军事行动教程], (Beijing: Academy of Military Sciences Press, 2013), pp.9–14.

[22] The book's title has no official English translation. The Chinese Military Encyclopedia translates the term "*jiaocheng*" (教程) as "course material," but given its usage in this instance, more properly connotes "textbook". The book's chief editor, Zheng Shouhua, is also the director of the MOOTW research center at AMS.

[23] Fu Zhanhe [傅占河], Zhang Ce [张策], and Yang Jianjun [杨建军], chief eds., *Research on the Command of Non-traditional Security Military Operations* [非传统安全军事行动指挥研究], (Beijing: PLA Press, 2008), pp.3–4.

[24] Song, et al., chief eds., *Military Operations Other Than War Case Studies* (2009), p. 9.

[25] Liu Yuejun [刘粤军], 'On the employment of military forces in peacetime' [论和平时期军事力量的运用], *China Military Science* [中国军事科学] 2013, No. 5, p.42; At the time of writing, the author was commander of the Lanzhou Military District.

[26] Song, et al., chief eds., *Military Operations Other Than War Case Studies* (2009), p.1.

[27] Song, et al., chief eds., *Military Operations Other Than War Case Studies* (2009), p.9–11.

[28] Fu, et al., chief eds., *Research on the Command of Non-traditional Security Military Operations* (2008), pp.3–4.

[29] Fu, et al., chief eds., *Research on the Command of Non-traditional Security Military Operations* (2008), p.2.

[30] Fu, et al., chief eds., *Research on the Command of Non-traditional Security Military Operations* (2008), pp.2–3.

[31] Liu, "On the employment of military forces in peacetime," *CMS* 2013, p.42. Liu Xiangyang [刘向阳], Xu Sheng [徐升], Xiong Kaiping [熊开平], and Zhang Chunyu [张春雨], "A study of non-war military operations" [非战争军事行动探要], *China Military Science* [中国军事科学] 2008, No. 3, p.3.

[32] Liu, et al., "A study of non-war military operations," *CMS* 2008, p.3.

[33] Fu, et al., chief eds., *Research on the Command of Non-traditional Security Military Operations* (2008), p.7.

[34] Fu, et al., chief eds., *Research on the Command of Non-traditional Security Military Operations* (2008), p.1.

[35] Liu, et al., "A study of non-war military operations," *CMS* 2008, p.3.

[36] Wang Guanzhong [王冠中], "Striving to build and consolidate the national defense and a strong army" [努力建设巩固国防和强大军队], *People's Daily* [人民日报], December 13, 2012.

[37] Zhou, "Discussion of guiding the vigorous improvement of MOOTW capabilities on the basis of Hu Jintao's military innovative theory," *Military Historical Research* 2009, p.25.

[38] Liu, "On the employment of military forces in peacetime," *CMS* 2013, p.43.

[39] Fu, et al., chief eds., *Research on the Command of Non-traditional Security Military Operations* (2008), p.17.

[40] Fu, et al., chief eds., *Research on the Command of Non-traditional Security Military Operations* (2008), p.12; In the view of the 2013 SMS, in the context of many types of MOOTW, the armed forces are primarily used as special, organized forces that only happen to have combat capabilities, emphasizing their organizational cohesion and discipline over their gross combat power. *SMS* 2013, p.164.

[41] SMS 2013, p.11; It also identifies MOOTW as one of the basic forms (alongside warfare and deterrence) by which the nation's military, political, economic, technological, and cultural strength is manifested. SMS 2013, p.6

[42] *SMS* 2013, p.155.

[43] *SMS* 2013, p.151.

[44] *SMS* 2013, p.157–158.

[45] *SMS* 2001, p. 500.

[46] *SMS* 2001, p.15–16.

[47] *SMS* 2013, p.154.

[48] From the *China Military Encyclopedia* (中国军事百科全书), quoted in Zheng, chief ed., *A Textbook of Military Operations Other Than War* (2013), p.1.

[49] Liu, et al., "A study of non-war military operations," CMS 2008, p.1.

[50] From the 2011 *junyu*, quoted in *SMS* 2013, p.154.

[51] Fu, et al., chief eds., *Research on the Command of Non-traditional Security Military Operations* (2008), p.16

[52] Essentially described as using exercises and other operations in a local area to intimidate, warn, or otherwise signal a target country.

[53] Song, et al., chief eds., *Military Operations Other Than War Case Studies* (2009), p.3–5; The order and precise wording differ slightly from the 2008 list, but are essentially the same: 1. Counter terrorism (反恐怖行动), 2. Maintaining social stability (维护社会稳定行动), 3. Emergency rescue and disaster relief (抢险救灾行动), 4. International peacekeeping (国际维和行动), and 5. Defending national rights and interests (维护国家权益行动).

[54] SMS 2013, p.162.

[55] SMS 2013, p.163.

[56] Ibid.

[57] Ibid.

[58] SMS 2013, p.164.

[59] To illustrate this, the source explicitly points to American restraint shown before the opening of hostilities during the Gulf War, though that conflict is not held up to be an example of MOOTW.

[60] The source points out that in the case of the United States, three years of peacekeeping in Yugoslavia cost $4.6 billion, while 43 days of war in the Persian Gulf cost $47 billion.

[61] Zheng, chief ed., *A Textbook of Military Operations Other Than War* (2013), p.7–8.

[62] The source notes that Russian efforts at counter-terrorism in Chechnya rapidly approached something close to a full-scale war, while MOOTW in Kosovo progressed to a full-scale war with Serbia when the United States became involved. Song, et al., chief eds., *Military Operations Other Than War Case Studies* (2009), p.5–6.

[63] Song, et al., chief eds., *Military Operations Other Than War Case Studies* (2009), p.5–6.

[64] Zhu, "On military operations other than war," p.84; Tang Liang [唐亮], "A new look at the characteristics and laws of MOOTW" [非战争军事行动特点规律新探], *Journal of the Xi'an Politics Institute* [西安政治学院学报] 2011, No. 2, p.125.

[65] SMS 2013, p.166.

[66] SMS 2013, p.165.

[67] SMS 2013, p.165.

[68] The source also emphasizes that the MOOTW command is very time-sensitive (指挥时效性强). With contingencies often emerging rapidly and unexpectedly, major command decisions must often be made within hours, especially in the case of disaster relief. Zheng, chief ed., *A Textbook of Military Operations Other Than War* (2013), pp.20–21.

[69] SMS 2013, p.166

[70] Zheng, chief ed., *A Textbook of Military Operations Other Than War* (2013), p.27–29.

[71] Quotation in Chinese: "非战争军事行动的实施易于谋划、易于控制、易于调节"; Tang, "A new look at the characteristics and laws of MOOTW," p.125.

[72] Zhu, "On military operations other than war," p.85.

[73] Liu, "On the employment of military forces in peacetime," *CMS* 2013, p.48.

[74] Zhu, "On military operations other than war," p.85.

[75] Liu, et al., "A study of non-war military operations," *CMS* 2008, pp.3–4

[76] Zheng, chief ed., *A Textbook of Military Operations Other Than War* (2013), pp.4–5.

[77] Zheng, chief ed., *A Textbook of Military Operations Other Than War* (2013), pp.4–5.

[78] *SMS* 2013, p.164.

[79] *SMS* 2013, p.165.

[80] *SMS* 2013, p.168.

[81] Song, et al., chief eds., *Military Operations Other Than War Case Studies* (2009), pp.6–7.

[82] Liu, et al., "A study of non-war military operations," CMS 2008, pp.4–5.

[83] Such operations are intended to enable the armed forces to play a role as a peaceful and constructive force. Nonetheless, it is acknowledged that confrontational MOOTW (especially when carried out against other states) have the potential to escalate toward war. SMS 2013, p.166.

[84] Zheng, chief ed., *A Textbook of Military Operations Other Than War* (2013), p.6.

[85] Quotation in Chinese: 尽管非战争军事行动常被某些霸权主义国家作为干涉他国内政的工具，但它同样也是许多国家反对霸权主义的工具; Nanjing 2003 p.85.

[86] CMS 2013 p.43–44.

[87] Zheng, chief ed., *A Textbook of Military Operations Other Than War* (2013), pp.6–7.

[88] Zheng, chief ed., *A Textbook of Military Operations Other Than War* (2013), p.8–9.

[89] Liu, et al., "A study of non-war military operations," *CMS* 2008, p.2.

[90] Zhou, "Discussion of guiding the vigorous improvement of MOOTW capabilities on the basis of Hu Jintao's military innovative theory," *Military Historical Research* 2009, p.25.

[91] Liu, et al., "A study of non-war military operations," *CMS* 2008, pp.3–4; This is true even for purely domestic instances of MOOTW. The emergency relief response to the 2008 earthquake was specifically seen as an opportunity to demonstrate effective command and control capabilities for modern warfare, utilizing diverse troop types engaged in a wide-range of tasks (especially by means of various satellite systems). Non-traditional security military command capabilities and operational command capability are described as an 'indivisible organism'. Fu, et al., chief eds., *Research on the Command of Non-traditional Security Military Operations* (2008), pp.17–18.

[92] Zhu and Wang, "A review of military operations other than war by the people's military," p.41.

[93] Tang Liang, "A new look at the characteristics and laws of MOOTW" (2011), p.126.

[94] Liu, et al., "A study of non-war military operations," *CMS* 2008, pp.2–3.

[95] Liu, et al., "A study of non-war military operations," *CMS* 2008, pp.5–6.

[96] Ministry of Defense, "Defense Ministry's regular press conference on April 30, 2015," available at http://eng.mod.gov.cn/Press/2015-04/30/content_4582738.htm.

[97] Andrew Erickson and Conor Kennedy, "China's maritime militia," paper presented at the Conference on China as a Maritime Power, Arlington, Va., pp. 28–29 July 2015.

Chapter 12: An Introduction to China's Strategic Military-Civilian Fusion

Daniel Alderman

"Expand Military-Civilian Fusion from its concentration in the realm of the defense science and technology industry, and broaden it into every area of the economy, science and technology, education, and personnel, etc., raising it from an industry and department-level issue to national strategic standing"

"把军民融合由主要集中在国防科技工业领域拓展到经济、科技、教育、人才等各个领域，由行业、部门层次提升到国家战略层次"

- Science of Military Strategy 2013[1]

China's national security propaganda is wallpapered with references promoting Military-Civilian Fusion (MCF), an important Chinese concept that has been routinely mentioned by Xi Jinping and frequently cited in seminal strategic works such as the 2013 edition of the *Science of Military Strategy* (SMS). Some authoritative Chinese sources go so far as to state that deepening Military-Civilian Fusion (MCF) is not merely a desirable outcome, but a national strategic objective. However, despite frequent mentions, foreign analyses of the PLA have not generally examined why China's leaders devote so much energy to this aspirational concept. This chapter attempts to answer a series of questions related to MCF as a strategic priority: What are its origins? What are its strategic goals? And how is it being implemented? This chapter begins answering these questions by analyzing the historic evolution, current meaning, and future prospects for MCF's implementation as it developed in China's strategic writings over the past fifteen years.

In order to define borders around the fairly broad Chinese concept of Military-Civilian Fusion, this chapter is divided into three sections. Section one analyzes previous efforts for civil-military integration, analyzing how China arrived at the concept of Military-Civilian Fusion (军民融合 / Junmin Ronghe) and why this differs in practice from Civil-Military Integration (军民结合 / Junmin Jiehe) and other previous PLA efforts at integrating civilian and military resources. Placing MCF in historical perspective, this section provides an overview of how Chinese leaders have historically addressed civil-military interaction, and why the goals of MCF are far more expansive than previous CMI efforts. Section two addresses the increased emphasis placed on MCF in recent authoritative Chinese sources, drawing upon China's larger strategic literature to note how these grand civil-military ambitions have evolved over time. It seeks to address why the Xi administration is now placing such importance on this concept and why they have so dramatically expanded their expectations in this realm. Finally, section three addresses the Xi administration's implementation of MCF, focusing on the organizations tasked to achieve this ambitious guidance, including the creation of an MCF Leading Small Group. This section highlights the unequal implementation of MCF and lack of clarity on how top-level leadership will be implemented. It concludes by noting that during the PLA's dramatic reorganization, the opportunity exists for significant changes as a result of top-level MCF policies. The full extent of these changes remains to be seen, determined by its prioritization within Xi's longer list of ambitious strategic objectives.

As a translation note, the two concepts of MCF (*Junmin Ronghe*) and CMI (*Junmin Jiehe*) are both often translated from Chinese as "Civil-Military Integration," unnecessarily blurring the significant differences between the two concepts. The term "Military Civilian Fusion" is an accurate English rendering of this Chinese-language PLA term of art, enabling a more nuanced discussion of how Chinese policy has evolved. However, Chinese sources with official English translations, such as the 2015 Defense White Paper, will not generally reflect this schema in their English versions. Sections two and three below analyze the transition in terminology and intent in greater detail.

Section One: Military-Civilian Fusion in Historical Context

This section provides an overview of the historical relationship between civilian and military resource sharing in China, including an examination of how the *Science of Military Strategy*'s previous 2001 edition addresses this issue in order to set a baseline for analysis of current efforts to recalibrate civil-military resource sharing. The first influential reference to Military-Civilian Fusion as a leading principle was Hu Jintao's urging to "take a path of Military-Civilian Fusion with Chinese characteristics" in his 2007 Party work report.[2] As longtime PLA analyst Ed Francis and others have noted, MCF is in many ways a continuation of a long line of concepts promoted by successive Chinese leaders to encourage cooperation between civilian and military resources in order to develop China's war fighting capabilities while also boosting civilian economic output.[3]

Dating back to the earliest days of the PRC, Chinese leaders have long sought more coordinated integration of military and civilian resources. This tradition included expansive propaganda campaigns by each successive head of state, accompanied by official slogans and pronouncements. In 1956 Mao put forward the concept of "handling military and civilian affairs together" (军民兼顾).[4] In 1982 Deng Xiaoping stated the often-referenced "16 character guiding principle," which is frequently referenced in MCF literature even today. Translated directly into English, these principles read: "civil-military integration, peacetime and wartime integration, giving predominance to military products, using the civilian to support the military" (军民结合,平战结合, 以军为主, 以民养军).[5] Jiang Zemin's ascendance in the 1990s brought the next generation of CMI policies with his promotion of "civil-military integration, locating the military within the civilian" (军民结合, 寓军于民).[6]

Each of these concepts spoke to the larger integration of defense and civilian resources and the goal of civilian support to military needs, but these successive campaigns were primarily focused on better integrating China's defense industry in order to guarantee that China's leading civilian scientists were directly supporting the military (and vice versa). With the introduction of Military-Civilian Fusion as a new guiding principle, Chinese ambitions expanded to include far more areas of the economy than simply the defense industry.

Hu Jintao's unveiling of MCF in 2007 marked a transition from primarily defense science and technology (S&T) focused CMI efforts to an attempt at larger scale coordination. In 2009, Hu described MCF as an effort to "establish and build a civil-military integrated weapons equipment research and production system, military talent training system, and military support system, while improving the national defense mobilization system," opening up "new prospects for Military-Civilian Fusion to occur."[7] The Xi administration later built on this base, continuing to push for deeper integration under the auspices of MCF. Interestingly, in the midst of this transition in 2012, defense industry officials directly stated that although CMI was still often referenced at the time as a defense industry-focused initiative for deeper integration, the industry was officially shifting focus from CMI to MCF.[8]

SMS 2001: Importance of the Masses

Looking back to the 2001 edition of the Science of Military Strategy, the volume's editorial board noted the importance of integrating civilians for support in war preparation and the defense industry's research, development, and acquisition (RDA) of weapons and equipment. However, SMS 2001 is light on specific areas for civilian integration, cooperation, and coordination with their military counterparts. Instead, it often provides vague references to the civilian "masses" (人民群众), which are instructed to provide broad, unspecified support to the military during the preparation and execution of military activities. This general call to the masses is accompanied by a heavier emphasis on the role of formal militias and reserve units as civilian contributors to the military's needs. Although the Chinese phrase for "masses" also appears in the SMS 2013 edition, its use appears primarily historical, not a reference to current efforts for support and integration.

SMS 2001's chapter on war preparations provides a representative window into its relative lack of depth in addressing civil-military integration efforts. The chapter directly addresses civilian participation in military efforts by broadly recognizing the need for civilian inputs into the economy and S&T development, but provides no specificity on how non-military organizations can directly assist military personnel.[9] Furthermore, when the chapter addresses wartime mobilization, it focuses exclusively on militia and reserve units with no emphasis on the role that purely civilian assets such as commercial ships, trucks, rail lines, and communication networks play in supporting mobilization. [10] Finally, when specifically addressing the strategic importance of sound logistics support, there is little nod to civilian support; nearly all the emphasis is placed on PLA activities.[11] As discussed in greater detail below, by the time SMS was updated in 2013, Chinese thinking had progressed far enough that civilian integration is now specifically referenced as a key factor in wartime preparation, including for logistics and mobilization, a far more intense level of cooperation than had been imagined a decade earlier.

The theme of broad support from the masses continues during the 2001 volume's discussion of political work and psychological work, which also receives a dedicated chapter. [12] Again, the editors emphasize the key role of the "masses," but do not detail any coordinated strategic interaction or goals. This more rudimentary analysis focuses on having the "masses" support the CCP/PLA with propaganda and support at home and abroad throughout a campaign, while also emphasizing the need for "mobilizing the masses for political work."[13] No additional detail is provided on what this political work should include or what government entities should be tasked with overseeing the coordination of these efforts across military and civilian lines. This type of broad, nebulous call for action is little more than safe 'boilerplate' language that was broadly used at the time in official pronouncements. Taken together with the omissions discussed above, it can be viewed as a reflection of the relatively low priority the Academy of Military Sciences placed on envisioning a role for civilians in supporting PLA operations in the early 2000s.

Beyond these broad calls to political support, however, the editors do posit a more direct role (albeit a somewhat narrow one) for civilian integration through militias and reserves, when describing the need for "Total Power of the People's War Under Modern Conditions."[14] Although militia units are not formally a part of the PLA, in the Chinese system they are taken together with the PLA and the People's Armed Police (PAP) as constituting "China's armed forces." AMS writing on this topic states plainly that "One central task is to mobilize, organize and arm the masses according to the requirements of the high-tech local war."[15] Little detail is provided on exactly what this means, but goalposts of a sort are provided in that this effort should "transform war potential into war power," with the important caveat that in most cases, the PLA should "do [its] utmost to avoid affecting the overall situation of the economic and social development of the country."[16]

At first glance, this imperative appears internally contradictory—expecting civilians to drop everything and contribute to the war effort on the one hand, and on the other hand exhorting them to continue as normal with their daily routines. This contradiction is overcome through an emphasis on the importance of militias and reserves. As the editors put it, "Arming the masses is realized by organizing and employing militia, reserve forces (units) and so on."[17] As noted below, the importance of reserve units continues as a theme in the 2013 volume, while the militia system receives significantly less emphasis.

In the viewpoints shown in SMS 2001, the "masses" are generally expected to offer broad support to wartime preparation and mobilization efforts, while militias and reserve units are expected to be the key elements of civilian society that deeply integrate or fuse with the PLA's wartime efforts. One key exception to this relationship is defense S&T, where civilians are expected to contribute fully in deeper integration with the defense sector, even being called upon in the books' final pages to "maintain our capability to get scientific, technical, and economic strategic resources from various international channels and in various ways."[18] This relatively narrow view of what civilian support entails was broadened via planning and policy over the subsequent decade, with SMS 2013 going into much greater detail on the key role of civilian fusion of resources in information security, mobilization, and talent development, in addition to continued emphasis on integration in S&T research and reserve forces.

Military-Civilian Fusion's Rise as a Strategic Concept

From its original promulgation midway through the Hu administration to Xi's ascent to power in 2012 and onward to the present day, MCF has evolved into a holistic strategic concept that reaches beyond the defense industry. Xi has put a prominent personal stamp on the concept, following in the tradition of previous supreme leaders. He has repeatedly called for "deepened reform," and his personal views on MCF are directly cited as the guiding philosophy for PLA strategists.[19] The rhetorical importance of this concept to leading Chinese bureaucrats is also evident, with one stating that Chinese leaders were previously called upon to make a "physical change" to implement civil-military relations through CMI, but with MCF they are now tasked with enabling a deeper "chemical reaction" between civilian and military resources.[20] SMS 2013 in particular offers an avenue for outside analysts to move beyond official rhetoric on MCF and truly understand China's goals for the concept.

In SMS 2013's vision of MCF, there is tremendous breadth in the types of activities envisioned as targets for "deeper reform," but three areas of emphasis stand out in its examination of the topic. First, SMS 2013 depicts network and information security as an increasingly important sphere that calls for direct civilian fusion with the military in actual combat roles. Second, SMS 2013 provides a detailed road map for civilian operational assistance with elements of mobilization and logistics during wartime preparation and implementation. Third, the defense industry, S&T research, and joint education all continue to be key areas of emphasis for greater cooperation between civilian and military assets. Across these three areas SMS 2013 continues to place importance on militias and reserve units, but greatly downplays the general idea of leveraging "the masses" in a military role as was previously seen in the 2001 edition.

SMS 2013 differs significantly from its 2001 predecessor by repeatedly calling for direct civilian integration and support of military operations, going so far as to call for the integration of civilian network warfare operators in combat roles. Whereas the 2001 volume makes no reference to purely civilian (non-militia/reserve) contributions to combat, the 2013 volume leans forward in promoting civilian assets for military use in network domain operations, whether during peacetime battlespace preparation or wartime activity. Much of this stance appears tied to Chinese strategists' belief that the network domain is inherently porous and therefore network operations by military and civilian actors are often difficult to distinguish. [21] It is important to note the significance of a decision to allow civilian actors to directly undertake combat activities, which has significant legal and strategic implications for potential adversaries.

In discussing how Chinese strategists can seize upon the porous network security landscape, SMS 2013's editors call for coordinated attacks by military and civilian entities, urging the use of civilians to shield military activities in network operations during peace and wartime. [22] This represents a significant departure from SMS 2001, in which civilians are never presented as likely combatants during wartime operations. Beyond network operations, this edition also goes on to note that civilians must be key participants in cross domain deterrence, including integrated deterrence efforts across the nuclear, space, and network domains.[23]

A second theme for MCF in SMS 2013 is a dependence on civilian logistics support for both peacetime planning and wartime mobilization. At the theoretical level, joint mobilization using civilian assets to rapidly move military personnel and supplies seems an obvious choice, as the civilian economy already has the planes, trains, automobiles, and basic supplies necessary to accomplish many mobilization activities in a peacetime environment. However, reliance on civilians for these critical needs is fraught with dilemmas, including a lack of operational security, challenges quickly transitioning peacetime assets to wartime footing, and coordination difficulties. Civilian contributors to wartime mobilization must carry out their routine operations in peacetime, and yet be trained, available, and willing to support the military at a moment's notice. Despite these challenges, SMS 2013 makes clear that civilian resources will be a critical participant in future wartime mobilization.[24]

SMS 2013 is explicit that the fusion of civilian and military resources is the key for rapid national mobilization through the existing civilian transportation infrastructure. Referring to MCF and local integration with the military, the authors define this fused system as an essential "strategic delivery" (战略投送) platform. [25] The need for an integrated platform between military and civilian assets is reiterated when discussing the need to develop an integrated military-civilian emergency monitoring mechanism.[26] As noted below, China's ability to construct a unified MCF command structure will likely be a key determinant of MCF's future success.

Discussion of how China's militia units fit into the PLA's mobilization and logistics modernization efforts is for the most part curiously absent from SMS 2013, despite it being frequently discussed in SMS 2001.[27] Despite this lack of focus, however, militias continue to be a key force in Chinese strategy, and the trend is toward their deployment as a quasi-military civilian force that can closely coordinate with defense goals but remain ostensibly commercial in their undertakings. This behavior is most prominent in the South China Sea, where maritime militias play a key role in China's coordinated effort to influence regions further afield.[28] Looking ahead, it will be critical to monitor how MCF impacts China's future use of militias further from home.

Finally, SMS also refers to the need for larger scale "development in fusion," including maintaining the areas of military-civilian integration that are working relatively efficiently, while also bolstering segments of MCF that are not as well developed. As this chapter's opening quotation makes clear, SMS 2013's editors wish to raise MCF from an industry-specific concept in the defense industrial base, to a much grander scale.[29] Key wildcards within this ambitious goal are economic fusion and talent development. On these fronts, PLA strategists recognize that the national economy must continue to remain healthy in order to allow the military to prepare and sustain itself in combat, but authoritative Chinese sources are quiet on the exact manner in which the military should take action on this front. In the meantime, joint development of defense S&T and technical education continue to be key areas of emphasis within MCF's now significantly broadened umbrella of strategic concepts.

Beyond SMS 2013, the ascendance of MCF as a strategic priority has also been evident over the last decade of China's national Defense White Papers. From 2006 to 2015, these papers show a discernable timeline of maturation as this concept evolved within Chinese strategic planning circles. In the 2006 and 2008 white papers there was an emphasis on CMI for its role in supporting defense S&T, as well as militias, reserve units, and a limited emphasis on mobilization, tracking closely with SMS 2001's emphasis on the same issues.[30]

Their emphasis on civil-military interactions expanded in 2010, with the Ministry of defense citing "logistical support" and personnel training" as emphases for MCF in addition to ongoing calls for greater civil-military defense S&T cooperation.[31] In the 2015 strategic defense white paper, MCF receives an extended treatment that emphasizes a broad, whole-of-government approach to increasing combat strength through civilian contributions across a sweeping number of spheres, including the need for a national-level MCF coordination organization, shared resources across technology and logistics, and deeper integration for national defense mobilization.[32] The evolution and expansion of MCF across China's strategic literature appears well coordinated, and this shift in strategic thinking can be mapped onto China's current plans for MCF's fuller realization.

The Future of Military-Civilian Fusion: Will Aspirational Policies be Forcefully Implemented?

As demonstrated above, MCF is an aspirational expansion of coordination between civilians and the military, with the explicit purpose of better preparing the military to fight and win wars. But how aggressively do Chinese leaders plan to implement these changes, and what organizations are responsible for overseeing its implementation? The 2013 SMS editorial team assists in answering this question by citing in their introduction that the volume is meant to assist in carrying out the spirit of the 18th National Congress and Chairman Xi's

"Strong Nation Strong Military" (强国强军) concept. This series of reforms, also known as the Third Plenum Reforms, contains a laundry list of key priorities that Xi's regime hopes to implement. Section 15, paragraph 57 of this guidance is entirely devoted to the implementation of MCF (深化国防和军队改革).[33] It reads:

> 57. *Deepening the integration between the military and civilian sectors.* To promote the integrated development of the military and civilian sectors, we will establish—at the national level—unified leadership, and institutions that coordinate between the military and local governments, link military demands to supplies, and share information. We will improve the national defense industry system and sci-tech innovation system serving national defense. We will reform the system and mechanism for the management of scientific research and production for national defense and armament procurement, and guide outstanding private enterprises into the fields of research, development, production and maintenance of military products. We will reform and improve the policies and systems for cultivating military personnel by relying on national education. We will open more areas of military logistics to ordinary enterprises. We will deepen the reform of national defense education, improve the national defense mobilization system, and the system of conscription during peace time and mobilization during wartime. We will deepen

> the reform of the militia reserve system, and
> adjust the management system of border defense,
> coast defense and air defense.[34]

Similar to SMS 2013, the Third Plenum guidance offers a detailed list of various forthcoming reforms that are intended in part to provide value to the military by more deeply integrating civilian resources. In evaluating the future prospects for the full range of MCF policies, one glaring void is a lack of information surrounding the creation of a national-level Military Civilian Fusion Leading Small Group (军民融合领导小组, or MCFLSG). This organization was discussed in an authoritative Party journal as early as September 2014, but its mission was still discussed in a planning phase in the 2015 Strategic Defense White Paper, without specifically being named. [35] [36] Although China created a State National Defense Mobilization Committee (SNDMC) as far back as 1994, it is not known whether this seldom-discussed and newly formed MCF Leading Small Group possesses a national coordination infrastructure to oversee the broad integration of shared resources envisioned in MCF.[37] It is known that the MCFLSG now has a national office associated with its mission and that some local governments and industries are creating their own MCF leading small groups.[38] However, it is not known whether Xi Jinping himself is overseeing the national level's push to provincial and local levels, or whether the MCFLSG's membership represents a broad spectrum of civilian entities at the national level. Considering the entrenched national and local bureaucracies at work, any indication that Xi is personally involved or is otherwise directing MCF implementation would be a significant departure and key signpost toward intensified sincerity in overcoming the lack of coordination between military and civilian entities at the national strategic level, flowing down to critically important local implementation.

In addition to the MCF Leading Small Group and its subsidiaries there are also two lower level sub-national entities devoted to the analysis and implementation of MCF-related initiatives. Within the military, the Academy of Military Science (AMS) is home to an MCF research center, which has the official English translation of "Civil-Military Integration Research Center" (军民融合研究中心).[39] Similar to the earlier mentioned translation confusion, this center's Chinese name references MCF and is an outgrowth of Chinese efforts to move beyond mere CMI, but the official English translation of the relevant portion of its name is nevertheless "civil-military integration". The Center, which was founded in late 2011 and is one of at least seven research institutes under AMS, is responsible for academic research on the implementation and optimization of MCF policies.[40]

This research center appears to be the PLA's closest thing to a "brain trust" for studying MCF, but based on its low ranking bureaucratic status and academic focus, likely lacks the political strength to significantly shift policies beyond offering recommendations. The Center does host China's largest annual conference on the implementation of MCF, and based on its call for papers on thirty different MCF topics, it is clearly examining a broad array of MCF related policies.[41] However, despite this deep academic interest, it not known whether the Center's work has directly affected policy outcomes. In determining the future of MCF-related reforms, this organization will be a key office to watch.

Within the civilian bureaucracy, the Ministry of Industry and Information Technology (MIIT) is home to a similarly low ranking office dedicated to MCF. Known formally as the Civil Military Integration Promotion Department (军民结合司, or CMIPD), this organization still references CMI (军民结合 / Junmin Jiehe) in its organizational title, not MCF (军民融合 / Junmin Ronghe).[42] Founded in 2008 during the creation of MIIT, CMIPD focuses on promoting the diffusion of dual-use technologies between civilian and military entities. Considering its home within the technology focused MIIT, it is unsurprising that this office is tightly focused on technology transfer, unlike its counterpart in AMS examines a wider variety of MCF policies. CMIPD is also unlike its AMS counterpart in that its role is largely functional, serving as a bridge between civilian and military technological actors, rather than that of an academic, theoretical institution researching the optimization of MCF policies. The larger policy impact from this office also appears minimal, but it remains a key organization to monitor for the future prospects of MCF.

In looking toward the future success of Military Civilian Fusion-related policies, the Military Civilian Fusion Leading Small Group remains the key entity to watch in determining the prospects for implementation of the ambitious stated objectives of Xi's priorities in MCF. At the heart of PLA reform, including the option of MCF, there is still only one person that formally straddles China's military and civilian bureaucracies, and that is Xi Jinping in his role as chairman of the Central Military Commission. In order to fully implement the numerous goals contained within MCF, the Chinese bureaucracy will have to work from within its existing structure in order to overcome entrenched bureaucratic interests that often work against resource sharing between civilian and military entities. Signs exist that this is beginning to change, but in the current absence of information regarding the MCFLSG's mission and membership, it appears likely that MCF objectives will be unevenly implemented among the long list of strategic objectives sought by Xi Jinping.

NOTES

[1] SMS 2013, pp. 271.

[2] "走出一条中国特色军民融合式发展路子" Xinhua, October 24, 2007. http://news.xinhuanet.com/newscenter/2007-10/24/content_6938568_8.htm.

[3] The author is grateful for the assistance of Ed Francis, who provided unpublished research on the history of Chinese CMI.

[4] Ling Shengyin, Peng Aihua, Zou Shimeng, "Retrospect and Enlightenment of the Development of Military and Civil Integration Concept," *China Military Science*, No. 1, 2009, Issue No. 103.

[5] Ling Shengyin, Peng Aihua, Zou Shimeng, "Retrospect and Enlightenment of the Development of Military and Civil Integration Concept," *China Military Science*, No. 1, 2009, Issue No. 103.

[6] "Retrospective and Thoughts on Our Country's Implementation of Civil-Military Integration, Locating the Military in the Civilian," *Defense Science and Technology Industry*, 2008, No. 12, page 30.

[7] "Hu Jintao: Follow the Path of Civil Military Fusion Type Development with Chinese Characteristics," Xinhua, September 5, 2010, http://news.xinhuanet.com/politics/2009-07/24/content_11768163.htm.

[8] "军民结合"到"军民融合" 管理体制亟待突破, Xinhua, April 15, 2012, http://www.cq.xinhuanet.com/2012-04/15/c_111782223.htm.

[9] SMS 2001, Chapter 7.

[10] SMS 2001, pp. 188.

[11] SMS 2001, pp. 353–357.

[12] SMS 2001, pp. 362.

[13] SMS 2001, pp. 369.

[14] SMS 2001, p. 454.

[15] SMS 2001, p. 455.

[16] Ibid.

[17] Ibid.

[18] SMS 2001, p. 472.

[19] Yu Chuanxin [于川信], 军民融合:牵住顶层设计这个牛鼻子

Center Perspectives [中心视点], Academy of Military Sciences Website, July 16, 2014, http://www.ams.ac.cn/portal/content/content!viewContent.action?contentid=152d848e-9bc5-4f35-8b97-2fc0b054ffb5. Esp. "习近平主席强调:"进一步做好军民融合式发展这篇大文章,坚持需求牵引、国家主导,努力形成基础设施和重要领域军民深度融合的发展格局。"

[20] Xu Dazhe [许达哲], "走军民融合深度发展之路," MIIT, July 7, 2015, http://www.miit.gov.cn/n11293472/n11294447/n15783164/n15783228/16695812.html.

[21] SMS 2013, pp. 131 and 196.

[22] SMS 2013, p. 130.

[23] SMS 2013, p. 169.

[24] SMS 2013, pp. 266–267.

[25] SMS 2013, p. 260.

[26] SMS 2013, pp. 262–263.

[27] SMS 2013, p. 272.

[28] James Kraska and Michael Monti, "The Law of Naval Warfare and China's Maritime Militia," *International Law Studies*, U.S. Naval War College, (2015) http://stockton.usnwc.edu/cgi/viewcontent.cgi?article=1406&context=ils.

[29] SMS 2013, pp. 270–272.

[30] "China's National Defense," [中国的国防] Xinhua, December 29, 2006, http://www.gov.cn/zwgk/2006-12/29/content_486759.htm, and "China's National Defense," Xinhua, January 20, 2009, http://www.gov.cn/zwgk/2009-01/20/content_1210224.htm.

[31] *China's National Defense in 2010*, http://www.china.org.cn/government/whitepaper/node_7114675.htm.

[32] China's Military Strategy [中国的军事战略] State Council Information Office [中华人民共和国国务院新闻办公室], May 29, 2015. http://www.scio.gov.cn/zfbps/gfbps/Document/1435341/1435341.htm.

[33] "授权发布:中共中央关于全面深化改革若干重大问题的决定," Xinhua, November 15, 2013, http://news.xinhuanet.com/politics/2013-11/15/c_118164235.htm.

[34] "Decision of the CCCPC on Some Major Issues Concerning Comprehensively Deepening the Reform," Xinhua, November 15, 2013, http://www.china.org.cn/chinese/2014-01/17/content_31226494_15.htm.

[35] 韩志庆, "论加快军民融合深度发展," *PLA Daily*, September 2, 2014, http://www.qstheory.cn/defense/2014-09/02/c_1112322874.htm.

[36] China's Military Strategy [中国的军事战略] State Council Information Office [中华人民共和国国务院新闻办公室], May 29, 2015. http://www.scio.gov.cn/zfbps/gfbps/Document/1435341/1435341.htm.

[37] Tai Ming Cheung, *Fortifying China: The Struggle to Build a Modern Defense Economy* (Ithaca, NY: Cornell University Press, 2009). p. 196.

[38] See for instance http://uav.fzexpo.cn/newsshow.asp?id=3195&big=42, http://www.jspxdj.gov.cn/html/rcgz/2016/0114/4357.html, and http://www.spacechina.com/n25/n144/n206/n216/c1010316/content.html.

[39] More information available at http://www.ams.ac.cn

[40] "军民融合研究中心成立," PLA Daily, December 9, 2011, http://mil.news.sina.com.cn/2011-12-09/0710676878.html.

[41] "第四届 '军民融合发展论坛' 征文通知" AMS, August 7, 2014, http://www.ams.ac.cn/portal/content/content!viewContent.action?contentid=d5e9c270-1293-4f2e-833f-59936be7cafc&contentType=szbf&imgName=tit_jmrh.png

[42]Website available at http://jmjhs.miit.gov.cn/n11293472/n11295193/index.html

ABOUT THE EDITOR

Joe McReynolds

Joe McReynolds is a Research Analyst at Defense Group Inc.'s Center for Intelligence Research and Analysis and the China Security Studies Fellow at the Jamestown Foundation. His research interests primarily center on China's approach to computer network warfare and defense science & technology development. Mr. McReynolds has previously worked with the Council on Foreign Relations and the Pacific Council for International Policy, and is a graduate of Georgetown University's School of Foreign Service and Graduate Security Studies programs. He speaks and reads Chinese and Japanese, and has lived and studied in Nagoya, Guilin and Beijing.

ABOUT THE AUTHORS

Dan Alderman

Daniel Alderman is a Deputy Director at the Defense Group Inc. where he manages a team of over 20 linguist-analysts at DGI's Center for Intelligence Research and Analysis. His research interests include China's science and technology policies, technology transfer efforts and civil-military relations. Alderman previously served as an assistant director at the National Bureau of Asian Research. A Chinese linguist, he received an MA in Asian studies at The George Washington University's Elliott School of International Affairs.

Dennis J. Blasko

Dennis J. Blasko, Lieutenant Colonel, U.S. Army (Retired), served 23 years as a Military Intelligence Officer and Foreign Area Officer specializing in China. Mr. Blasko was an army attaché in Beijing from 1992-1995 and in Hong Kong from 1995-1996. He also served in infantry units in Germany, Italy, and Korea and in Washington at the Defense Intelligence Agency, Headquarters Department of the Army (Office of Special Operations), and the National Defense University War Gaming and Simulation Center. Mr. Blasko is a graduate of the United States Military Academy and the Naval Postgraduate School. He has written numerous articles and chapters on the Chinese military and defense industries and is the author of the book, The Chinese Army Today: Tradition and Transformation for the 21st Century, second edition (Routledge, 2012).

Michael Chase

Michael S. Chase, Ph.D., is a Senior Political Scientist at RAND and an adjunct professor in the China Studies and Strategic Studies Departments at Johns Hopkins University's School of Advanced International Studies (SAIS) in Washington, DC. A specialist in China and Asia-Pacific security issues, he was previously an Associate Professor at the U.S. Naval War College (NWC) in Newport, Rhode Island, where he served as director of the strategic deterrence group in the Warfare Analysis and Research Department and taught in the Strategy and Policy Department. Prior to joining the faculty at NWC, he was a Research Analyst at Defense Group Inc. and an Associate International Policy Analyst at RAND. He is the author of the book Taiwan's Security Policy and numerous chapters and articles on China and Asia-Pacific security issues. His current research focuses on Chinese military modernization, China's nuclear policy and strategy and nuclear force modernization, Taiwan's defense policy, and Asia-Pacific security issues.

Morgan Clemens

Morgan Clemens is a Research Analyst at Defense Group, Inc., where his work focuses on the Chinese armed forces and defense industry. He holds an MA in Asian Studies from George Washington University and a BA in History and Government from the College of William and Mary. He has previously studied at Tsinghua University in Beijing and the Zhejiang University of Technology in Hangzhou.

John Costello

John Costello is Congressional Innovation Fellow for New American Foundation and a former Research Analyst at Defense Group Inc. He was a member of the US Navy and a DOD Analyst. He specializes in information warfare, electronic warfare and non-kinetic counterspace issues.

Andrew S. Erickson

Dr. Erickson is Professor of Strategy in, and a core founding member of, the U.S. Naval War College's China Maritime Studies Institute. He serves on the Naval War College Review's Editorial Board. Since 2008 he has been an Associate in Research at Harvard University's John King Fairbank Center for Chinese Studies. Erickson is also an expert contributor to the Wall Street Journal's China Real Time Report and a term member of the Council on Foreign Relations. In 2012 the National Bureau of Asian Research awarded Erickson the inaugural Ellis Joffe Prize for PLA Studies. He is the author of the volume Chinese Anti-Ship Ballistic Missile Development (Jamestown, 2013) and coauthor of two additional books: Gulf of Aden Anti-Piracy and China's Maritime Commons Presence (Jamestown, 2015), as well as

Assessing China's Cruise Missile Ambitions. He has published extensively in such peer-reviewed journals as China Quarterly, Journal of Contemporary China, Asian Security, Asia Policy, Journal of Strategic Studies, and Acta Astronautica. Erickson received his Ph.D. and M.A. from Princeton University and studied Mandarin at Beijing Normal University's College of Chinese Language and Culture.

M. Taylor Fravel

M. Taylor Fravel is Associate Professor of Political Science and member of the Security Studies Program at MIT. He is currently writing a book entitled Active Defense: Explaining the Evolution of China's Military Strategy. He can be followed on twitter @fravel.

Cristina Garafola

Ms. Garafola is a Project Associate-China Specialist at the RAND Corporation. She holds an M.A. from the Johns Hopkins School of Advanced International Studies and a certificate from the Hopkins-Nanjing Center for Chinese and American Studies. Cristina has previously worked at the Department of State, the Department of Treasury, and the Freeman Chair in China Studies at the Center for Strategic and International Studies. She is fluent in Mandarin.

Timothy R. Heath

Timothy R. Heath is Senior International and Defense Analyst at the RAND Corporation and a recognized expert on Chinese strategy and political-military topics. He served for five years as the senior analyst in the United States Pacific Command (USPACOM) China Strategic Focus Group and has over fifteen years of experience in the US government as a specialist on China. Mr. Heath has authored many articles and a book chapter on topics related to Chinese security and political issues. He earned his MA in Asian Studies from George Washington University and speaks fluent Mandarin Chinese.

Peter Mattis

Peter Mattis is a Fellow in the China Program at The Jamestown Foundation. He edited Jamestown's biweekly *China Brief* from 2011 to 2013. Prior to The Jamestown Foundation, Mr. Mattis worked as an international affairs analyst for the U.S. Government. He received his M.A. in Security Studies from the Georgetown University School of Foreign Service and earned his B.A. in Political Science and Asian Studies from the University of Washington in Seattle. He also previously worked as a Research Associate at the National Bureau of Asian Research in its Strategic Asia and Northeast Asian Studies programs. He is currently researching a book on Chinese intelligence.

Kevin Pollpeter

Kevin Pollpeter is a Research Scientist at the Center for Naval Analyses (CNA). He previously served as the Deputy Director of the East Asia Program at Defense Group Inc (DGI) where he managed a group of more than 20 China analysts. He is widely published on China national security issues, with a focus on China's space program. His most recent publications include, "The PLAAF and the Integration of Air and Space Power," in Richard P. Hallion, Roger Cliff, and Phillip C. Saunders, The Chinese Air Force: Evolving Concepts, Roles, and Capabilities (NDU, 2012) and "Controlling the Information Domain: Space, Cyber, and Electronic Warfare," in Ashley J. Tellis and Travis Tanner, Strategic Asia 2012-2013: China's Military Challenge (NBR: 2012). His other publications include "Upward and Onward: Technological Innovation and Organizational Change in China's Space Industry" in the Journal of Strategic Studies (June 2011), "China's Space Doctrine" in Andrew S. Erickson and Lyle J. Goldstein, eds., Chinese Aerospace Power (Naval Institute Press, 2011), as well as numerous articles in China Brief. A Chinese linguist, he holds an M.A. in International Policy Studies from the Monterey Institute of International Studies.

Jonathan Ray

Jonathan Ray is a Research Associate at Defense Group Inc. (DGI), where he conducts research and analysis using Chinese-language sources on foreign policy, national security, and science and technology issues. Previously he was a contract researcher at the National Defense University, where he wrote Red China's "Capitalist Bomb": Inside the Chinese Neutron Bomb Program.